Vichy's Afterlife

Vichy's

History
and
Counterhistory
in
Postwar
France

Afterlife

Richard J. Golsan

University of Nebraska Press

Lincoln & London

Acknowledgments for the use of
previously published material appear
on pages x–xi.

Library of Congress
Cataloging-in-Publication Data
Golsan, Richard Joseph, 1952–
Vichy's afterlife : history and counterhistory in postwar
France / by Richard J. Golsan.
p. cm.
Includes bibliographical references and index.
ISBN 0-8032-7094-1 (pa: alk. paper)
1. France—History—German occupation, 1940–
1945—Historiography.   2. Vichy (France)—Politics
and government—Moral and ethical aspects.
3. Historians—France—Attitudes.   4. War crime
trials—France—Public opinion.   5. Public opinion—
France.   I. Title.
DC397 .G59 2000
944'.597—dc21   00-024203

𝒩

This book is dedicated with love

to my mother, Lucy Broyles Golsan,

and to the memory of my grandmother,

Mary Jones Broyles

Contents

Acknowledgments

I have been interested in the history and memory of Vichy for many years, and it has been my great pleasure during that time to share that interest with a number of friends and colleagues, all of whom have taught me a great deal and have generously offered their advice and support on a number of occasions.

In France, Annette Lévy-Willard of *Libération* has been a most generous friend and a valuable source of contacts, documents, information, and, most of all, conversation. Without her help on many occasions, this book would not have been possible. I have learned much from Henry Rousso, who has shared his remarkable knowledge and insights into the memory of Vichy with me on several occasions and has been most generous in making the resources of the Institut d'Histoire du Temps Présent available to me. Tzvetan Todorov has over the last several years shared his unique and rich perspectives on contemporary France and Europe with me, as has Marc Dambre and Jean-Jacques Fleury. From Rémy Desquesnes I have learned to appreciate in a visceral sense the sacrifices of war on visits to the Normandy beaches and cemeteries. My friends Pat and Hervé Picton have offered me their hospitality on my numerous trips to France.

In England, Chris Flood has been a constant friend and intellectual companion for many years.

In the United States, my debts are many. Lynn Higgins and Bob Soucy offered much helpful advice in the revision of this manuscript, and I hope neither is too disappointed by the final version. I have also learned a great deal about film and literature from Lynn and about fascism from Bob, and I have benefited as well from many conversations over the years with Mary Jean Green, Rosemary Scullion, Dina Shirzer, Jean-Pierre Cauvin, Leah Hewitt, Jeffrey Schnapp, Richard Wolin, Bert Gordon, Tom Hilde, and Van and Mary Kelly. In the mid-1980s I had the great pleasure of attending Steve Ungar and Dudley Andrew's NEH seminar on French fiction and film between the wars at the University of Iowa. The experience launched me along the intellectual trajectory I have followed ever since.

Closer to home, Nathan Bracher, Frank Baumgartner, and Bob Schandley have shared a passionate interest in the Vichy past that has fueled team-taught courses, NEH seminars, and many spirited discussions. Terry Anderson, Doug Goodgame, and Larry Reynolds have taught me more about good tennis than I ever needed to know. They have been good friends as well.

Most of all, I want to thank my family. My sisters Maryanne and Katie and my niece, Sonia, share my love of France, and so many other things as well. But it is my wife, Nancy, and our sons, Jody and James, who have to put up with me all the time. They remain, as always, the reasons why.

Versions of several of these chapters have been given as talks at the Universities of Iowa and Kansas and Cornell University in this country, and at the Universities of Southampton and Surrey and Kingston University in Britain. I wish to thank those responsible for inviting me. Portions of this book have been previously published as: (chapter 1) "Memory and Justice Abused: The 1949 Trial of René Bousquet," *Studies in Twentieth Century Literature* 23, no. 1 (winter 1999): 93–110; (chapter 3) "*Lacombe Lucien,* the *Mode Rétro,* and the Vichy Syndrome," in *Identity Papers: Contested Nationhood in Twentieth-Century France,* ed. Steven Ungar and Tom Conley (University of Minnesota Press, 1996), 139–55, copyright 1996 by the Regents of the University of Minnesota; (chapter 4) "*Hotel Terminus* via the Vélodrome d'Hiver: Collaboration and Aesthetics of Denial," *L'Esprit Créateur* 33, no. 2 (spring 1993): 75–84; (chapter 6) "Reflections on Mitterand's Années Noires: Pierre Péan's *Une Jeunesse française: François Mitterand, 1934–1937,*" *Contemporary French Civilization* 19, no. 2 (summer/fall 1995): 292–311; (chapter 7) adapted from the introduction to *The Future of a Negation: Reflections on the Question of Genocide* by Alain Finkielkraut by permission of the University of Nebraska Press, © 1998 by the University of Nebraska Press; (chapter 8) "From Sarajevo to Vichy: French Intellectuals and the Wages of Commitment in the Balkans," *L'Esprit*

Créateur 37, no. 2 (summer 1997): 79–89; and (chapter 9) "Mémoires à Rétardement: Maurice Papon, Crimes against Humanity, and 17 October 1961," *Journal of European Studies* 28, nos. 109–10 (March/June 1998): 153–72. I wish to thank the editors concerned for their kind permission to republish here.

Vichy's Afterlife

Introduction

The Body in the Basement

In 1987, at the outset of *The Vichy Syndrome*—his now classic study of the memory of the Occupation years in postwar France— Henry Rousso proposed a somewhat macabre surgical metaphor for his discovery that Vichy, far from being a past that had truly passed, was in fact a living, breathing entity: "In the late 1970s, I began work on the history of the Vichy regime, obviously still a subject of heated controversy. Nevertheless, in all innocence, I thought sufficient time had passed to allow me to wield my scalpel. But the corpse was still warm. It was too soon for the pathologist to do an autopsy; what the case called for was a doctor qualified to treat the living, not the dead."[1] Five years later, at the conclusion of an article also dealing with Vichy's afterlife, the journalist Éric Conan offered a strikingly similar metaphor to evoke the continuing vibrancy of this troubling past in French political and cultural life: "Like Ionesco's Amédée, Vichy is a cadaver that continues to grow as we speak of it, a cadaver that invades everything, and that we no longer know how to get rid of."[2]

It is perhaps appropriate that two of France's most visible commentators on what has now widely come to be known as "the Vichy Syndrome" should invoke the same image of an ever-present, indisposable, living, growing corpse in order to describe a past that continues to haunt the French more than fifty years after the Second World War. Exasperated and convinced that this national obsession with Vichy was largely attributable to media hype that dealt in spectacular rumor and innuendo rather than in historical truth, Conan and Rousso joined forces in 1994 to write a provocative book, *Vichy: An Everpresent Past,* which in essence called for a moratorium on such scandal mongering in favor of a more sober analysis of the facts and realities of the period. But at the time *Vichy: An Everpresent Past* appeared in the fall of 1994, the scandal surrounding President François Mitterrand's own Vichy past erupted and submerged the nation in another onslaught of the Vichy Syndrome. The ghost of Vichy was indeed a living presence that sought to perpetuate itself through controversy despite Conan and Rousso's appeal. Their admonishments were, for all intents and purposes, lost in the shuffle, and the memory of *les années noires*—the Dark Years between 1940 and 1944—continued to make its presence felt in a variety of forms and circumstances.

The most spectacular of these manifestations was the trial for crimes against humanity of Maurice Papon, which got under way at the Bordeaux assizes court in October 1997. Papon, former secretary-general of the Gironde prefecture, was charged with organizing convoys and deporting some fifteen hundred Jews from the Bordeaux region to death camps between 1942 and 1944. After numerous delays due for the most part to Papon's illnesses, the trial finally ended some six months later, the longest trial in French history. The verdict and sentence satisfied few.[3] Papon was found guilty of complicity in the Final Solution—and, therefore, of crimes against humanity—but innocent of the charge of having knowingly sent his victims to their deaths. He was sentenced to ten years in prison, not twenty years, as the prosecutor had requested.

Among those who criticized both the verdict and the sentence was Papon's lawyer, Jean-Marc Varaut, who argued that the court had "cheated with the truth" in rendering a "bastard decision."[4] On purely practical grounds, however, Varaut should not have protested the assizes court's treatment of his client. At the outset of the trial, the presiding judge, Jean-Louis Castagnède, released Papon from custody for health reasons. According to French law, Papon could not therefore be jailed, even *after* sentencing, until all appeals were exhausted. As a result, Papon remained, until very recently, a free man. In October 1999, shortly before his appeal was to be heard in Paris, Papon fled to Switzerland. An international warrant for his arrest was issued and he was caught in a hotel in Gstaad. He was returned to France and imprisoned at Fresnes prison. One newspaper remarked caustically concerning his flight, "For once Papon did not collaborate." And as Nicolas Weill has bitterly remarked in a recent essay on the significance of the Bordeaux proceedings, Papon attended his own trial for crimes against humanity as one might attend a colloquium. This colloquium was certainly "a little solemn, [and] undoubtedly disagreeable, but [it was] nevertheless devoted entirely to him!"[5]

If the verdict and sentence were unsatisfactory—not to say unsettling—to many, so too was the fact that a trial that was intended to put into relief Papon's role as a Vichy functionary ended up meandering through the details of his postwar political career—a career carried out for the most part under the banner of Gaullism. The trial dealt with Papon's role as prefect of Paris police in the late 1950s and early 1960s and touched on his stint as minister of budget under Valéry Giscard d'Estaing, when revelations of his Vichy past brought his career as a high functionary to an end. Instead of clarifying the specificity of Vichy complicity with the Nazis and the nature and extent of Papon's crimes, the trial succeeded, on occasion, in conflating Vichy's excesses with those of the Gaullist years. The muddying of historical waters in this and in other instances in the trial led Rousso to argue in an interview that the trial marked a "regression" in historical knowledge and that it was of no pedagogical value whatsoever, historically speaking.[6] Some have strongly disagreed with Rousso's assessment. Nicolas Weill, for example, argues that such global dismissals of the trial obscure the fact that many of the charges against Papon were firmly established in Bordeaux and that, in this sense, justice was done. Weill also laments the fact that what he describes as the "intellectual be-littling" of and "hypercritical attitude" toward these trials for crimes against humanity, once the exclusive property of "a certain right nostalgic for Vichy," have now emigrated to a misguided "national-republican" left.[7] Clearly, the debate over the value, meaning, and significance of the Papon trial and, more broadly, of crimes against humanity in France is not over yet.

The summer before the Papon trial got under way, another scandal associated with the Occupation made the headlines. In a book titled *Aubrac: Lyon 1943*, the journalist and historian Gérard Chauvy accused Resistance hero Raymond Aubrac of having been "turned" by the Gestapo in Lyons and providing information that led to the arrest of Resistance martyr Jean Moulin.[8] Outraged, Raymond Aubrac sued Chauvy for defamation of character, a suit he eventually won in 1998, but he and his wife did not stop there. At the urging of the Aubracs, a committee of distinguished historians and others including François Bédarida, Jean Moulin's biographer and former secretary, Daniel Cordier, and Henry Rousso, met with the Aubracs on 17 May 1997 to discuss the events at issue under the auspices of the Parisian daily *Libération*. The discussions that ensued satisfied no one. Questions about the Aubracs credibility in all the details of the affair remained (as did questions about what actually happened in Lyons in 1943), and some felt that the role of the historians had been compromised in agreeing to serve as "inquisitors." These critics apparently chose to overlook the fact that the Aubracs themselves had called for the creation of the roundtable to get the support of the historians in the first place. Ironically, that same summer, a popular film about the unalloyed heroism of Raymond and Lucie Aubrac was doing well in movie houses.[9]

In many ways, the Aubrac affair was little more than an epiphenomenon in the ongoing debates surrounding the Resistance that centered for the most part on martyred hero Jean Moulin. Moulin was arrested, tortured, and murdered in 1943 by the ss chief in occupied Lyons, Klaus Barbie. In December 1964, Moulin's remains were transferred to the Panthéon in one of Gaullism's most celebrated efforts to

4   *Introduction*

ratify its version of history, according to which the vast majority of the French, following de Gaulle's example, heroically resisted the Nazis. The ceremonies lasted two days, and on the second day the events were broadcast on national television, the highlight of which was André Malraux's famous eulogy to "the people of the night."

But Moulin did not rest in peace. His legacy has been challenged in the 1990s, first in 1993 by the journalist Thierry Wolton, who accused Moulin of being a Soviet spy in his book *Le Grand Recrutement*. Wolton's charges stirred considerable controversy. In addition, and to the consternation of many, the distinguished historians François Furet and Annie Kriegel lent their support to Wolton's theses in the pages of the major weekly magazines *Le Nouvel Observateur* and *Figaro Magazine*, respectively. Taking the opposite view, Pierre Vidal-Naquet considered Wolton's charges scandalous and dangerous enough to be attacked and dismantled in his book, *Le Trait empoisonné: Réflexions sur l'affaire Moulin*. Vidal-Naquet described Wolton's method as that of "amalgamation," a method he argued was perfected by Stalinists in trials in Moscow, Budapest, and elsewhere. According to Vidal-Naquet, the method involves simply asserting: "You knew X who has been identified as a traitor and you are therefore yourself a traitor." Because Moulin was linked to French political figures who favored a Franco-Soviet rapprochement, Wolton would have it that Moulin must have favored this rapprochement as well.[10]

The arguments of Vidal-Naquet and others put to rest only temporarily Wolton's claim that Jean Moulin was a Communist mole and the broader controversy surrounding his true political allegiance. The Resistance hero's image suffered another blow in the fall of 1998 when another book claiming to offer "new" revelations concerning Moulin argued that Barbie's most famous victim was in fact an *American* agent. Controversy once again ensued, and the debate became so heated that it appears at this writing that the differences between the book's author and at least one of his critics will be settled in court. But no matter what the outcome of these legal proceedings will be, it is clear that Moulin's history will continue to be rewritten. At about the same time that the book accusing Moulin of being an American agent was published, yet another biography of the Resistance martyr was released, this one titled *Vies et mort de Jean Moulin*. Claiming to be "swarming with revelations," *Vies et mort de Jean Moulin* enjoyed one advantage the others did not—the celebrity of its author, Pierre Péan. No stranger to the scandals surrounding the Vichy past, Péan had previously published *François Mitterrand: Une Jeunesse française* in the fall of 1994, which touched off the controversy over Mitterrand's service to Vichy.[11] (*Une Jeunesse française* will be discussed in detail in chapter 6.)

If the Papon trial, the Aubrac affair, and the ongoing controversies surrounding the figure of Jean Moulin are among the most spectacular recent manifestations of Vichy's afterlife, they are far from being the only ones in the last few years. As Vichy historian Robert Paxton notes, other manifestations include "new 'revelations' concerning the probable French manufacture of Cyclone-B gas for the Nazis . . . and the discovery of additional war time police files of Jewish names and addresses in provincial archives." Other sources of controversy include the "hitherto taboo subject with immense destructive potential" of "the disposition of Jewish property confiscated during the Occupation, or bought at knock-down prices, and neither returned nor re-imbursed after the Liberation. A corner of the veil was lifted in early 1997 when it turned out that French national museums still possess considerable seized Jewish property."[12]

The scandalous memory of the Dark Years has also, of course, long been associated with the publication of novels and especially the release of films. This trend has continued into the 1990s, although none of these recent works can be said to have had the impact on the collective memory of the period or the national conscience that films like *Le Chagrin et la pitié* and *Lacombe Lucien* or novels like Modiano's *La Place de l'étoile* and Michel Tournier's *Le Roi des Aulnes* (The ogre) had more than two decades ago.[13] At least where film is concerned, the general tendency has been to consider post-1970s works to be indicators of the state of the memory of Vichy at the time the work appears rather than pathbreaking works containing new historical insights or significant revelations about the period. Thus it has been argued, for example, that François Truffaut's *Le Dernier Métro* reflects a widely held desire in the early 1980s to submerge the Second World War past and paper over its most insidious features.[14] More recently, works like *Le Docteur Petiot* have reflected what Conan and Rousso, among others, refer to as the "judeocentrism" of the Vichy Syndrome: the increasing focus on the fate of the Jews, Vichy anti-Semitism, and French participation in the Final Solution. Claude Berri's adaptation of Marcel Aymé's *Uranus*, at least in Conan's view, reflects the argument central to the "return" of Pétainist ideology in the1990s, which is that all Frenchmen—*collabo, attentiste,* and *résistant*—were alike in their *veulerie*, or abject cowardice.[15] Other films in more or less the same vein include Jean Marboeuf's *Pétain*, whose star, Jacques Dufilho, is a convinced Pétainiste.

Fiction dealing with the Dark Years published in the 1980s and 1990s has certainly also tapped into the ongoing fascination with the period. However, with few exceptions—most notably Marguerite Duras's extraordinary 1985 work, *La Douleur*—the novels published are less reflective of changes in the public memory of Vichy than they are of a desire to exploit a pseudohistorical public fascination with figures and events from the period—figures and events that still enjoy an aura of taboo. For example, the central figure of Michel del Castillo's 1987 novel, *Le Démon de l'oubli*, is a literary collaborator in Paris who rubs shoulders with the likes of Pierre Drieu la Rochelle, one of France's most infamous fascist writers and the wartime editor of *Nouvelle Revue Française*. In a similar fashion, Marc Lambron's 1997 novel, *1941,* serves up in often excessive detail fictional portraits of Vichy's political leaders. (One has the impression that Lambron is more interested in showing off his historical knowledge than writing a compelling novel.) Patrick Modiano's latest novel, *Dora Bruder*, while it resembles his earlier works dealing with the Occupation in theme and structure, is certainly more compelling than the works of Lambron and del Castillo, among others. (*Dora Bruder* will be discussed in chapter 2.)

If the preceding remarks suggest some of the more obvious and direct ways in which the Vichy past and, more generally, the memory of the Second World War make their presence felt in French public life, other aspects of *l'actualité*, or the current scene, also reflect the power of the memory and legacy of the Dark Years, albeit in a more indirect fashion. The continuing success of the National Front at the polls and the presence in the Front's ranks of former arch *collabos* like François Brigneau and Roland Gaucher suggest to many the return of Pétainist racism and xenophobia at their most virulent, or worse.[16] *Le négationnisme*, or the French version of the Holocaust denial, also reared its head again in the spring and summer of 1996, when the renowned Catholic cleric Father Pierre lent his support to a *négationniste* book written by his old friend, Roger Garaudy. In another instance, Alain Finkielkraut, Bernard-Henri Lévy, Jacques Julliard, and other intellectuals denounced France's and Europe's passivity in the face of Serb aggression in the Balkans in the early 1990s. They considered this passivity reminiscent not only of French *attentisme* under Vichy, but of a generalized European apathy comparable to the paralysis of Europe's democracies in the 1930s that paved the way to Munich, Vichy, and the conflagration of the Second World War. Sounding an apocalyptic note, Julliard titled his 1994 book of ruminations on the topic *Ce fascisme qui vient* . . . (This fascism that is coming . . .). Whether the analogies deployed by Julliard and his colleagues actually led to a better understanding of the Balkan conflict is open to debate, but it is certainly true that references to Vichy and the events that made it possible were bound to grab the public's attention and help channel it toward the events in Croatia and Bosnia.

The obvious question, then, is why Vichy, and all that the name entails, fascinates and even obsesses the French the way it does, inflecting not only discussions of the past but of the present as well. According to Paxton, there are several overriding reasons, the first being that French national identity is at stake. At a time when the French are suffering "acute anxiety about the decline of their culture, language, and way of life under the onslaughts of economic and cultural globalization," to lose "the memory of having earned a legitimate place among the victors of World War II would be particularly hard to bear." A second reason is that "there are still a few skeletons in the closet." Finally, and perhaps most significant, is the fact that "mastering the past raises issues which are hardly grasped by the public, let alone resolved."[17] Restating Paxton's final reason somewhat differently, Rousso observes: "What France has difficulty facing today is not so much its [Vichy] past but the fact of having to live with the rupture [it embodies], a rupture that no trial, no commemoration, no speech can fix. Facing up to, accepting the irreparable is, in my opinion, the real issue at stake for our generation and for future generations as well."[18]

There are, of course, other reasons that help explain the current obsession. The first of these is that the memory and public perception of the Vichy period have undergone a number of drastic and often disorienting changes under the pressure of subsequent events. In *The Vichy Syndrome*, Rousso argues that these changes can be summarized and systematized in a series of four "stages" or "phases." For ten years following the war, Rousso asserts, the nation was caught up in a period of "unfinished mourning," when it was forced to "deal directly with the aftermath of civil war, purge and amnesty."[19] This first stage was followed by a second stage of seventeen years of "repressions," when the Gaullist myth of Resistance—which held that the vast majority of the French had resisted and the collaborators were a small handful of scoundrels and misfits—held sway, and the result was a comfortable period of collective amnesia.[20] In 1971, the third stage began. In the aftermath of the student revolts of May 1968, the "mirror broke," initially as a result of the change in generational perspective signaled by the "events of May" and the sensation caused by the release *Le Chagrin et la pitié*. The publication of Paxton's *La France de Vichy* in 1973, as well as other events, consolidated this shift in mood and outlook. In 1974, according to Rousso, the final, or "Obsession," phase began. This phase was marked primarily by the reawakening of Jewish memory, which had been repressed in the postwar years by, among other things, the Jewish community's desire to reintegrate itself into the national mainstream and not to set itself apart by emphasizing what happened to it at German *and* French hands during the Occupation.[21] Since 1974, the "Obsession" phase has, Rousso argues, continued more or less unabated. Moreover, it has now swelled to the point where, coupled with the nation's supposed "duty to memory"—an issue to which we shall return shortly—it must now be considered an "impasse." The "overfullness" of memory, as Rousso labels it, has become as much a problem as the denial of memory.[22]

If popular memory and public perceptions of the Vichy period have undergone a number of occasionally contradictory and always unsettling changes, the same can be said, to a significant degree, of the scholarly historiography of the period. At least until the mid-1960s, scholarly studies tended to focus on the role of the Resistance and German oppression, not on the Vichy regime itself and certainly not on Vichy anti-Semitism, the Final Solution, and the deportations of the Jews. Lucette Valensi, for one, attributes this to the climate of the postwar years themselves:

> It took a long time in France to be willing to undertake the study of Vichy. . . . A tacit agreement had been reached, from the moment of the Liberation, between the different currents of public opinion, to remain silent about the defeat of 1940 and the Vichy regime itself. Motivated by a variety of different interests, Gaullists, Communists, Jews, former Collaborators, ordinary citizens all got together to construct a myth of a massive and victorious Resistance and of a heroic national memory. *In this context, the professional historian, like his fellow citizens, did not seek to underscore or sustain the Franco-French animosities that marked the war years* [my emphasis].[23]

As Rousso notes, the thrust of the work done by Henri Michel and his colleagues at Comité d'Histoire de la Deuxième Guerre Mondiale (CHDGM—later to become the Institut d'Histoire du Temps Présent IHTP)—in the 1940s, 1950s, and early 1960s was to focus on the Resistance, the role of the Germans, and the deportations (although not of Jews). He argues as well, however, that works such as Michel's own *Vichy, année 40*—which, according to Jean-Pierre Azéma, contributed toward disproving the Aronian thesis that Vichy acted as a "shield" to the French and was pressured into collaboration against its will—also helped pave the way for the reassessments of Eberhard Jäckel and especially Robert Paxton.[24]

Pascal Ory is not as generous as Rousso in his assessment of the work of Michel and the CHDGM: "Henri Michel steered the work of his industrious CHDGM toward the almost exclusive analysis of the Resistance and its repression. Official heroization, and the damnation of memory: all was for the best in the best of all possible historiographies, even if this meant abandoning the history of the Vichy regime to a moderately Pétainist reading, Robert Aron's reading, founded on the now altogether classic parallel of Pétain the 'shield' and De Gaulle the 'sword.'"[25] Without delving too deeply into the role of Henri Michel and CHDGM or of Rousso and Ory's contradictory assessment of it, it is clear that even the historians are not in agreement about the historiography of Vichy, at least in this instance. This is perhaps, then, a good example of the complexity of issues referred to earlier by Paxton that marks the troubled legacy of Vichy and makes it all the more difficult for the general public to comprehend and digest. Several other examples will be explored in this book.

If the work of Henri Michel and the CHDGM constitutes a source of disagreement if not controversy, the next—and most crucial—development in the historiography of Vichy lends itself to other forms of controversy and confusion as well. First, the German historian Eberhard Jäckel's study, published in France in 1968 as *La France dans l'Europe d'Hitler*, and then Paxton's more significant *La France de Vichy*, published in 1973, fully exposed the extent of Vichy complicity with the Germans. Paxton's book, in fact, sparked considerable controversy shortly after its publication and was dismissed by a number of French historians as prejudiced and ill informed.[26] It succeeded, nonetheless, according to Azéma, in confirming that "Vichy never ceased to pursue a policy of collaboration of State and never practiced the slightest 'double game' nor, *a fortiori,* did it facilitate the efforts of the Allies in any way."[27] *La France de Vichy* thus put the final—and biggest—nail in the coffin of Aron's "shield" theory.

Paxton is the first to admit his indebtedness to Jäckel and to French predecessors like Yves Durand (whose work, like Jäckel's, never received the attention received by *La France de Vichy*), but the succès de scandale of his own book, and the belatedly recognized work done by

Jäckel, helped foster the belief that it took *foreigners* to get at the real truth about Vichy.[28] And this, in turn, implied at least to some that the French historians were involved in some sort of cover-up. When, in the early 1980s, the first major studies on Vichy anti-Semitism and participation in the Final Solution were written either by foreigners—this time Paxton and his Canadian colleague and former student Michael Marrus—or the amateur historian, lawyer, and "memory militant" Serge Klarsfeld, the impression seemed to some to be confirmed. Indeed, as Lucette Valensi notes in her essay "Présence du passé, lenteur de l'histoire," the first major academic colloquium in France to deal directly with Vichy and the Jews occurred in 1992—a full fifty years after the implementation of the Final Solution in France.[29] Earlier colloquia, and especially the landmark Le Gouvernement de Vichy: 1940–1942 held at the Fondation Nationale des Sciences Politiques in 1970, had virtually nothing to say about the persecution of the Jews.[30] The same is true of the 1990 colloquium, "Le Régime de Vichy et les Français," organized by the IHTP.[31]

To be sure, as Valensi also affirms, there are very good reasons why historians, and not just French historians, have found (and should find) it difficult and fraught with risks to work on a subject as historically and morally complex as the Holocaust, an event whose intricacies and implications have in fact often been best explored by *non-historians* (Valensi cites Raul Hilberg, a political scientist, and Claude Lanzmann, the maker of the film *Shoah*, among others). These reasons include the fact that traumas of the dimensions of the Holocaust by definition present multiple levels of signification. As a result, the "truth" of the events, as Valensi labels it, is never fully revealed and what *is* known only reveals itself over time. A second reason is that in dealing with "massive collective traumas," the historian does not simply produce "cold hard knowledge" but participates in the construction and the transmission of "social memory." The stakes are of course thereby raised, since, as Saul Friedlander asserts, by definition the historian is working in an area where "moral and cognitive categories are fused."[32] And since in France at least, according to Valensi, history has "a civic function" and the historian is a "sentinel on duty," she or he must be especially careful in presenting his or her discoveries.

As if these difficulties facing the historian were not enough—difficulties of which the public is, no doubt, not generally aware—for historians dealing with Vichy and the Dark Years there are other quandaries as well. In *La Hantise du passé*, Rousso devotes a number of pages to the role the historian has been expected to play in the recent trials of Paul Touvier and Maurice Papon. In both trials, distinguished historians presented themselves at the bar to testify about the realities of the Vichy regime and the workings of the deportations. In the trial of Touvier, this occurred in a context where historical reality had to be denied or at least seriously doctored in order to secure a conviction. (This will be discussed in detail in chapter 5.) This was clearly not the most auspicious forum in which an historian could express his or her views. In the Papon trial, the stakes and difficulties involved were somewhat different. Although the historians were called as "expert witnesses," the moment of their appearance, as Rousso notes, was symbolic of their real status. They were called *along with all the other witnesses*, and their testimony ultimately carried no more weight than that of their fellows. But as Rousso also asserts, it could hardly have been otherwise; unlike the judges and lawyers, most of the historians did not have access to the massive amount of documentation assembled in the case. The one "historian" who had had the greatest access to the files and documents was Michel Bergès, who was not even an historian by training. A political scientist who had originally unearthed the incriminating archival evidence against the accused, Bergès had at the outset lent his support to those who wished to prosecute Papon. But he had subsequently changed sides. At Papon's trial, Bergès testified for the defense, although by that time his integrity was in question.[33] From an historical standpoint, the situation could hardly have been more confusing and unsettling.

So what role should the historian have played in these trials? Although he does not criticize his colleagues who chose to testify before the court, Rousso states that for his part he refused to testify, first when called as a witness for the prosecution (or, to be more accurate, the "civil parties" attached to it) in the Touvier case and later, as a witness for the defense in the Papon case. In the first instance, this was, Rousso acknowledges, refusing to help the "good cause," but he reasons that once the historian accepts the role of *participant*, his or her role as detached purveyor of objective truth is open to challenge, at least within the context of the trial. This is precisely what happened to Robert Paxton in the Touvier trial. According to Touvier's lawyer, Jacques Trémolet de Villers, Paxton's views on Vichy, as expressed in court were, like the views of all historians, nothing more than "a matter of opinion." In the context of a legal proceeding, Trémolet was, unfortunately, not entirely wrong.

It appears, then, that one of the distinctive features of the Vichy Syndrome is that it has exacerbated the dilemma facing the historian in present-day France, which, as Gérard Noiriel describes it in *Sur la "crise" de l'histoire*, consists in being caught between a duty to the "community of memory"—the historian's public function—and a duty to "the community of knowledge." Some, like Paxton, have paid the price for their willingness to fulfill their public function by having their expertise denigrated by the likes of Trémolet. Others, like Sorbonne Professor François-Georges Dreyfus, have played a more insidious public role. In a widely publicized book lauded by the extreme right titled *Histoire de Vichy* (1990), Dreyfus relaunched the Aronian "shield" thesis of Vichy's passive resistance to the Germans during the war, a thesis, as noted earlier, long since dismissed by what Noiriel labels the "community of knowledge." Given, then, that the most respected historians of Vichy have had their views publicly attacked while other, less reputable ones find success in certain quarters in resuscitating discredited versions of the past, it is not surprising that an authoritative, definitive version of the Vichy past has had some difficulty in imposing itself on public imagination and understanding. Moreover, the historians' role is not likely to become less complex or vexed in a country where history plays such an important role in defining the national community and where the intellectuals, including the historians, are expected, as Jacques Julliard has remarked recently, to serve, among other things, as mediators between the state and the people.[34]

As if the historical and historiographical context were not complicated enough, there is also the issue of memory. In general terms, as Pierre Nora among others has argued, memory and history often work at counterpurposes, and it is therefore not surprising that they should come into conflict over the Vichy past. The historian's measured reconstruction of the past, always by definition "problematic and incomplete" according to Nora, can hardly avoid running afoul of the living memories of those who have survived, memories which are themselves subject to "the dialectic of remembering and forgetting," to manipulation, and to distortion.[35] In *Vichy: An Everpresent Past*, Conan and Rousso assert that the national state of mind concerning the Dark Years is suggestive of a situation in which the victims and heroes, not to mention all the others, are still not satisfied with the place they have assumed in the nation's past, in *history*. In their efforts to rectify the situation and to inscribe *their* memories of the war on the nation's history, Jewish victims of the Shoah have of course been at the forefront of efforts to bring individuals like René Bousquet, Paul Touvier, and Maurice Papon to justice. This, they argue, is a *national* "duty to memory." So, too, are efforts to combat the work of the *négationnistes* by legal means.

But here, "the duty to memory" runs into a new obstacle—the law. Legislative measures to block the public circulation of the theses of the *négationnistes* have produced considerable controversy, but the conflict between memory and the law is most evident in the context of the trials for crimes against humanity.[36] In the 1980s, the debate leading up to the trial of Klaus Barbie focused at a critical juncture not on Jewish memory but on that of former *résistants*, who did not want to see *their* suffering effaced by exclusive emphasis on Barbie's role in the Final Solution. The resulting modification of France's crimes against humanity statutes to include Resistance victims only served to complicate enormously the legal issues at stake in the case. In the long run, it also hindered efforts to come up with a coherent and workable definition of crimes against humanity in French law. Similar legal "adjustments" preceding the trials of Paul Touvier and Maurice Papon in the 1990s also made matters worse.[37] And during the Papon trial especially, the conflict between the demands of memory and the law was evident not only in the legal contortions necessary to bring Papon to trial in the first place, but also in a number of events that occurred within the courtroom as well as on the steps outside.

In his journal of the trial, Éric Conan notes that when judge Jean-Louis Castagnède decided to release Papon from detainment at the outset of the trial because of Papon's ill health, the decision was in keeping with the spirit of the law. But for the survivors of the deportations and family members of those who had died at Auschwitz and elsewhere, the judge's decision seemed the height of injustice.[38] The struggle between the exigencies of the law and what might be described as "courtroom decorum" on the one hand and the commemorations required by memory on the other was also evident in disagreements between the judge and the lawyers of the victims as to whether or not photos of the victims could be projected in the courtroom when requested. Finally, the entire courtroom proceedings took place against the backdrop of the protests of the "memory militants" camped in front of the courthouse. In reading the names of Papon's victims over loudspeakers, among other activities, the protesters made clear their intent to influence the proceedings within.

Apart from the difficulties just alluded to, there are moral, ethical, and even political dilemmas and pitfalls associated with the "duty to memory" that have surfaced in relation to the Vichy past. Addressing the moral and ethical dimensions of the problem, Tzvetan Todorov argues in *Les Abus de la mémoire* that memory may be "exemplary" and serve as a guidepost for moral actions in the future. But Todorov warns that it may also be too "literal," thereby becoming a sterile obsession that really teaches nothing about the past while encouraging the one who remembers to indulge in the futile satisfaction of claiming the righteous role of the victim. Discussing the Papon trial, Paul Thibaud underscores another unfortunate moral consequence of the duty to remember. For Thibaud, the danger lies less in assuming the victim's role than it does in judging the crimes of the past from the secure and impregnable position of the present. The result is a smug and artificial moral superiority that benefits neither the judges nor those being judged. We shall return to these issues in subsequent chapters.[39]

For Alain Finkielkraut, the dangers associated with an excessive preoccupation with the Vichy past are primarily political. In his 1992 book on the conflict in the former Yugoslavia, *Dispatches from the Balkan War,* Finkielkraut argued that the obsessive concern with the duty to remember Vichy's crimes and victims was nothing more than the latest form of national "navel contemplation" that blinded the French to the realities in the Balkans. (As noted earlier, and as will be discussed in some detail in chapter 8, this did not prevent Finkielkraut from trotting out the ghosts of Vichy and Nazism for his own purposes in goading the French to action on behalf of the Croatians.) Shortly after the opening of the Papon trial in 1997, Finkielkraut reiterated his views on the futility of the duty to memory in an editorial in *Le Monde* titled simply "Papon, trop tard"—"Papon, too late."

In a sense, Finkielkraut's views bring us full circle. They imply that, rather than indulge in an obsession with the Vichy past or even attempt to understand the reasons for it, the French should simply put it behind them. Alongside and even superseding the duty to memory is, then, an "imperative to forget." Nicolas Weill goes a step further, asserting that all the talk of "syndromes," "phantasms," and the like concerning this past have not helped identify a real national malady, malaise, or obsession but rather have served to *create* one in the public mind.[40] In effect, the metaphor *is* the illness, and the "body in the basement" of my title is there because some say it is. To approach this line of reasoning from another angle, one could argue that Vichy is a kind of Girardian scapegoat that holds Memory—the "last civic religion" according to Bernard-Henri Lévy—together.

I do not share this perspective, and the present study constitutes an effort to explore the very real complexities of some of the most provocative episodes of Vichy's curious afterlife in France. In these pages I also hope to offer a perspective different from those presented above as to why the memory of the Dark Years has proven as troubling and obsessive as it has. Simply stated, my thesis is that each of these episodes, events, or scandals constitutes a veritable crossroads where history and what I would describe as "counterhistory," or competing or different versions of the past, or even different *pasts*, encounter one another, often with explosive and even destructive consequences. What I am proposing here bears some resemblance, of course, to Nora's idea of a "site of contested memory," and so why not simply refer to the notions of memory and "countermemory," notions that have already been given a certain intellectual currency and legitimacy by the likes of Michel Foucault and Natalie Davis, among others? If one follows Nora's definition(s) of memory, memory is "life," a "phenomenon of emotion and magic," and "thrives on vague, telescoping reminiscences, on hazy general impressions or specific symbolic details." Countermemory, on the other hand, may be a "private fetish or a public injunction to forget—a decree of amnesty would be an instance of a politics of forgetting." According to Foucault, "[C]ounter-memory designates the residual or resistant strains that withstand official versions of historical continuity." But what I mean by history and counterhistory are divergent *narratives* or "representations of the past." According to Nora, any such "representation of the past" falls clearly into the category of history.[41]

I should stress, however, that where the legacy of Vichy is concerned, "representations of the past" can obviously include, or be included in, scholarly and popular histories of the period or in biographies of important figures linked to Vichy. But they can also be found in documentary as well as fictional films, novels, court decisions, and even in essays and polemics treating subjects that have no real or tangible connection to the Vichy past. Moreover, as noted earlier, it is of course one of the peculiarities of Vichy's afterlife that historical, fictional, and legal discourses concerning the period have been confused, deliberately or not, or substituted for each other, usually in attempts to better understand an individual linked to that past or to summarize a stage in Vichy's memory. Thus, for example, as we shall see, at the height of the 1994 Mitterrand scandal the French president was compared to well-known fictional heroes and villains by way of explaining his character and especially his political trajectory. After René Bousquet's 1993 murder, the former chief of Vichy police became a character in potboilers, while Maurice Papon made the transition from history to fiction in Didier Daeninckx's detective novel *Meurtres pour mémoire*. And Paul Touvier, achieving a more international fictional notoriety, became a remarkably sinister con man and murderer in Brian Moore's *The Statement*. As for the crossing of historical and fictional boundaries where the memory of Vichy is concerned, the best example can be found in Stanley Hoffmann's 1992 assertion that after the demise of the Gaullist myth of Resistance, in the mid-1970s France succumbed to a countermyth according to which everyone collaborated. Hoffmann labeled this myth the "*Lacombe Lucien* myth," thereby damning a film that I shall attempt to rehabilitate here.

As the preceding remarks should suggest, the subjects discussed in these pages will include not only historical events and scandals, but also documentary and fictional films, novels, and essays ostensibly having little to do directly with Vichy and its legacy. The range of issues, events, and objects discussed will, I hope, allow me to demonstrate the variety of ways that history and counterhistory work against each other in very different ways and contexts. The resulting complexities and ambiguities have surely done their part to create public confusion and a lack of comprehension which, as noted earlier, have contributed in Robert Paxton's opinion to the French national obsession with the Dark Years.

The most obvious clash of history and counterhistory can be found in events like *le négationnisme*, discussed here in relation to the 1996 scandal surrounding Father Pierre's support of Roger Garaudy's *négationniste* book, *Les Mythes fondateurs de la politique israélienne*. But history and counterhistory can also confront each other in less obvious ways, even in circumstances where efforts are supposedly being made not to deny the historical realities or establish a competing version of the truth but to *disclose* these realities. When François Mitterrand went on French television in 1994 to discuss his Vichy past, among other things he asserted that Vichy persecuted only *foreign*

Jews. Mitterrand also claimed that his friend René Bousquet had been judged for *all* his actions as a Vichy functionary during the Occupation, including his alleged crimes against humanity, during his 1949 trial. Both claims were blatantly false, but coming from the president of the republic, they certainly appeared more credible than they might otherwise have appeared. Moreover, in making his comments about Bousquet's being tried for all his crimes in 1949, Mitterrand inadvertently pointed to yet *another* counterhistorical discourse or version of history—Bousquet's own false account of his actions during the Occupation given in his defense before the High Court. Bousquet's misrepresentation of his role in the implementation of the Final Solution in France set the stage, of course, for other legal quandaries associated with Vichy's afterlife.

The role of the French courts in getting at the truth concerning the Dark Years has also led to egregious examples of counterhistorical discourses. When the Paris court of appeals dropped charges of crimes against humanity against Paul Touvier in April 1992, it justified its decision on the basis of a reading of the Vichy regime totally at odds with the facts: the regime, the court argued, was not anti-Semitic and never practiced a policy of "ideological hegemony." Moreover, when Touvier did stand trial in 1994, he could only be found guilty if he could be considered an agent of the Germans—a dubious claim to say the least.[42]

Counterhistory also means the deviation or misdirection of history or, in one instance, what might be described as its "deflation," or annihilation. As an example of the former with relation to the Vichy past, at the outset of the Papon trial, efforts to get at the heart of the matter—Papon's role in the deportation of Jews from Bordeaux—were derailed by attention being shifted to another controversial moment in France's—and Papon's—past, the Algerian War. So brutal were the actions of Papon's Paris police in 1961 in suppressing Algerian protesters that many have compared these events to those during the Occupation and wondered whether charges of crimes against humanity against Papon were not justified in *both* cases. Such comparisons could only deflect the focus from the Vichy past and, more significant, blur the specificity of the Final Solution and the young Papon's role in carrying it out.

Another example occurs in Marcel Ophuls's film *Hotel Terminus*, which deals with the Barbie Affair. For while focusing in part on Barbie's crimes in Lyons during the Occupation and his trial in the 1980s, the film succeeds, perhaps inadvertently, in *diminishing* French complicity in Barbie's crimes and, more broadly, those of the Nazis, by honing in on postwar German amnesia and America's misguided postwar support of former Nazis in the name of the struggle against communism.

If events and aspects of *les années noires* can be obfuscated and their disclosure or analysis derailed by "counterhistorical discourses" such as those described above, the memory of Vichy linked to the obsessive search for historical truth where that memory is concerned can also become a distorting mirror itself. Such is the case, I argue here, in the conflicting and often misguided interpretations of Louis Malle's classic film *Lacombe Lucien*, which is as much a victim of the Vichy Syndrome as pathology as it is a symptom of it. Another good example of Vichy as a potentially distorting mirror can be found, as noted earlier, in the attempts of French intellectuals to comprehend and analyze the events in the Balkans in the early to mid-1990s. As provocative as the analogies they proposed in comparing the Balkan war to Vichy and Nazism were, it is not necessarily the case that these comparisons illuminated the realities of the wars in Croatia and Bosnia.

Finally, the evocation and representation of the Vichy past have led, at least in the early, influential works of Patrick Modiano as well as in his latest novel to a kind of deflation or annihilation of history, where the Dark Years are mirrored in their corruption and decadence by other historical periods surrounding them—the France of the interwar years and of the Liberation. Here, the legacy of Vichy is the affirmation of the destructive, leveling weight of History. Given Modiano's remarkable popularity, his fictional evocations of the period certainly cannot have helped clarify the specificity of the Vichy past in the public view.

If the Vichy past is peculiarly vulnerable to the contradictory and conflicting discourses of history and counterhistory as I argue here, the obvious question is why this is the case. One could argue with Nora that in the postmodern culture that is contemporary France all past moments are "equidistant"—equally available and equally remote from the present. In an historical field leveled in this fashion, it would seem only natural that multiple, often contradictory versions or narratives about specific moments in the past would circulate freely, without one version necessarily being able to impose its authority over another. My own preference, however, is to view the problem from a different angle. Especially where the Vichy past is concerned, there has been, as the previous remarks suggest, a confusion (conflation?) of *roles* as regards those who have narrated or represented the events and realities at issue. Historians are thrust into the public limelight as journalists, television commentators, and even as witnesses in a court of law. Conversely, judges have become involved in the interpretation of ideology and even in the writing of history, as, for example, in the Touvier case. Presidents of the republic, documentary and feature filmmakers, and journalists have also played a part. Under these circumstances, it is easy to see why an authoritative or definitive version or representation of Vichy and its legacy has failed to impose itself and, therefore, why Vichy's afterlife has lasted so long.

The chapters in this book have been organized chronologically, although not with the intent of suggesting a progression or evolution in the relations between history and counterhistory where the legacy of Vichy is concerned. Generally, I certainly agree with Henry Rousso's assessment in *The Vichy Syndrome* that there have been, broadly speaking, a succession of "stages" or "phases" in the memory of Vichy. But Rousso's approach to the legacy of Vichy, viewed through the optic of the continuum of postwar French history, is not the approach taken here. My own focus is on a series of specific events, films, and texts tied together by a series of historical, legal, ethical, and moral concerns that each event, film, or text reflects in different but often related ways. In this sense, my approach is synchronic rather than diachronic, and therefore rather than refer to the metaphor of a "syndrome" or malady so closely linked with Rousso's chronological or diachronic approach to the memory of Vichy, I will speak here of Vichy's "afterlife." The *Random House Dictionary* defines "afterlife" as both "the life after death" and "the latter part of one's life." What better expression for the paradox that is the memory and legacy of Vichy in postwar France?

1 : Memory and Justice Abused

The 1949 Trial of René Bousquet

On the morning of 8 June 1993, one Christian Didier arrived at 34 rue Raphael, a posh apartment building in Paris's sixteenth arrondissement and the residence of René Bousquet, former head of Vichy police. Claiming to be a messenger from the ministry of the interior bearing important documents concerning Bousquet's imminent trial for crimes against humanity, Didier was admitted into the building. After climbing the stairs, Didier knocked on Bousquet's door and was greeted by Bousquet himself. On the pretext of removing the documents in question, Didier reached into his bag and extracted a revolver. According to his own account, he then shot Bousquet four times at point-blank range, three times in the abdomen and once in the head. The four shots were necessary, Didier explained, because the first few shots failed to slow Bousquet, who advanced on his assailant, called him a bastard, and tried to hit him. After the murder, Didier exited the building, crossed the Ranelagh Gardens, and took the metro at La Muette. From there, he traveled to a small hotel at Lilas on the outskirts of Paris. He then called members of the press, whom he regaled with accounts of the murder until the police arrived to arrest him. In justifying his crime, Didier stated that Bousquet "incarnated evil" whereas he himself "incarnated good." He likened his crime to "killing a serpent."[1]

The murder of René Bousquet in the summer of 1993 brought to a dramatic conclusion one of the most troubling and significant episodes of Vichy's disturbing afterlife in contemporary France. But, as commentators were quick to point out, Bousquet's death was as premature and frustrating in historical and legal terms as it was spectacular. René Bousquet had come to symbolize in the public mind the Vichy regime's complicity with the Final Solution. Many believed that his imminent trial for crimes against humanity for actions undertaken against the Jews while serving as secretary-general for police in Vichy's ministry of the interior from April 1942 to December 1943 would have exposed the full horror of Vichy anti-Semitism and shattered once and for all the myth that Vichy resisted the implementation of the Final Solution. In its 9 June 1993 story on the murder of Bousquet, the headline in the Communist daily *L'Humanité* did not mention Bousquet's name but simply affirmed: "The trial of Vichy remains to be carried out." Other newspapers, citing the need for such a trial, called for an acceleration of proceedings against Paul Touvier and Maurice Papon, the two surviving Frenchmen charged with crimes against humanity for their actions against Jews during the Occupation.

When Touvier, the first of the two to be tried, finally appeared before the Yvelines Court at Versailles in the spring of 1994, however, many felt his trial was just a poor substitute for the Bousquet trial that never took place. In *Vichy: An Everpresent Past*, Éric Conan and Henry Rousso referred to the sentiment shared by many that Touvier was tried faute de mieux—for lack of a better choice. They also claimed that "the impossibility of trying Bousquet cast a shadow" on the courtroom.[2] In the spring of 1996, in an interview with Annette Lévy-Willard published in the Parisian daily *Libération*, Maurice Papon stated that he saw "only advantages" in putting Vichy on trial, but that he had no wish to serve as a "scapegoat" for those he considered to be the real guilty parties. According to Papon, the culprits were those who put French forces, and the French police in particular, at the disposal of the Nazis. Obviously, Papon was pointing the finger at Bousquet.[3]

There are a number of misperceptions attendant upon the notion that the trial of René Bousquet would, or could, somehow have constituted a symbolic, necessary, and indeed cathartic trial of Vichy, complete with a clear-cut and unambiguous verdict. First, to the extent that one can try a regime by prosecuting representative individuals, Vichy had already been tried, albeit imperfectly, during the postwar Purge.[4] Among those tried and convicted, moreover, was Bousquet himself, who went before the High Court in 1949 for his actions as head of Vichy police during the Occupation. It was this trial to which François Mitterrand conveniently and misleadingly referred in the fall of 1994 when his own Vichy past and his postwar friendship with Bousquet created a national scandal (see chapter 6). Given that Bousquet had already been tried and sentenced for his actions during the war, Mitterrand argued, a new trial would have constituted a clear case of double jeopardy. What Mitterrand failed to mention was that Bousquet had *not* been tried for crimes against humanity in 1949, since no statutes governing crimes of this nature existed in French law before 1964.[5] Bousquet's role in the deportations of the Jews—which would later form the basis of charges of crimes against humanity against him—was, therefore, hardly central to the case. Moreover, as we shall see, the presentation before the Court of Bousquet's role in the deportations was seriously distorted by testimony of the chief witness, the defendant himself.

Another misperception is that a second trial of Vichy's head of police was necessary for the full truth of French complicity in the Final Solution to emerge. In an interview published in *Le Figaro* the day after Bousquet's murder, the lawyer and Holocaust historian Serge Klarsfeld acknowledged that Vichy's role was already fully known and that no major new revelations would have been forthcoming had Bousquet been tried. Klarsfeld noted, however, that the trial would have had great pedagogical value not only in debunking Bousquet's own version of events but in making it possible to contrast the horrors resulting from Vichy cooperation with the Nazis with official resistance to these policies in other countries.[6]

Klarsfeld's comments about the pedagogical function of a second trial of Bousquet are certainly reasonable but perhaps overly optimistic, given a final series of legal and historical complications that almost inevitably would have arisen during the course of the proceedings. For example, it is easy to overlook the fact that the second trial of Bousquet would have preceded the spring 1994 trial of Paul Touvier and the 1997–98 trial of Maurice Papon. Therefore, many of the broader legal and moral issues raised in the Touvier and Papon trials would certainly have been aired in the trial of Bousquet. Those uncomfortable with the retroactive application of the statutes concerning crimes against humanity in the subsequent trials in all likelihood would have felt the same way about their application to Bousquet, although Bousquet was ultimately responsible for many more deaths than was Touvier or Papon. In terms of the importance of his position, moreover, Bousquet was certainly not insignificant "political rabble," as François Mitterrand disdainfully labeled Touvier.[7] Nevertheless, like Touvier and Papon, Bousquet would be standing trial for crimes committed fifty years earlier, and many wondered if the aging and reclusive retiree was even the same man as the zealous young bureaucrat of 1942–43. Following Bousquet's murder, in fact, one newspaper, attempting to cover the "human" side of the story, reported on the neighbors' perception of Bousquet as a thoughtful and kindly old man unjustly persecuted.[8]

In historical terms, a second trial of Bousquet would also have involved more than simply a refutation of Bousquet's version of events—his counterhistory—or even a comprehensive elaboration of the full implications of Vichy's complicity in the Final Solution. From the time of his 1949 trial, Bousquet had done extremely well as a banker and businessman, and he had even become something of a political powerbroker to the degree that for many years he controlled the powerful Toulousian newspaper *Dépêche du midi*. His control of the newspaper resulted from his relationship with the widow of a former radical-socialist mentor and ally, Jean Baylet. It was Baylet who, not coincidentally, sat on the jury during Bousquet's 1949 trial and, according to Bousquet's biographer, Pascale Froment, made sure his protégé received the lightest of sentences. Moreover, Bousquet's radical-socialist connections through Baylet and others not only helped ensure his postwar successes but also greased the skids for his rapid rise through the ranks of government in the interwar years.[9] The renewed public exposure of these connections in the context of the trial would certainly have highlighted a troubling *continuity* extending from the 1930s through Vichy and into the postwar years. As a result, the pedagogical function of the trial as exemplary of Vichy and Vichy alone would have been all the more difficult to sustain.

That these connections would have been fully exposed during the trial might have shocked some, but it was Bousquet's other political connections, also linked to *Dépêche du midi*, which, when aired in the context of the uproar over Mitterrand's past, contributed to a national scandal in September 1994. As Pierre Péan's biography of Mitterrand and other sources revealed, Bousquet made sure that the newspaper supported Mitterrand's unsuccessful 1965 presidential candidacy, even to the tune of contributing 500,000 francs to the campaign. The two men became fast friends, and Bousquet became a regular dinner guest at the Élysée palace even into the mid-1980s. Later, after Bousquet was charged with crimes against humanity in 1989, Mitterrand did his best to protect his friend from prosecution. In October 1990, the state prosecutor Pierre Truche, who had secured the conviction of Klaus Barbie, asked the indictments division of the Paris court of appeals to declare itself incompetent to handle the Bousquet case. Truche argued that it should be handled by the High Court of the Liberation, which had originally heard Bousquet's case in 1949. The proposal was patently absurd because the High Court had been dissolved for several decades and most of its members were now dead. Efforts to reconstitute the Court in any guise would take years, and Bousquet in all likelihood would have died of old age before being tried. Clearly a delaying tactic, Truche's maneuver was, many sources suggest, originally proposed by the new special delegate to the ministry of justice, George Kiejman, who also happened to be François

Mitterrand's personal lawyer. The hand of God, or Dieu, as Mitterrand was then referred to by the French public, was clearly in evidence.[10]

It is likely that a second trial of René Bousquet would have focused a harsh and distracting light on the ways of power in prewar and especially postwar France, in much the same way that during the trial of Maurice Papon the defendant's postwar tenure as prefect of Paris police in the late 1950s and 1960s came to preoccupy the court, at least early on. And in these instances at least, the scandal surrounding Vichy is not due to its status as an anomaly, as Rousso suggests, but to its *connection* to the postwar past. But the central and fundamental issue in Bousquet's trial, of course, would nevertheless have remained the accused's role in the Final Solution and the manner in which this issue was addressed in the 1949 trial. Any number of distorted and distracting versions of the past have circulated in recent years on both scores, both after Bousquet's murder and, as noted earlier, during the scandal surrounding Mitterrand's Vichy past in the fall of 1994. Even as late as the spring of 1995, in fact, and in conversations with Elie Wiesel no less, Mitterrand continued to affirm that Bousquet had been tried for all his actions during the Occupation, despite all the evidence to the contrary.[11] He went on to claim that French justice was "particularly severe" at the time, although any number of reliable historical sources confirm that the opposite was in fact the case. For instance, in her biography of Bousquet, Pascale Froment affirms that at the moment Bousquet's case was placed on the docket of the High Court, "the great wind" of the Purge had subsided, and if amnesty's moment had not fully arrived, it was nevertheless in the air.[12] A form of "countermemory," to use Foucault's expression, was seeking to impose itself. In fact, during the course of Bousquet's trial, the government of Henri Queuille announced a first large-scale amnesty plan for those guilty of collaboration, a plan with which the jurors, all legislators themselves, were certainly familiar. The government spokesperson announcing the plan was, moreover, the young secretary of state for information—one François Mitterrand.[13]

The amnesty issue and its evident impact on the 1949 trial underscore the need for further historical contextualization, especially where the extent and nature of the deliberations over Bousquet's— and Vichy's—participation in the Final Solution are concerned. It is important to keep in mind, for example, that for the Court the crucial issue was not Bousquet's role in organizing the deportations but his conduct vis-à-vis the Resistance. The reasons for this are first of all legal, since no statutes for crimes against humanity—which directly address the persecution of the Jews—existed in French law at the time, and also because the Purge as a whole concerned itself primarily with treason, intelligence with the enemy, and other such crimes. In sociological terms, the subject of the deportation of the Jews was generally taboo at the time.[14] For non-Jewish French, amnesia was the most comfortable mental state to adopt—an amnesia beautifully described in Michel Tournier's autobiography.[15] And for the Jews themselves, reintegration into French society was the order of the day. Moreover, few wished to seek justice from a legal system and a police force that had been involved in their deportation a few short years before. These factors, of course, help explain the High Court's hurried and remarkably uncritical response to Bousquet's account of his role in negotiating and carrying out the roundup of the Jews.

If the Court showed leniency to Bousquet in questioning him about his role in the Final Solution, this was part of a broader, benevolent, and indeed generally indulgent attitude on the part of the Court that shocked many of those who witnessed the trial, especially journalists. Vichy's "pin-up boy," as *France-Soir* labeled him, dominated the proceedings through a combination of eloquence and arrogance. In the pages of *Combat* the setting was likened to that of a schoolmaster giving lessons to children.[16] Regally attired and seated at a desk befitting a minister, Bousquet lectured the jurors arrayed in their *pupitres*, or student desks. At the end of the trial, when the Court's attitude was made abundantly clear in the leniency of its sentence—five years of *dégradation nationale* ("national shame," involving the loss of one's civil rights) suspended immediately for acts of resistance—the bitterness felt by many was expressed by journalists who had been present. Writing in *Libération*, Madeleine Jacob remarked caustically, "One minute of national degradation for Bousquet. Resistance credentials come very cheap this year."[17] The headline in *L'Humanité* announced: "The Resistance Flaunted." Another commentator remarked: "The Republic showed herself to be 'a very good girl' this year. I say that so as not to say something else."[18]

In looking into possible political motives for the Court's leniency in dealing with Bousquet, it is easy to single out the presence on the jury of the aforementioned Jean Baylet. But it is important to note as well the influence of Bousquet's other friends and acquaintances, some very much indebted to him, who also made their presence felt in one form or another. For example, members of Mitterrand's Resistance organization of former prisoners of war testified on Bousquet's behalf. Although he did not intervene in the proceedings, Queuille paid close attention to Bousquet's fate, since Bousquet had apparently done him the great service during the Occupation of warning him of his imminent arrest, thus allowing him to flee.[19] Members of the Court were undoubtedly aware of Queuille's interest in the case.

Political cronyism was not the sole political factor that softened the Court's attitude toward Bousquet. Among the jurors and magistrates Communists were no longer present, the Communist Party having decided that the High Court was too lenient in its treatment of collaborators. Justice, they believed, could no longer be served.[20] Since Bousquet had apparently been ruthless in his pursuit of Communists during the Occupation, this could only be to his advantage.[21] Moreover, anti-Communist sentiment among many members of the Court cast Bousquet in a more sympathetic light.

At the same time, hostility toward Vichy was at a rather low ebb. Madeleine Jacob noted that one of the jurors proudly wore his Francisque—the highest honor Vichy conferred—on his lapel, and Pascale Froment affirms that the Court frequently used stationery whose original letterhead, "État Français," was marked through and "République française" written in.[22] As many commentators have remarked, the general sentiment at the time was to put the recent past behind.

In turning, finally, to the actual Court proceedings and specifically those portions dealing with Bousquet's role in the Final Solution, several things are immediately apparent. The first is that virtually the entire discussion is orchestrated and carried out by Bousquet himself. Other than the reading into the record of a few telegrams signed by Bousquet, the remainder of the discussion consists almost entirely of Bousquet's version of events—in effect, Bousquet's counterhistory. Apart from questions from the president of the Court at the outset concerning the meaning of Bousquet's signature on the telegrams mentioned earlier, *no* questions are asked at the conclusion of Bousquet's testimony either by the prosecutor or by members of the jury. Bousquet's version of events stands as fact. The only additional statement made before the Court is adjourned for the day is the reading of a letter from Bousquet to Helmut Knochen, head of German security in France, in which Bouquet affirms that for the French police and for the French administration "the fact of being Jewish does not constitute a presumption of responsibility either in political matters or in common law. Nor can it be viewed as adding to this responsibility, when a Jew is pursued, in the application of our penal legislation, for a crime or other offense." No mention is made, of course, of Vichy's own anti-Jewish statutes, either in Bousquet's letter or by those listening in Court. Read by Bousquet's attorney, Maurice Ribet, the letter constitutes, in Ribet's view, proof of Bousquet's courage, given that it was written one month before Bousquet's departure from his post at Vichy in November 1943. Ribet's assessment goes unchallenged, and the session ends on a clearly upbeat note for the defense. Bousquet even promises not to call witnesses who could testify concerning his role as chief of Vichy police "so that the debates can be accelerated." No one suggests, as would Laurent Greilsamer in *Le Monde* the day after Bousquet's murder, that Bousquet was in fact belatedly covering his tracks in anticipation of a potential German defeat in writing the letter.[23] His previous actions as head of police certainly support Greilsamer's view, since Bousquet had already helped send 60,000 Jews to their deaths by the time he left his post. By contrast, Bousquet's supposedly more fanatical successor, Joseph Darnand, managed to deport "only" 15,000 Jews in 1944.

Crucial facts and grizzly statistics such as these, however, were not part of the testimony and deliberations of the High Court in 1949. As noted earlier, the portion of the trial dealing with the deportations opens with the president of the Court, Henri Noguères, asking Bousquet to comment on a number of telegrams dated summer and fall 1942, signed by the defendant. The subject matter and language of the telegrams are most revealing. In the first telegram cited, dated 22 August 1942, regional prefects are instructed to personally take charge of the roundups of foreign Jews and not to hesitate to "break down all resistance that you may encounter." The telegram goes on to instruct the prefects to proceed with the severest of measures, including the use of "sizeable detachments of police," to "liberate" their territories from the presence of foreign Jews. A subsequent telegram, dated 30 August, calls the prefects' attention to the disparity between the number of foreign Jews known to be in particular regions and the number arrested. To overcome this disparity, the prefects are instructed to use all police and gendarmerie personnel available to carry out identity checks, roundups, and searches of residences wherever necessary. Those arrested, the telegram concludes, will be sent to the Rivesaltes concentration camp and then transferred by "subsequent convoys." Another telegram, dated 11 September, informs the prefects that certain police commissioners are known to be distributing certificates of nonappurtenance to the Jewish race to potential detainees, clearly with the intention of helping them avoid arrest. These certificates, the telegram warns, can only be distributed by the Commissariat Général aux Questions Juives (CGQJ), or Commissariat-general for Jewish Affairs.

What is fascinating about the discussion of these telegrams following their being read into the record is that their content, and the terrible and obvious implications of the events they refer to, are not even addressed in the exchanges that ensue. Bousquet quickly diverts the Court's attention by focusing on technicalities: he did not sign them, he states, but simply "certified" or "countersigned" them—the French verb he uses is *viser*. He is thus simply a passive cog in the massive machinery of state. In other instances, Bousquet explains that although he was obliged to transmit instructions, he was able to introduce coded formula into these instructions, which, he implies, allowed him to intervene to protect those menaced by these instructions. Thus Bousquet claims that "Could you speak to me about . . . " or "Could you see if . . . " really meant "Could you do nothing until I am fully apprised of the situation." After explaining the "real" meanings of these codes and the innocuous signification of the presence of his "countersignature" on the telegrams, Bousquet affirms that "if it gave him pleasure," he could bring to the Court hundreds and hundreds of Jews, French and foreign, who could testify to his having protected them from danger.

Equipped with 20/20 hindsight, it is easy to be appalled at the blatant speciousness of the details of Bousquet's self-exculpating narrative and the lack of even the slightest protest from the Court. But what is even more troubling is the fact that following testimony such as this, Bousquet's subsequent account of his protracted dealings with the Germans on the deportations also goes unchallenged. According to this account, at every turn Bousquet's actions in effect countered the German plan for France which, he argued, was only entirely divulged following the war during the Nuremburg trials. The particulars of the plan were, according to Bousquet, to prepare public opinion; break down, if necessary, the resistance of the French government and the police; infiltrate the French police; and support the CGQJ and Darquier de Pellepoix.

Regardless of the accuracy of Bousquet's assessment of the German plan, on all four counts his claims are preposterous. On the first point, the preparation of public opinion, Bousquet's efforts only assisted Nazi designs, since the use of French police for the roundups in 1942 and 1943 allowed the occupier to avoid the onus of being seen rounding up and deporting innocent and helpless human beings. As to breaking down the resistance of the French government and police, the Germans could have had no better ally than Bousquet, who, as we shall see, secured the active support of the entire French police force in carrying out German aims both in the case of the roundup of Jews and in the struggle against Vichy and Germany's "common enemies." This is the spirit and intent of the infamous Bousquet-Oberg Accords of late summer 1942.[24]

As to the third German objective, the infiltration of the French police, other testimony at the trial suggests that Bousquet was most helpful to the Germans here as well. In the context of what was referred to as the "mission Desloges," testimony confirmed that Bousquet had helped the Nazis infiltrate and destroy Resistance communications networks by providing them with false French identity papers and allowing them to use official police radio communications in relaying information to Germany.[25] French police were also assigned to assist the Germans in their endeavors. Even if episodes such as this had not occurred, it is hard to imagine why such infiltration would even make much of a difference, given the practical and even ideological alliance between the two police forces established at the behest of Bousquet.

In turning to the final Nazi objective as defined by Bousquet, the support of Darquier de Pellepoix and the CGQJ, the defendant is explicit in his claim of having weakened Darquier and his agency by suppressing the anti-Jewish police and marginalizing the CGQJ in detaching it from the ministry of the interior. Although the statement contains inaccuracies, the implied motive—the frustration of Nazi aims—is misleading in the extreme. Bousquet wanted full power over all French police forces and to achieve this, he needed to weaken Darquier. But as to stymieing the CGQJ in its murderous *chasse aux juifs*, Court testimony already confirmed Bousquet's complicity. In the telegram of 11 September cited earlier, far from undermining the authority of the CGQJ, Bousquet reconfirms it in writing to his prefects in stressing that the CGQJ alone, not police officers, has the right to issue certificates of nonappurtenance to the Jewish race.

In his testimony Bousquet also discusses at great length two other issues that would have proven crucial had he been tried for crimes against humanity in the 1990s. These are his personal dealings and negotiations with the Germans and the question of his own attitudes toward the Jews. Here again, distortions abound. Rather than admit to his central and indeed pivotal role in negotiating and organizing the deportations or to his cordial and frequently warm relations with the Germans, Bousquet diminishes his function and powers and often professes ignorance as to what was occurring. When asked, for example, why he did not intervene at various stages of the process where he might have been able to improve the situation, Bousquet states helplessly: "It was the law. I could not have done otherwise." In discussing his initial contacts with the Germans over the issue of the Final Solution, Bousquet presents himself as being introduced into the game late, a game in which the hands were already dealt by the Germans and Darquier. His first official contacts with these figures, he claims, were at the behest of Pierre Laval, who sent him to Paris to "see what was going to happen."

Throughout his testimony Bousquet asserts that his relations with the Germans were uniformly hostile and that he opposed them at every turn. In an unpleasant meeting with Theodor Danneker, in which the German representative claimed to be deporting Jews with the "humane" end in view of providing them with their own state, Bousquet affirms that he exposed Nazi hypocrisy by suggesting that if humaneness was the German intent, then perhaps the Red Cross should be placed in charge of the deportations. Bousquet goes on to claim that he offered to secure the participation of the Red Cross in the process, an offer declined or ignored by his German interlocutor.

But it is in negotiating the French role in the actual roundup of the Jews that, according to Bousquet, the Germans were at their worst. Claiming that he initially opposed all the roundups of French and foreign Jews alike, Bousquet states that Nazi representatives then resorted to "frightful and abominable blackmail." Thus Bousquet asserts that Danneker informed him, "If, very quickly, you do not hand over German Jews in the Unoccupied Zone, we will arrest French Jews in the Occupied Zone." Faced with this ultimatum, Bousquet asserts, his hands were tied.

As the historical record shows, the vast majority of Bousquet's testimony is sheer fantasy. Despite his claims of having been a hostile and persistent opponent of the Nazis and their plans, Bousquet in fact curried favor with them and, almost without reservation, supported Nazi intentions from the outset. Karl Oberg, head of the ss in France, described Bousquet as a "precious collaborator" and, at the moment of the Liberation in 1944, sent two of his personal cars to transport "his friend" Bousquet, his family, and their belongings to Germany. Once there, the family resided in a villa that had formerly housed Mussolini's foreign minister, Count Graciano Ciano.

If in his testimony Bousquet misrepresented the spirit of his personal dealings with the Nazis, such distortions pale in comparison with the extent to which he deceived the Court on the subject of his negotiations with the Nazis concerning the deportations of the Jews, as well as the real consequences of those negotiations. The roundups of the Vélodrome d'Hiver in July 1942 in which some 13,000 people were arrested and deported are completely elided. So, too, are the roundups of the Old Port area in Marseilles in January 1943.[26] There is, moreover, no mention of the fact that when Catholic cardinals and bishops protested the inhumanity of the summer 1942 roundups, Bousquet had the ingenious idea of threatening to eliminate state subventions to parochial schools in order to silence them.[27] But perhaps the biggest lacuna, and the one that would eventually make possible a trial for crimes against humanity, was any reference to or testimony concerning a meeting between German representatives and Bousquet, the sole French representative present, on 2 July 1942. It was the German minutes of this meeting, not included in the 1949 criminal dossier, that provided the most damaging evidence against Bousquet in the 1990s.[28]

What the account of the meeting confirms first of all is that Bousquet never sought to protect foreign Jews interned or hiding in France. In fact, he readily volunteered French police to carry out the arrests in the Unoccupied Zone, a task that, as Robert Paxton and others have argued, would have been impossible for the Germans to handle alone.[29] The sticking point in the negotiations was the implementation of similar operations in the Occupied Zone. For the sake of appearances, the Germans wished to avoid carrying out the arrests, and when Oberg insisted that Hitler himself would be upset if the operation was not handled by the French, Bousquet acquiesced. The French police under his authority would handle the roundups of foreign Jews throughout France. The next day, the agreement was ratified at Vichy.

In his statements before the High Court, Bousquet claimed that he was blackmailed into deporting foreign Jews, and he implies that as a result, French Jews were spared. Documents from the time suggest, however, that the Germans never really disguised their intention to eventually deport French Jews and that Bousquet was fully aware of this. Moreover, Bousquet would later claim that he was unaware of the fate of the deportees, an assertion contested by Robert Paxton.[30] Finally, and perhaps most damning, is the fact that once the deportations were under way, Bousquet lifted restrictions imposed by the Germans themselves concerning the deportation of very young children and old people. The result was the deportation of children sent alone in cattle cars after their parents had already been deported and exterminated in Auschwitz. Needless to say, no testimony along these lines was heard by the Court in 1949. When the final draft of the indictment for crimes against humanity was completed just before Bousquet's murder, telegrams concerning this action were cited along with the German record of the 2 July 1942 meeting.

If, with the help of historical documents, it is possible to dismantle Bousquet's testimony concerning his negotiations with the Germans and fill in the holes in his account of what actually occurred once the Final Solution was under way in France, understanding his motives and his attitudes toward the Jews is much more difficult to sort out. During the interrogation leading up to the 1949 trial, Bousquet stated unequivocally, "For me, during the Occupation, there was not and could never be a 'Jewish problem.' I am not and was not an anti-Semite." As in so many other instances, the Court and its representatives took Bousquet at his word. Many historians have in fact echoed this view and attributed his actions to motives other than racial hatred. Robert Paxton, for one, sees Bousquet as "a functionary, a bureaucrat, who was primarily interested in the continuity of the French state." He was, Paxton continues, "perhaps the purest example of the phenomenon so characteristic of Vichy called *collaboration d'état*—i.e., cooperation with the Germans for reasons of state as distinguished from collaboration for reasons of ideological sympathy."[31] What Bousquet sought to achieve in exchange for his cooperation was increased power and autonomy for French police in both zones. He sought more training schools, more powerful arms, and more men. But any concessions he obtained from the Germans ultimately proved illusory and in fact meaningless. Codified in the Bousquet-Oberg Accords, what the negotiations ultimately accomplished was, as Philippe Burrin has noted, simply the establishment of a new level of ideological complicity—henceforth Nazi police and French police would fight together against their "common enemies."[32]

Before we accept too quickly the notion that Bousquet was simply a zealous technocrat whose maneuverings ultimately came to naught, however, it would perhaps be wise to look more closely at perceptions of the man and his motives. It is here, in fact, that a more complex and contradictory picture emerges, one that might well have been clarified by a second trial. In his *Prison Journal*, Edouard Daladier describes a visit from Bousquet to his cell at Bourassol on 16 September 1942. Daladier describes Bousquet as a man both "intelligent and kind" who served the Vichy government out of a firm conviction that German might would eventually win out.[33] Unlike most of the French (in his opinion), Bousquet saw himself as a clear-sighted pragmatist motivated by a keen awareness of historical realities. The impression we are left with is to a tangible degree that of the Sartrean collaborator, the self-deluding "realist" who mistakes treason for a tough-minded acceptance of things as they are.

In his *Mémoires* Fernand de Brinon paints a different portrait of Bousquet—not as someone who deals with the Germans out of simple pragmatism but out of shared affinities. Brinon states that Bousquet, recognizing the increasing authority of the ss in the spring of 1942, had sought them out and expressed, on occasion, a genuine admiration for the ss and their "courage." Brinon concludes by remarking on the *warmth* of relations between Bousquet and the head of Reich central security, Reinhard Heydrich, a view that clearly does not coincide with Bousquet's description during the 1949 trial of testy negotiations with Heydrich. For Brinon, the two men were in fact quite similar. Brinon mentions as well the premature end of the burgeoning friendship between the two with the assassination of Heydrich by Czech resistance in May 1942.[34]

In other circumstances, Bousquet expressed a similar attraction for Italian fascism, this time to the Italian consul in Reims in 1941 while Bousquet was prefect of Champagne. According to the Italian consul, Bousquet on occasion praised the notion of a single-party system, without which the kind of authoritarian regime he longed for would not be possible. The Italian consul concluded that Bousquet's political conceptions were well adjusted in principle to an accord with the Axis.[35]

The expression of sentiments such as these suggests that another look at the issue of Bousquet's anti-Semitism is in order. In one of the most chilling evocations of Bousquet during his tenure as head of Vichy police, Joseph Barthélemy in his memoirs describes Bousquet as an *arriviste* pretty boy and dandy who took an infantile pleasure in discussing the number of people he had had arrested, as if they were so many hunting trophies.[36] That the majority of those arrested were Jews goes without saying.[37] In other memoirs, such as those of the Protestant pastor Marc Boegner who went to see Bousquet to protest the deportations, Bousquet is reported to have said, "Whatever the outcome of the war, the Jewish problem will have to be resolved." He went on to assert that he himself was only interested in French Jews but that even these would be subject to "strict obligations" and "limited rights."[38] Comments such as this would lend credence to the claim made by Serge Klarsfeld after Bousquet's murder that Bousquet was in fact an anti-Semite and a xenophobe.[39]

Conflicting testimonies concerning Bousquet the individual and contradictory theories proposed to account for why he played the role he did in implementing the Final Solution in France suggest that on this score as well, a second trial could have been illuminating. Following the trial of Paul Touvier in the spring of 1994, most historians concluded that little new in historical terms had been disclosed and that the issue of Vichy's status in legal terms was not really resolved. But what had emerged was a much clearer understanding of Touvier the individual. No "French Schindler" as his lawyer claimed, no Christian martyr or French patriot unjustly persecuted, Touvier revealed himself through slips of the tongue, lies exposed, and memory lapses to have been nothing more than a vicious anti-Semite with no remorse and no greater wisdom gleaned from fifty years on the run. Similarly, during Papon's trial, the accused expressed no remorse and gave proof of the same bureaucratic zeal and arrogance that had paved the way to his actions and successes during—and after—the war.

So what could a second trial of René Bousquet have accomplished? An optimistic view of what might have occurred is, first of all, that Bousquet's version of events would have been put to rest historically *and* legally. It was, after all, this version of events, this counterhistory, that the High Court accepted *as history* in delivering its verdict in 1949. A second trial might also have shed a definitive light on Bousquet the individual, much as the trials of Touvier and Papon, despite their numerous shortcomings, afforded clearer insights into the respective personalities and politics of the accused. Because those involved in the Final Solution often appear, ultimately, as little more than faceless, passive cogs in a huge, inhuman machine, a better understanding of René Bousquet, his motives, attitudes, and sentiments could have proven valuable and instructive. It would also have coincided with a relatively recent trend in coming to terms with the Holocaust in giving a real, human face to the perpetrators, evident in works such as Christopher Browning's *Ordinary Men*, Raul Hilberg's *Perpetrators, Victims, Bystanders*, Judith Miller's *One, by One, by One*, and Daniel Goldhagen's spectacularly successful *Hitler's Willing Executioners*.

But this is perhaps putting too optimistic a spin on the trial of René Bousquet that never was. It is also possible that the trial of the former chief of police under Vichy, even more than that of his subordinate in Bordeaux, Maurice Papon, would have become bogged down in polemics about the value and meaning of such belated trials for crimes against humanity. In the case of the Papon trial, Nicolas Weill has argued that the facts of the case against Papon simply "disappeared" under the weight of ubiquitous dismissals of the trial or inflated interpretations of its function as "a vast psychodrama where the Providential State is the only real target."[40] Given the symbolic, historical, and legal magnitude of a trial of Bousquet in the 1990s, it is entirely plausible that the rectification of history vis-à-vis Bousquet's wartime record—a counterhistory to his own counterhistory—would simply have been submerged under the weight of similar grandiose interpretations, debates in the media, memory militancy, and so on.

There is one final danger that might also have derailed the trial of René Bousquet. As noted earlier and as will be discussed in detail in chapter 9, even before it got fully under way, the Papon trial was sidetracked by its delving into the role of the accused as prefect of Paris police in 1961 and in the brutal suppression of Algerian protesters. In effect, excavating the troubled Vichy past unearthed *another* past, also with potentially explosive consequences to the national psyche today—France's colonial past. Among Bousquet's postwar activities were lucrative stints on the board of directors of the Bank of Indochina, the Indo-Suez Bank, and the Indo-Chinese Water and Electric Company, as well as several other powerful positions in the Far East. Would the issue of colonization and its abuses (albeit in Indochina) have surfaced in the trial of Bousquet and conflated and confused two pasts, as they did in the Papon trial?

There is, of course, no way to answer this question, nor is it possible to know if a trial of René Bousquet in the 1990s would have served the interests of justice and history in relation to the Vichy past alone. Without the trial, what we are left with is something of an enigma: Who, after all, was René Bousquet? The final images in the public mind of the prewar government functionary, Vichy police chief, and postwar entrepreneur are as infelicitous as they are crassly spectacular. From Mitterrand's ludicrous portrait of an honorable man of real stature, to Christian Didier's demonically evil murder victim in an overblown melodrama, to, most recently, a cardboard character in a political potboiler, Bousquet becomes increasingly fictitious and intangible and not, sadly, the reverse.[41] In this sense at least, René Bousquet, like many of Patrick Modiano's shadowy figures from the Dark Years, may, after all, have made his getaway.

2 : History as Counterhistory

Modiano and the Occupation

In 1997 the popular and critically acclaimed writer and novelist Patrick Modiano published his twenty-seventh book, *Dora Bruder*, a brief, often moving account of Modiano's attempt to trace the destiny of a young Jewish girl living in Paris at the outset of the Occupation. Initially interested in Bruder after discovering a missing persons announcement dating from December 1941 and placed in the newspaper *Paris Soir* by her parents, Modiano discovers that some time before the placing of the newspaper announcement, the girl had mysteriously fled the Catholic school where she was safely hidden away, only to be arrested and then deported to Auschwitz several months later.

As the narrative unfolds, Modiano also reveals details of his own family and background, including his relationship with his father, whose abusive treatment and final abandonment of his son contributed greatly to the writer's profound sense of rootlessness and to his fascination/obsession with the Occupation. Like other Jews of his generation, Modiano's father, in his son's view, had been indelibly marked by the horrors of French and Vichy anti-Semitism, especially the implementation of the Final Solution in France. Rather than despise his father for abandoning him, however, Modiano's tendency, especially in *Dora Bruder*, is to sympathize, indeed, to empathize with him and all those among his contemporaries who suffered so terribly simply for being born Jewish. For the writer, it was this generation that, "just before my birth, had exhausted every conceivable form of pain and suffering in order to permit us [Modiano's generation] to suffer only small sorrows."[1] Modiano shares a deep and binding tragic solidarity with this generation, so much so that he tends to imagine their community of suffering in physically proximate terms. He describes his father's arrest and transportation in a paddy wagon in which his father notices a young girl of Dora's age, and Modiano is quick to conclude that this is perhaps Dora. When this proves not to be the case, the writer explains his urge to link his father and the wayward teenager in the following terms: "Perhaps I wanted them to cross paths, my father and her, in this winter of 1942. As different as they were, one from the other, they had both been classified in the same category of outcasts."[2]

But perhaps the ultimate gesture of sympathy, or empathy, on the part of the writer for his father and those who shared his destiny is, as Modiano reveals in *Dora Bruder*, that his first novel, *La Place de l'étoile*, was an act of defiance and indeed retaliation against "all those people whose insults wounded me because of my father." The people in question were the French anti-Semites who, during the Occupation, had written books condemning the Jews, books Modiano's father had purchased apparently to understand "what they reproached him with." On the "terrain of French prose," Modiano affirms, he had wanted "to stick it to them once and for all" ("leur river une bonne fois pour toutes leur clou"), but he had later come to understand the "childish naïvete" of his own gesture: "[M]ost of these authors had disappeared, having been shot or exiled, or had become senile and died of old age. Yes, unfortunately, I came too late."[3]

Of all French writers and novelists born in the postwar years, Patrick Modiano is certainly the best known of those who have devoted their writing to the evocation of the troubled memory of the

Dark Years and to assessing the impact of Vichy's afterlife on those who did not experience the Occupation directly. In the 1970s Modiano's early works helped to launch and define the *mode rétro* (to be discussed in detail in the next chapter), and in the 1980s and 1990s his novels continued to hover obsessively around the period, while, for the most part, dealing less directly with it. What makes *Dora Bruder* in particular so fascinating is, first, that it appears to be a kind of memoir or historical investigation rather than a work of fiction, as are the vast majority of Modiano's other works, and second, that it reengages directly, and indeed virtually exclusively, with the Occupation period and specifically the horror of the Final Solution and the deportation of the Jews. In this sense, in the broader cultural context, *Dora Bruder* is reflective of what Conan and Rousso have described as the "judeo-centrism" of the Vichy Syndrome in the 1990s.

But these apparent differences between *Dora Bruder* and Modiano's earlier works should not, on the one hand, obscure profound similarities and *continuities* between the 1997 book and its predecessors nor, on the other hand, should it lead one to conclude that the apparent distinctiveness of *Dora Bruder* means that it marks a new and perhaps definitive stage in Modiano's meditations on and representation of the legacy of the Dark Years in postwar France, especially its relation to the substance and meaning of history itself. First, as concerns the distinctiveness or perhaps uniqueness of *Dora Bruder,* Colin Nettelbeck points out that Modiano's *Remise de peine*, published in 1988, was also a kind of memoir, in this case about his childhood and his brother Rudy; only later did Modiano designate the work a novel. Moreover, the title *Dora Bruder*, given by Modiano as the name of a real person, is itself somewhat suspicious because, as Nettelbeck also points out, the name "Dora" is anagrammatically "adore," while "Bruder" is German for "brother." Together, the two words cannot help but evoke the "adored (and deceased) brother" and in so doing, blur the boundary between historical fact and fiction that is so typical of Modiano's writing.[4]

Leaving aside questions concerning the historical existence of the girl Dora Bruder and the book's status as historical investigation, memoir, or novel—specific answers to which may never be forthcoming—the fact remains that, as Nettelbeck affirms, *Dora Bruder* deploys "the same thematic material and the same literary strategies that he [Modiano] uses in his narrative fiction."[5] Foremost among these is the blurring of the boundaries between (historical) reality and fiction evident, most obviously, in the status of "Dora Bruder." Also prominent is what might be described as the conflation of historical epochs, so many superimposed geological or archaeological beds whose many traces can be detected in the present. Behind the facade of present-day Paris, for example, lurks the Paris of the Dark Years: "I have the impression of being alone in drawing the link between the Paris of those times [the Occupation] and the Paris of today. . . . Sometimes, the link becomes more tenuous [*s'amenuise*] and risks breaking, but on other evenings, the city of yesterday appears to me in furtive reflections behind the city of today."[6] But the shadowy presence of Occupied Paris, hidden most often and for most people beneath a "bed [couche] of amnesia," does not serve to orient the writer by providing a point of historical reference. Instead it *disorients* him, as if, in discovering this past through memory, Modiano finds himself "on the edge of a magnetic field, without a compass to capture its waves."[7]

The Occupation is not the only past that emerges or, in some ways, merges into the present in *Dora Bruder*. In pursuing the traces of the deported girl in the streets and neighborhoods of Paris, Modiano finds himself confronted with other pasts, other troubled times in history, which his memory calls up but fails to integrate into any coherent vision or understanding of what has gone before. For example, he recalls "the Boulevard Barbès and the Boulevard Ornano, deserted, on a sunny Sunday afternoon in May 1958. On each corner were groups of Mobile Guards, because of the events in Algeria."[8] Here, as in so many other manifestations of Vichy's afterlife in the 1980s and 1990s, from the Barbie trial to the trial of Maurice Papon, efforts to come to terms with the memory and legacy of the Dark Years—whether in fiction or in real historical events—are linked to, and somehow must pass through, the equally troubling memory of the Algerian War.

History as Counterhistory

In *Dora Bruder* especially, Modiano is at pains to describe the role, indeed the privileged function, of the writer, who possesses the gift of clairvoyance, allowing him or her "brief intuitions 'concerning past and future events.' "[9] But the writer is also to a very real degree the one who *preserves* the past—and the individuals belonging to that past— through the act of writing it: "If I wasn't there to preserve them in writing, there would be no more traces of this unknown woman [Dora], or of my father, in a paddy wagon in February 1942, on the Champ-Élysées. There would only be persons—dead or alive—who one places in the category of unidentified individuals."[10]

If in *Dora Bruder* Modiano has made progress in articulating the function of the writer, the repetition of the "thematic material" and "narrative strategies," as Nettelbeck labels them, the unresolved status of the Dark Years and of history itself caught in vortex where fiction and reality overlap, all these elements suggest that returning to the origins of Modiano's writing, to his *literary* past, might prove helpful in integrating the apparently disparate features of his vision and his work. More important for the purposes of this study, they should contribute to our understanding of why the memories of the Dark Years remain obsessive and scandalous for a writer who did not experience them. Moreover, this is not a subject of literary interest alone. For thirty years Modiano's literary works have contributed greatly to shaping France's imagination and understanding of its Vichy past, and I will argue that Modiano's nihilistic vision of history, glimpsed through the prism of the Occupation, functions as a kind of counterhistory that undermines any effort to come to terms with the Dark Years and put their memory to rest. The proof, so to speak, is in Modiano's own inability to move on.

Where to begin? Modiano's first three novels, *La Place de l'étoile*, *La Ronde de nuit*, and *Les Boulevards de ceinture* make up what is often called Modiano's Occupation trilogy, and as such they provide the appropriate focus for our purposes here. Of the three, however, *La Place de l'étoile* had, as discussed above, a very specific origin in Modiano's desire to avenge himself on the anti-Semitic writers whose works contributed greatly to the wartime persecution of his father and other

Jews of his generation. As such, Modiano's first novel is less germane to a general understanding of Modiano's vision of the Occupation and of history, and so it is to a consideration of the second and third novels of the Occupation trilogy, especially the implications of their juxtaposition, to which I shall now turn.

Shortly before vanishing into the night at the end of *La Ronde de nuit*, Swing Troubadour, the novel's narrator and protagonist, stares into a mirror in the hope that the reflection he finds there will provide him with the reassuring image of his authentic self. What he discovers instead is most disconcerting. The face gazing back at him is not his own but that of a youthful Marshal Philippe Pétain. As Troubadour continues to study the reflection, it undergoes a sudden metamorphosis and becomes the face of King Lear. Drawing back from the mirror, Troubadour completely loses his bearings. Objects disintegrate around him and he wonders if the piano music he has just heard was played by Le Khédive, one of his fellows in a band of French collaborators working for the Nazis, or a certain Mademoiselle Mylo d'Arcille, who, Swing tells us, died sixty years earlier.

The scene just described provides an appropriate climax to a novel in which time and space are distorted, reality—or, more precisely, history—and fiction overlap and dissolve into one another, and the identity of the narrator remains an enigma. Ostensibly a narrative whose action occurs exclusively during the Occupation, *La Ronde de nuit* incorporates the 1930s and especially the postwar period in such a fashion as to completely undermine any notion of chronology. For example, Troubadour discusses his own trial for collaboration while describing what will then be written about him and by whom. Such clairvoyance is astonishing, not only because he should have no way of knowing what the outcome of the war will be or what its aftermath will be like, but also because, as he himself confirms, he will be killed by his fellow French Gestapo members before the Occupation ends. The reader can only conclude that the two historical periods are somehow superimposed, that they occur simultaneously.

Temporal distortions in the novel are accompanied by a vertiginous juxtaposition of history and fiction. Troubadour, whose reflec-

History as Counterhistory

tions in the mirror include the head of the Vichy government and Shakespeare's tragic hero, is also the son of the 1930s swindler Sacha Stavisky. He works with a band of fictional collaborators and thugs headed by two men known as Le Khédive and Monsieur Philibert. But are these characters fictional? Nettelbeck among others has suggested that they are inspired by the infamous Bonny-Laffont gang of the Rue Lauriston, and Modiano's text is studded with details that confirm the connection. Like Henri Laffont, Le Khédive drives a white Bentley and seduces aristocratic women whom he encourages to participate in the gruesome interrogations at the Rue Lauriston.[11] He frequents Fabienne Jamet's brothel "One Two-Two," one of Paris's most famous hot spots before and during the Occupation and named after its address at 122, rue de Provence.[12] Monsieur Philibert is, like his historical double Pierre Bonny, a former Paris police inspector from the prewar period. In Le Khédive and Philibert's group are characters who go by such names as Darquier de Pellepoix and Pierre Constantini. Historically, Darquier was of course the notorious anti-Semite and head of Vichy's ministry of Jewish affairs during the later stages of the Occupation, while Constantini headed his own neo-Nazi group, the Ligue Française, and received his paychecks from the Germans.[13]

In such a witches' brew of history and fiction, past, present, and future, it is hardly surprising that Swing Troubadour should have a difficult time deciding exactly who and what he is. Is he saint or sinner, hero or traitor? Is he indeed Swing Troubadour or the mysterious Princesse de Lamballe? His confusion is at the same time moral, political, and gender related. Even his name, Swing, itself an alias, suggests a hopeless oscillation between labels that are all ultimately inadequate to self-definition.[14] Only one thing is certain—he is a double agent. As Swing Troubadour, he works for the French Gestapo, and as the Princesse de Lamballe he is an agent for the Resistance group Réseau des Chevaliers de l'Ombre (Network of the knights of the shadows). Even if he were to choose one group over the other, however, his choice would not resolve his dilemma, since both groups, for him at least, boil down to the same thing. The Resistance fighters may favor a rhetoric of heroism and the *collabos* a language of tough pragmatism, but these superficial distinctions only serve to mask the duplicity and ultimate corruption common to both groups. Like their pro-Nazi counterparts, the members of the Réseau des Chevaliers de l'Ombre most frequently travel under assumed names, and despite their aspirations to purity, demand the same "dirty work" of Swing—that he infiltrate and inform on the enemy. In short, an affiliation with either group or with *both groups* perpetuates Swing's own duplicity and intensifies his identity crisis. In the novel's final pages, Swing laments his definitive anonymity and concludes, "I do not exist."[15] He dismisses *collabos* and Resistance fighters alike as "maniacs" and leaves it to another maniac, Patrick Modiano perhaps, to decipher the riddle of his identity and assign a meaning to his story and that of all of those who lived through the "troubled period" of the Occupation. He authorizes his biographer to call him simply "a man" and wishes him "courage."

Readers of *La Ronde de nuit* will recognize in the novel as described here all the distinctive features of Modiano's writing from *La Place de l'étoile* to *Dora Bruder*: enigmatic central characters, dispossessed anonymous first-person narrators without personality, all bearing a striking resemblance to the fictional antiheroes Nathalie Sarraute described in 1950 as inhabiting the fiction of the "age of suspicion"[16]; a hallucinatory Occupation period, a vortex conflating fact and fiction and making a mockery of time and space; and finally, on the fringes, an author who is never either completely within his fiction or external to it but hovers over it as if it held the key to his own identity.[17] How all these elements fit together, how they generate one another, is the subject of a good deal of criticism written on Modiano and his work. According to Colin Nettelbeck and P. A. Hueston, memory itself holds the key. They argue that for Modiano, memory is a "force of dispersion," unpredictable in its durability, which "dissolves the boundaries between individual lives and the collectivity."[18] Thus the identity of the individual becomes fragmented, overlaps with other identities in time and space, and in the process, the barrier between fact and fiction crumbles. Modiano's statements in works such as *Livret de famille* certainly lend credence to this line of argument. He claims to possess, for example, a memory that predates his birth: "I was only twenty one years old, but my memory preceded my birth. I was sure, for example, of having lived in Paris during the Occupation because I could remember certain figures from the period as well as tiny, troubling details, things that no history book mentions."[19]

Just as memory allows Modiano to project his own existence indefinitely, to multiply his past selves, it also allows him to extend infinitely his network of fictional and historic relations. For example, at the end of *Livret de famille*, Modiano claims as his sister Corinne Luchaire, the collaborationist actress who died shortly after the war ended and who serves as a model for several of Modiano's fictional femmes fatales.

As a thread to guide the reader through the labyrinth of Modiano's fiction, however, memory ultimately proves to be inadequate because it fails to account for the novelist's fixation on the Occupation period. Given Modiano's background, a Jewish father persecuted during the war, and "a Flemish-speaking Belgian actress mother who spent the war in Paris working for a German film company," his fascination with the period is natural enough.[20] A number of critics argue that it is in fact Modiano's knowledge of the Occupation and his deep understanding of its aftermath that make him write the kind of fiction he does. Marc Lambron, for example, asserts that "Modiano's major intuition . . . is that the Occupation has not ended because the fathers have not reappeared."[21] So time has stopped, past and present overlap, and individuals have no identity because their roots have disappeared with their fathers. In a similar vein, Gerald Prince accounts for the dislocations in time, memory, and narrative voice in Modiano's texts in the following fashion: "Something happened. That's the story. The Occupation. Drancy. Auschwitz."[22]

But is the Occupation *all* that happened, and what exactly is it that the Dark Years between 1940 and 1944 represent to Modiano? Prince's statement, with its reference to Drancy and Auschwitz, would seem to suggest that the horrors perpetrated by the Nazis and their French minions have stripped away the moral and ethical foundations on which traditional definitions of "the human" have rested. No new definitions have been forthcoming, and Modiano's anonymous characters, and perhaps the writer along with them, wander vainly searching for their identities in an alien world in which time and history have stopped with the death camps.

There are two problems with this reading of Modiano, both of which are evident in *La Ronde de nuit*. First, the moral and ethical bankruptcy of the Occupation period cannot be accounted for entirely by calling up names such as Auschwitz and Drancy that evoke, respectively, the worst of Nazi and Vichy excesses. Swing Troubadour's experience, at least, is much more ambiguous. Both *collabos and* Resistance fighters demand that he compromise himself by working with others under false pretenses while arranging to betray them. In Troubadour's view, both groups ultimately fall under the sign of "Moral decomposition." The *collabos* may well be "rats who take over a town after the inhabitants have been decimated by the plague,"[23] but the *résistants* at the moment of their arrest are hardly presented in a more favorable light: "But little by little the varnish of their faces peels away, they lose their arrogance and the beautiful certainty that illuminated their faces is extinguished like the flame of a candle one blows out."[24] No Gaullist myth of a noble (or widespread) resistance to the Nazi occupant prevails here, since the Resistance fighters are ineffective and weak and their enemies are not the Germans but their fellow countrymen.

A more significant difficulty is that, as the text itself suggests, the Occupation does not mark the beginning of the decline but itself forms part of a larger process extending indefinitely into the past. Swing, for one, believes "the dice were already loaded" before the arrival of the Germans. As his personal quandary intensifies toward the end of *La Ronde de nuit*, he seeks answers to the riddle of his identity and the reasons for his moral collapse in reflecting not only on his own experiences during the Occupation, but on the shattered aspirations of his father, Sacha Stavisky, during the 1930s. Swing's ruminations remain inconclusive, however, as he is forced to flee Le Khédive and his cohorts at novel's end. The importance of the link between father and son is confirmed, but its significance remains obscure.

Similarly, the connection between the Occupation and the 1930s, specifically the turbulent events of 1933–34, is established, but Modiano fails to illuminate the connection in *La Ronde de nuit*. For the novelist, what do the activities and mysterious death of a swindler, the fall of the Chautemps government, and the riots of 6 February have to do with the Occupation? To find the answer, one must employ a favorite strategy of many of Modiano's characters, that is, to locate one's lost father. The search does not take long; Stavisky appears, albeit using an alias, in Modiano's next novel, *Les Boulevards de ceinture*.

On first reading, *Les Boulevards de ceinture* appears to be much less ambiguous in its treatment of moral decay and corruption during the Occupation period than its predecessor. Serge Alexandre, the novel's young narrator, sets out to find his father, who has disappeared some ten years earlier. He discovers him living under an assumed name, Baron Deyckecaire, and working with a group of collaborators who are for the most part professional journalists associated with the newspaper *C'est la vie*. Modiano informs the reader at the outset that these figures are entirely fictional, but this assertion is surely made tongue in cheek, since many of them are easily recognizable as prominent members of the collaborationist press or their associates. The editor of *C'est la vie* is Jean Muraille, who aspires to the position of head of the Paris Press Corporation. His daughter, Annie Muraille, is a famous movie starlet. The historical models for these two figures are undoubtedly Jean Luchaire, editor of *Les Nouveaux Temps*, and his daughter Corinne, alluded to earlier. In Muraille's circle are a certain Robert Lestandi, whose first name alone distinguishes him from the editor of the vicious anti-Semitic paper *Au Pilori*, Jean Lestandi, and Alain Gerbère, a clone of the editor of *Je suis partout*, Robert Brasillach.[25] The name "Gerbère" would itself appear to be a variation on the title of yet another pro-Nazi publication, *La Gerbe*, founded by Alphonse de Chateaubriant and funded by the Germans.[26]

Like Le Khédive's gang in *La Ronde de nuit*, the members of Muraille's circle are corrupt in every conceivable way. They steal, indulge in all forms of sexual debauchery, and are verbally and even physically abusive with outsiders as well as members of their own circle. The young narrator, Serge Alexandre, by and large an ingenue when he enters Muraille's circle, is himself eventually debased through his contact with the group. He begins to drink heavily and sleep with prostitutes while writing columns for *C'est la vie* whose titles, "Via Lesbos" and "Confessions of a Worldly Chauffeur," confirm his vocation of pornographer. Experiencing within himself the "crisis of values without precedent" that he finds all around him, Alexandre begins to lose sense of who he is.[27] He affirms that he has lost his identity papers. In a desperate attempt to reappropriate his past and his sense of self and in an effort to strike back at the individuals and the situation that have deprived him of these necessities, Alexandre kills a member of Muraille's circle and convinces his father to flee with him. Their escape is short-lived, however; they are captured by the Gestapo and led away to be executed at the end of the novel.

As the preceding remarks suggest, the moral framework of *Les Boulevards de ceinture* appears at first glance to be straightforward and unambiguous. The lesson, as it were, is clear. Political treason, collaborationism, and immorality are firmly and inextricably linked to one another. All those who come into contact with the collaborationist milieu, in this case innocents like Alexandre and his father, are contaminated, losing their morals, their sense of themselves, and even their lives. Since most Frenchmen were affected by the capitulations of the Vichy regime and the treachery of many of their fellows, the Occupation is a nightmare that refuses to go away.

But is this the moral of the tale? Alexandre, the cornerstone on which its moral edifice is constructed, turns out to be no ingenue after all. Historians of the Stavisky affair point out that Sacha Stavisky was prone to using aliases, among them Serge Alexandre, in reality his first and middle names. Indeed, as William Shirer noted years ago, when the arrest order for Stavisky was issued in 1933, it bore the name "Serge Alexandre."[28] Modiano's choice of names for his protagonist ultimately subverts the moral lesson that the plot structure of *Les Boulevards de ceinture* authorizes. Serge Alexandre cannot be corrupted because he already is corrupt. Thief, womanizer, confidence man,

History as Counterhistory

yes, but innocent, no. The cornerstone will not hold, and the edifice collapses.

If the novel's moral lesson is compromised by the ghost of Stavisky, what of its historical and political implications? The Occupation is not a unique and sudden catastrophe that brings history to a close and destroys the human, but it is itself a function of a larger past, of previous events that must be understood if its full significance is to be grasped. Through the intermediary of Alexandre, Modiano juxtaposes two scandals, one of the 1930s and the other of the 1940s, to draw conclusions about History itself. The result is most disheartening. Like his fictional namesake, the real Sacha Stavisky moved in what Eugen Weber describes as "that shadowy half world where fashionable people, crooks, adventurers and politicians mixed without asking one another many questions except about current credit."[29] His friends, or more precisely those who shared in and benefited from his schemes, included newspaper men such as Albert Dubarry, editor of the left-wing *La Volonté*, Jean Chiappe, head of the Paris police, and left-wing politicians such as the Bayonne deputy Joseph Garat and even the minister of colonies and former minister of justice, Albert Dalimier. All these men were caught up in the municipal bond scandal that eventually cost Stavisky his life, brought about the fall of the Radical Chautemps government, and led finally to the right-wing inspired riots of 6 February 1934.

But what exactly is the connection between the 1930s scandal and the Occupation? In essence, the periods turn out to be mirror images of each other, in which right and left in political terms are reversed but the reflection itself remains the same. That reflection is one of corruption, degradation, and brutality—a world in which the human, morality, and ethics have no place. The "mirroring of epochs," which according to Marc Lambron levels time and history from 1940 on in Modiano's novels, appears to extend back to the 1930s and perhaps beyond. In the final analysis, history collapses on itself, and its events and individuals have no substance or meaning.

This is why Modiano's characters are interchangeable in time and space, why they freely cross the boundary between history and fiction. The fictional protagonist of *Les Boulevards de ceinture* and the real Sacha Stavisky are both annihilated by the engine of History, which relentlessly flattens everything in its path. What is true for his characters, moreover, is true for the artist as well. Modiano hovers on the edge of his texts and intervenes in them in his own name and through his characters because he, too, is subject to the destruction of History and he, too, must seek his identity in the shattered world it leaves in its wake. His starting point is always the Occupation, as virtually all of his novels attest, because the Dark Years are the window through which he first glimpsed the void, through which he first heard the voice of History. It is Swing Troubadour, however, paraphrasing the wisdom of Macbeth, who best sums up its message: "The world [is] decidedly full of sound and fury. No importance."[30]

At the end of *Dora Bruder*, Modiano speculates on the final enigma of the Jewish girl who, during the Occupation, had run away from a Catholic boarding school to embark on a journey that would lead to her death in Auschwitz. Why had she done it? Typically, Modiano offers no definitive answers, other than to speculate that the act of running away is itself a form of suicide or, at least, a flight from time: "And it happens that at the end of the morning, the sky is light blue and nothing weighs on you. The hands on the clock in the Tuileries gardens are immobile forever. An ant never finishes crossing a patch of sunlight."[31]

But it is not simply time that weighs on Bruder, as the above passage implies, but the crushing burden of History itself, privileged access to whose meaning is provided by the experience of the Dark Years. Dora's secret, Modiano informs us, is all that is left to her, all that cannot be stolen by "the torturers, the regulations, the so-called authorities of the Occupation, the depot, the barracks, the camps, History, time—all that soils and destroys us."[32] Even the writer cannot retrieve it.

It is the spectator who creates cinema,
much more so than the reader does a book.
The spectator is the movie maker.
—*Marguerite Duras*

3 : Collaboration and Context

Louis Malle's *Lacombe Lucien* and the *Mode Rétro*

Of the major films dealing with the Occupation produced in post-Gaullist France, none has proven more controversial than *Lacombe Lucien*, Louis Malle's portrait of a wily peasant boy caught up in the worst excesses of collaborationism in southwestern France shortly before the Liberation. Hailed by both the right and the left after its initial release in January 1974—prominent leftist critics like Jean-Louis Bory praised it as "the first true film . . . about the Occupation," while *Le Figaro* and *Rivarol* lauded it, respectively, as "a beautiful film of high moral standing" and as "a work of great quality"—*Lacombe Lucien* soon fell on harder critical times.[1] Beginning around February of the same year, a series of lengthier assessments of the film, uniformly negative, began to appear in newspapers and reviews reflecting a broad range of political and ideological perspectives. In the extreme right-wing periodicals *Minute* and *Aspects de la France*, the film's young peasant protagonist was condemned for his lack of political idealism—an idealism, these reviews contended, that typified those Frenchmen who joined Vichy's Militia or chose to serve Hitler and the Nazi cause. Assessments on the left were equally hostile, if more subtle and wide ranging in their criticisms. These commentaries, in fact, deserve closer scrutiny because they provide significant insights into the *mode rétro*, the wave of nostalgia for the 1940s and the Occupation in particular that swept France in the mid-1970s and of which Malle's film is considered a prime example.[2] They also raise troubling questions concerning the accuracy and legitimacy of aesthetic judgments of the film. Finally, when considered in conjunction with more recent commentary, these assessments suggest that *Lacombe Lucien* and its critical reception can teach us more about postwar views of the Occupation and French self-perceptions since the war than about the history of the period itself. In effect, the history that the film purports to represent is overwritten by a critical discourse that imposes a *divergent* historical meaning on *Lacombe Lucien*, and it is the tension between Malle's "history" and the critics' "counter-history" that makes the film scandalous even up to the present time. So, in a sense, *Lacombe Lucien* is less a symptom of Rousso's Vichy Syndrome than its victim.

In several articles and interviews dealing with *Lacombe Lucien* appearing in the summer of 1974 in the pages of prestigious leftist reviews including *Les Temps modernes* and the *Cahiers du cinéma*, criticisms of Malle's film were inseparable from more ubiquitous condemnations of the *mode rétro*. Critics including Christian Zimmer and Pascal Bonitzer as well as leading intellectuals like Michel Foucault attacked Malle's film as symptomatic of a broader and dangerous malaise sweeping the nation in the wake of the recent election of Valéry Giscard d'Estaing as president. For these critics, the *mode rétro* represented not only a "snobbish fetishism of old things" but a "derision" or "false archeology of history."[3] What the *mode rétro* sought to accomplish, they believed, was a sinister rewriting of history, specifically the history of the Occupation, in order to challenge and indeed to undermine the image of heroic and widespread resistance to Nazism, an image nurtured by the recently defeated Gaullists: "Gone the *grand designs*: the Resistance was one, and so was Gaullism. . . . Gone also virtuous indignation, intransigence, fidelity."[4] In the place of this

Gaullist myth of resistance was substituted a more "realistic" image of the period in which the role of ideology and political commitment were downplayed and the choices and actions of individuals were attributed to the vagaries of chance or "fate" and "human nature" itself. A more accommodating attitude toward former collaborators and even the Nazis themselves was in the air. Christian Zimmer asserted: "[T]he hour has come to familiarize oneself, in the most affective sense of the term, with the ex-enemy, and books appear on Hitler—the man, not the politics, and the bookstores are now selling collections of *Signal*, the Nazi weekly for French readers."[5] The moral of this new version of the past, according to Zimmer, was that there were ultimately no heroes or villains, only everyday human beings who were the victims of circumstances, which is to say, of History itself. In this scenario, little if anything separated *résistant* from *collabo* in historical terms and, in any event, if the truth were really known about the period, one would be forced to admit that "the French people didn't give a damn about fascism."[6]

Whitewashed in this fashion, fascism, and Nazism in particular, could assume an erotic charge in that it constituted the expression of "obscure forces" and "buried 'instincts'" that slept in the souls of all human beings, criminals, "honest people" and victims alike.[7] The inevitable result of this line of reasoning, according to Pascal Bonitzer, was that fascism and human nature were conflated, and to deny the connection would be to deny falsely the existence of some of humankind's most basic (if darkest) impulses.

For Michel Foucault, the *mode rétro* eroticized power not only in works such as *Lacombe Lucien*, but in Liliana Cavani's *Night Porter*, where an ex-Nazi officer reasserts his sexual dominance over a former victim who is all too willing to go along with her tormentor. For Foucault, what was most disturbing about these representations of the eroticism of (fascist) power was that they found an echo in contemporary politics as practiced by Giscard: "It is certain that Giscard built his campaign in part not only on his physical presence but also on a certain eroticization of his person, of his elegance."[8]

By linking representations of Nazi eroticization of power in the cinema to Giscardian politics of the mid-1970s, Foucault underscored the degree to which the *mode rétro* derived from important changes in the French political landscape after the fall of Gaullism. French critics at the time, including Foucault, Bonitzer, and Zimmer, and more recently British critics like Alan Morris, have all viewed the *mode rétro* as embodying the bourgeoisie's effort to rid itself and the nation of a heroic image of resistance with which it felt uncomfortable and which failed to coincide with its own historic role during the Occupation.[9] At the same time, it supposedly represented the Pétainist, collaborationist right's effort to "come out of the closet" and vindicate itself in the eyes of History, or more precisely, to rewrite its own history, after hiding behind Gaullism during the postwar period.[10] According to Foucault, the events of May 1968 lent a real urgency to this revisionism, since the student uprisings had brought home the fact that popular revolutionary upheaval was not something that took place only in other countries but something that could occur under the noses of the French ruling classes. In order to disarm the potential for popular struggle in advance, it became necessary to empty even the most controversial moments in the nation's history of their conflictual content:

> The struggles became not part of the present but part of the eventual future of our system. It was thus necessary to place them at a distance. How? Not by interpreting them directly, because this would expose them to all sorts of denials, but in proposing a historical interpretation of old popular struggles that took place among us, to show that in fact they [these struggles] never existed! Before 1968, it was "That won't come here because that kind of thing takes place elsewhere": now, it's "That won't come here because it never took place! And look, even something like the Resistance, about which many people have thought so much, look a little closer. . . . Nothing. Empty, it rings hollow!"[11]

Thus the Occupation, rather than being a period of grand ideological confrontations, popular struggles, and heroic endeavors, was transformed into a time when a few troublemakers caused ripples on the surface of the nation's well-being but failed to affect its depths.

Collaboration and Context

Given the critique of the *mode rétro* sketched out here, it is easy to see how discussions of *Lacombe Lucien* became inscribed and indeed subsumed in a broader polemic against Giscardism and its implications for French political and cultural practice. Malle's hero was considered the perfect example of an essentially apolitical, insignificant, and indeed mediocre individual who happens by chance to join up with the French Gestapo because he gets a flat tire on his bike and is caught after curfew by his future cohorts.[12] The fact that the young Lucien could just as easily have joined up with the Resistance is confirmed by the fact that, earlier in the film, he had already been turned away by the local Resistance leader and schoolteacher, Peyssac (whom he later betrays to the French Gestapo), before setting out on his ill-fated bicycle trip. Ideological distinctions between the two camps are lost on Lucien who, at various points in the film, naively asks who the Jews and the masons are, implying that he has no idea why they are persecuted and why they are "France's enemies."[13] Lacking a core of political beliefs that would bind him to his fellow French Gestapo members, Lucien remains with them because he enjoys an almost unlimited power that allows him to impose himself on the Horn family, wealthy Parisian Jews attempting to flee persecution and reach the Spanish border and safety. He enters the Horn household, treats the father disrespectfully and, on occasion, abusively, and seduces the daughter, France, who is unquestionably drawn to a man she should absolutely loathe. Lucien's animal magnetism apparently confirms his status as a prime example of the *mode rétro*'s disturbing emphasis on the link between (fascist) power and eroticism. Indeed, France Horn, Lucien's sexual partner, is entirely at his mercy throughout the film.

Condemned as a work fitting the broad parameters of the *mode rétro* as elaborated by Foucault and others, *Lacombe Lucien* became the target of related criticisms that also sought to tie the film to reactionary politics and aesthetics. In the leftist *Charlie Hebdo*, Delfeil de Ton blasted *Lacombe Lucien* as an attempt to "to make innocent those who furnished the victims of the Nazi organization" in presenting the young peasant as a fundamentally sympathetic and "normal" adolescent.[14] In an exchange with Malle in the pages of *L'Humanité dimanche*, the former Resistance leader René Andrieu argued that the film's lack of verisimilitude was confirmation of a reactionary apologetics. According to Andrieu, it was highly unlikely in historical terms that someone frustrated in their effort to join the Resistance would immediately swing to the other extreme and sign on with the Gestapo, or that a Jewish girl would voluntarily sleep with "a torturer for the Militia."[15] Andrieu also protested what he perceived to be a condescending portrait of peasants in the film as "crude, weak, greedy, [and] incapable of generosity."[16]

Rather than criticize *Lacombe Lucien*'s supposed lack of historical verisimilitude or its hostile characterization of the lower classes, Christian Zimmer dismissed the film in its entirety as a reactionary chef-d'oeuvre structured on the duality of formal perfection and a cynically pessimistic vision of human imperfection and corruptibility. The film's negative worldview, Zimmer continued, affirmed "the impossibility of changing man and the world," while its seamless purity of form made such a vision seem ineluctable.[17] In other words, the perfection of art confirmed the imperfection of humanity. History itself, as a force of change, was once again stripped of all meaning and significance.

In his own commentaries on *Lacombe Lucien* at the time of the film's succès de scandale, Malle generally failed to counter many of the charges against his film, and in several instances he in fact confirmed, perhaps inadvertently, the bases upon which these charges were made. Speaking with Andrieu in *L'Humanité dimanche* of the role of chance in Lucien's *engagement,* Malle stated that "without the flat tire nothing would have happened to him, he would have remained at the hospice." He also described Lucien as "extremely normal," thus, in a certain sense, legitimizing the latter's actions, no matter how repugnant, by making them appear part of the natural order of things.

Malle did challenge claims that *Lacombe Lucien* was riddled with historical inaccuracies and distortions, basing his responses in part on his and cowriter Patrick Modiano's knowledge of the period as well his own personal experience of the Occupation.[18] Responding to Andrieu's charge of the improbability of Lucien's political trajectory,

Malle noted that "there is a part of the population which does not possess a political conscience."[19] For such individuals, presumably, a radical shift of this sort would not seem particularly incongruous or inconsistent, and it is certainly borne out by historical examples in recent French history, especially around the time of the Occupation.[20] Moreover, in an interview with Gilles Jacob in *Positif*, Malle also emphasized that given the hardships and privations of the period, "[a lot of] people found themselves in the Militia because they simply had nothing to eat."[21] It was completely understandable, therefore, that "there was a little of everything in the Militia, people on the lam as well as minor provincial noblemen, workers as well as former members of fascist leagues."[22] Malle insisted on the authenticity of Hippolyte, the black member of the Gestapo group with whom Lucien becomes involved, noting that other "non-Aryans" such as Arabs were recruited into the French Gestapo by the infamous Bonny/Laffont gang near Limoges. (See the preceding chapter for their activities in Paris.) Finally, in response to Andrieu's charge that the France-Lucien liaison seemed highly improbable, Malle asserted that in Toulouse, Jewish girls were known to have slept with their enemies in order to save their families.[23]

Malle's comments in interviews given around the time of the release of *Lacombe Lucien* certainly help vindicate the film where charges of historical inaccuracy are concerned. Conversely, more recent remarks, particularly concerning recollections of his childhood and family life during the Occupation, lend themselves to serious misinterpretation, especially when the supposed "ideological underpinnings" of *Lacombe Lucien* are at issue. In *Louis Malle par Louis Malle*, a collection of reflections on his life and films published in 1978, Malle describes the bad faith and hypocrisy of his own wealthy bourgeois family in dealing with the history and memory of the Occupation: "My family, like many French people, had confidence in Pétain at least until 1942. Pétain was the great warrior, the hero of 1914, a person the bourgeoisie respected. When I was with the Jesuits in Paris in 1941, they made us sell in the streets, from shop to shop, portraits of the Marshal. . . . When I recall this episode, I anger my family! Like everybody, they have a selective memory. But at the time, they needed to reassure themselves."[24] In effect, Malle's commentary on his own family confirms a crucial motivation attributed to the *mode rétro* as defined by its critics in that it depicts a reactionary bourgeoisie eager to ignore its own dubious past and that would be receptive to and indeed likely to promote the deheroicized version of the Occupation presented in *Lacombe Lucien*, a film made, not coincidentally, by one of its own. Moreover, Malle's reflections on his own attitudes at the time are suggestive of the degree to which the family's conservatism had tainted his own views. Speaking of a local Resistance member with whom he and his schoolmates became familiar, Malle notes that "given our social origins, this resistance fighter was on the other side of the fence."[25]

Louis Malle par Louis Malle also deals at length with the director's rather amoral and apolitical adolescence, an adolescence concerned more with rebelling against parents and other authority figures than with coming to grips with the political realities of the day. It is this adolescence, in fact, upon which Malle sought to draw in developing the character of Lucien: "In working on *Lacombe Lucien*, I tried to recall what I felt at the time."[26] The crafty Quercy peasant, it would appear, is also the alter-ego of the coddled bourgeois, Malle himself. To the degree that Lucien is presented in a sympathetic light in the film, therefore, it could be argued that through its central character, *Lacombe Lucien* constitutes an apology for the decadence of the bourgeoisie.

My intent here is not to suggest that *Lacombe Lucien* does indeed embody the reactionary ideology attributed to the *mode rétro* or that, in making the film, Malle was complicitous with the historical revisionism attributed to his class. On the other hand, it could be argued, I believe, that Malle's comments on *Lacombe Lucien*, at least in *Louis Malle par Louis Malle*, suggest an inability on the filmmaker's part to separate his "family romance" from his conceptualization of the Occupation and his representation of it on film. For this reason, he remains blind (or perhaps indifferent) to charges that *Lacombe Lucien* embodies a reactionary and revisionist bourgeois ideology because the issues these charges raise are for him linked less to broad, impersonal ideological issues than to intensely personal and familial concerns. In fact, Malle does not exorcise his personal ghosts where the Occupation is concerned until 1987, with the making of *Au revoir les enfants*. In this film, which has proven much less controversial than its predecessor, Malle at last deals directly with his most significant memory of the war, the arrest by the Gestapo and deportation of a Jewish boy being hidden by priests in the Jesuit school Malle had attended. At the same time, he confronts the decadence and indifference of the bourgeoisie in the representation of the film's young protagonist, Julien Quentin's spoiled, superficial, and politically naive mother, and her son's quasi-incestuous attachment to her. Indeed, the introduction of the theme of incest personalizes *Au revoir les enfants* not only in relation to Malle's biography but in relation to his career as a filmmaker as well, since it recalls the principle theme of the 1971 film *Le Souffle au coeur*. In this sense *Le Souffle au coeur*, *Lacombe Lucien*, and *Au revoir les enfants* form a trilogy in which the troubled and conflated memory of family relations and childhood experiences during the Occupation are worked through and resolved over a period of almost twenty years. It is not surprising, therefore, that many of Malle's most astute and impersonal observations about *Lacombe Lucien* were made after the completion of *Au revoir les enfants*.[27]

The convergence of *Lacombe Lucien*'s critical reception and Malle's reading of his own experiences and background into the work do suggest that during the 1970s, the film became trapped in a cultural, historical, and political context that created a scandal around the film and ultimately distorted and foreclosed discussion of its qualities as a work of art. In his study of the *mode rétro*, Alan Morris notes that any number of works prior to Malle's film and to the fall of Gaullism had already blurred the distinction between collaboration and resistance and emphasized the role of chance, opportunism, or some other nonpolitical motive implicit in the choice of one over the other. These works include Marcel Aymé's novels *Uranus* and *Le Chemin des écoliers*, Jean Genet's *Pompes funèbres*, Jacques Laurent's *Le Petit canard*, Pierre de Boisdeffre's *Le Fins dernières*, and Roger Nimier's *Les Épées* and *Le Hussard bleu*. In Genet's work, the central character, like Lucien, joins one side simply because the other side turned him down. In *Le Petit Canard*, the hero fights the Nazis and is eventually killed for them, not out of ideological conviction but out of despair over losing his girl-friend. The young heroes of Nimier's novels are by and large equally ideologically uncommitted, and it is even possible that they helped inspire the character of Lucien. As Malle stated in an interview with Marc Dambre in 1988, Malle had decided to ask Nimier to collaborate with him in writing the script for the 1958 film *Ascenseur pour l'échafaud* because he "liked Nimier's novels very much."[28] Even Lucien's oppor-tunistic and juvenile amorality, or moral "idiocy," as one critic de-scribed it, had long since been on display in the maudlin, simple-minded, and real-life memoirs of the collaborationist actress Corinne Luchaire.[29] None of these works, however, has proven as controver-sial as Malle's film, in some cases because they simply lacked artistic merit, but for the most part because the climate of the times, domi-nated as they were by the myth of Resistance, simply made the revi-sionist message of these works fall on deaf ears.

If *Lacombe Lucien* has in fact been "freeze-framed" by the historical context in which it first appeared, it is important to examine both what has been "edited out," so to speak, and to examine the film's subsequent reception to determine if changing historical and political contexts have allowed the film to recuperate a certain autonomy as a work of art. Artistic autonomy is of course a dangerous and debatable proposition. In the case of *Lacombe Lucien*, however, it is an important and indeed crucial consideration because the evaluation of the film as a work of art has always been tied to its supposed ideological bent or how well or "correctly" it treats the historical period it purports to represent.[30] In other words, judgments of *Lacombe Lucien* have always been precisely that. Assessments of the film have either been "for" or "against," with no middle ground possible. The critic must either attack or defend it, and the film itself must be shown to reflect a specific ideology that determines plot as well as characterization.[31] There can be no room for *ambiguity*. The critic who accepts the film's ambiguities and willingly suspends judgment is guilty of a cowardly critical blindness and paralysis, and probably revisionist politics as well.[32] For example, to acknowledge the ambiguities of Lucien's character, to allow for both his cold brutality and his apparent capacity for love is to permit "the recuperation . . . of a bastard," while to embrace "the duality of human ambivalence," which, some argue, characterizes the vision of *Lacombe Lucien*, is to be seduced by the work's reactionary ideology.[33]

And yet, as many scenes confirm, the film is nothing if not ambiguous, both when important insights into the central characters are provided and when crucial moments in plot development occur. For example, Lucien's brutality, his potential for sadism, is strongly suggested in a number of scenes early in the film. In the opening segment Lucien kills a bird with his slingshot, apparently for the sheer pleasure of it. Later, he massacres rabbits with the cold precision of an executioner and kills chickens with the same dispassion. In a scene carefully placed just before the massacre of the rabbits, however, Lucien helps remove the carcass of a dead horse from the family barn. When the others leave to take a drink without so much as a second look at the horse, Lucien stays behind with the animal, clearly affected by its death. Which is the real Lucien? The issue, of course, becomes much more important later in the film, when Lucien's dealings with other human beings are at stake. Is the real Lucien the sadistic killer, the *collabo* who betrays, tortures, and in a scene remarkable for its exquisite cruelty, destroys the model ship of the Resistance doctor's son just to witness the latter's anguished incredulity, or is he the concerned but ineffectual adolescent who tries to lead Horn away when Horn, no longer able to tolerate a life of fear and degradation, essentially signs his own death warrant by showing up at the Hôtel des Grottes, the Gestapo headquarters? Finally, is the real Lucien the crude and thoughtless adolescent who foists himself on the Horn family, or is he the savior of France and the grandmother, whom he rescues from a German soldier and leads to a rustic and almost idyllic country retreat at the end of the film? Even this choice is not clear, because the film leaves the spectator in doubt as to whether Lucien *intentionally* decides to save France and the grandmother in killing the German soldier or kills the latter to get a gold watch he wanted.[34]

Any number of similar ambiguities and ambivalences can be cited in relation to other major characters and scenes. Despite the *mode rétro* critics' assumptions concerning a clear connection between eroticism and power in the film, the attraction between France and Lucien cannot be reduced to such abstract, totalizing concepts. Not only are Lucien's own feelings where France is concerned too complex, but so, too, are hers vis-à-vis Lucien. Nowhere is this more evident than near the end of the film, when France holds a rock over the head of the sleeping Lucien but cannot make up her mind whether or not to kill him. This episode occurs, moreover, when France and Lucien appear to be happily and unproblematically in love with each other during the "country idyll" at the end of the film, when political power, at least, is no longer an issue.

Ironically, *Lacombe Lucien* is *least* ambiguous in its portrayals of secondary characters whose function is precisely to represent particular political groups or viewpoints. Lucien's fellow Gestapo members, clearly adapted primarily from the characters in Modiano's *La Ronde de nuit* and *Boulevards de ceinture*, are unequivocally corrupt and malicious. They include the fanatical fascist and anti-Semite, Faure, who has Horn deported; the sleazy aristocrat, Jean-Bernard de Voisins; his cruel, superficial, and stupid actress girlfriend, Betty Beaulieu; and the alcoholic leader of the group, Tonin.[35] By contrast, the characters who represent the Resistance, the *instituteur* Peyssac and Professor Vaugeois, who is tricked into revealing his Resistance sympathies when Jean-Bernard pretends to be a wounded Resistance fighter in need of medical attention, are notable for their courage and dignity.

To the degree that the film takes a political stance, then, it would appear to be *pro-Resistance* and *anticollaborationist,* but this has been ignored by critics whose readings of the film's politics are predicated on condemnatory and occasionally faulty interpretations of the actions of the film's more central characters. To mention only one example, the character whom Malle himself considers to be the most "positive" in the film is Albert Horn, who, according to Malle, is notable for his "dignity" and "integrity."[36] But Naomi Greene, among other detractors of Horn, remarks first on the fact that he is doubly stereotypi-

Collaboration and Context

cal and hence "improbable": "[H]e combines the image of the Jewish immigrant (who [like Horn] often worked in the garment trade) with that of the Jew as wealthy cosmopolitan." Greene then condemns Horn as "improbable" (psychologically? historically?) on another score as well, which is that after having tried to save France by fleeing to Spain with her and her grandmother, he then "abandons" his "beloved daughter" when he turns himself in to Lucien's cohorts "in a crisis of despair."[37] As the film as well as the screenplay of *Lacombe Lucien* confirm, this is not what happens. At the French Gestapo headquarters, it is clear that Horn's act of desperation is designed to *save* France, not to abandon her. The drama of his arrival is intended to shake Lucien into taking action to save France (if not the whole family) by helping her flee to Spain. The exchange between the two men is as follows:

Lucien *(astonished)*: "You went out?"
Horn: "France told me you could get us into Spain . . . "
Lucien *(astonished)*: "Me?"
Horn: "Yes. . . . You see Lucien, I wanted to speak to you man to man. . . . We have never spoken together . . . "
Lucien: "To speak about what?"
Horn: "About France."
Lucien *(getting up)*: "I don't have the time, M. Horn . . . I have my work."[38]

In this scene, despite Greene's claims, Horn's actions are both laudable and *consistent* with his character. They are hardly "improbable."

To return to the film's ambiguities, in an interview with Melinda Camber Porter in the mid-1980s, Malle stressed the degree to which his art is centered on the representation of the irrational, the illogical, in human behavior. This interests Malle not out of a sense of perversity, but because "each time I come to a turning point in my life, either in work or personally, I make irrational decisions."[39] Such illogic, such irrationality certainly lend themselves to inconsistency and therefore to ambiguity, but to renounce his commitment to these tropes would be to betray his art. Discussing *Lacombe Lucien* in a more recent interview, Malle notes that, as in all his films, "I did not want to simplify, I did not want simply to paint a portrait of a traitor. Rather I was looking to analyze an individual in all his contradictions."[40]

Malle realizes, nevertheless, that it is precisely the renunciation of the irrational, the ambiguous, that the public wants: "People want fiction to be more 'real' than life which means they want to eliminate the illogical."[41] During the 1970s, this was especially true, of course, of *Lacombe Lucien*, where political and ideological ambiguity and "irrationality" were clearly unacceptable. For Malle, the result was not only a willful ignorance of the subtleties of his art but a necessary foreclosure of discussion of the film's most profound political insights. According to Malle, such insights are not to be gained in unambiguous and heavy-handed *films engagés*, because these films "drive their nail in so heavily that they permit no serious political reflection."[42] Although Malle does not elaborate on what "serious political reflection" inspired by *Lacombe Lucien* might reveal, one possibility is suggested in the interview with Camber Porter. Malle notes that in beginning a film, "I take my starting point as an unacceptable, impossible, and shocking idea and try to render it acceptable."[43] At the time of the making of *Lacombe Lucien*, this would entail not the creation of a countermyth to the Gaullist myth of Resistance, the latter having already been seriously undermined by Marcel Ophuls's 1971 documentary *The Sorrow and the Pity*, but by challenging the mythmaking process itself by offering ambiguities to reflect on rather than dubious certainties and another, equally false version of the history the Occupation—precisely what the critics of the *mode rétro* accused *Lacombe Lucien* of doing.

If Malle's intention in making *Lacombe Lucien* was to demythify the Occupation rather than create a countermyth to Gaullist resistancialism, few if any commentators in the post-*rétro* era as well are willing to consider the film in this light. In fact, in a 1992 essay on Vichy's legacy, "Cinquante ans après" (Fifty years later), Stanley Hoffmann specifically refers to what he labels "the *Lacombe Lucien* myth," successor to the Gaullist myth, which paints the portrait of "a weak and complicitous France, where there would only have been a handful of

resistance fighters, where the regime could not only further the desires and pressures of the occupier, but could count on the support of
debased people."[44] That the *"Lacombe Lucien* myth" embraces social,
political, and historical issues well beyond the scope of Malle's film
is only the most obvious of the ways in which it misrepresents it.
But then, the very context of Hoffmann's remarks confirms that the
movie *Lacombe Lucien* has long since surpassed its role as a work of art
about the Occupation to become incorporated into the *historical* discourse of the memory of the period itself. Any effort to judge the film
must first extricate it from its own myth and, to a degree, the discourse
of postwar history itself.

One wonders, in fact, if more recent assessments of *Lacombe Lucien,* such as Hoffmann's, are judgments of the film or of the myth it
has inspired. To be sure, these judgments are uniformly negative. In a
recent interview, Marcel Ophuls dismisses *Lacombe Lucien* as "rather
ludicrous," without further comment.[45] In his preface to the May 1992
issue of *Esprit* titled "Que faire de Vichy?" (What can be done with
Vichy?), Éric Conan refers to the "nihilism" of *Lacombe Lucien* while
condemning it for presenting a "simplistic account" and ignoring the
complexities of the period. Such a description is certainly more in
keeping with straightforward claims of the myth than the ambiguities
of the film.

In this country as well, Malle's film remains largely trapped in its
own myth, in the false version of history it supposedly recounts. In
Landscapes of Loss, Naomi Greene continues to see in the character of
Lucien an apology for the collaborator rather than the portrait an ambiguous and ambivalent adolescent, and her reading of the film therefore echoes the views of the *mode rétro* critics of twenty-five years ago.
For Greene, Lucien betrays a "childlike simplicity and vulnerability,"
especially in his love for France. And when Lucien rescues France and
her grandmother (in a scene whose ambiguities have already been
noted), it is "the redemptive quality of his love" that leads him to provide for France and the old woman in the film's final scenes. According to Greene, we are supposed to believe that the "good" Lucien has
finally triumphed. And so when *Lacombe Lucien* abruptly concludes

with the statement on screen that Lucien has been executed for his wartime crimes, Greene echoes the Italian critics Eduardo Bruno and Ciriaco Tiso in arguing that the abruptness of this final transition from idyllic life to the announcement of Lucien's death is intended to stir regret and a sense of injustice in the spectator. Through Lucien, the collaborator is vindicated.[46]

It is curious that the "myth," or what I would prefer to call the counterhistory of *Lacombe Lucien*, originally proposed by critics at the time of the film's release but still articulated in similar terms today, should for so long have been able to counter or undermine the actual vision of the history of the Occupation presented in Malle's film. Works of art, especially those that are as deliberately ambiguous in many instances as is *Lacombe Lucien*, certainly lend themselves to multiple interpretations, and this fact may well explain the widely divergent assessments of the film presented here. But it is also true that the film has long since transcended its status as "merely" a work of art (if such a status can be said to exist) to become a site of contested memory in Vichy's long afterlife. As such it remains, a quarter of a century after its release, a source of scandal, debate, and controversy. For Louis Malle, at least, this would have been the true mark of *Lacombe Lucien*'s success.

4 : Revising *The Sorrow and the Pity*

Marcel Ophuls's *Hotel Terminus*

If Louis Malle's *Lacombe Lucien* created a scandal upon its release in 1974 and earned subsequently, as I argued in the last chapter, an undeserved reputation as a procollaborationist apology for the bourgeoisie, there is no doubt that the ground for the controversy surrounding Malle's film was prepared by the release of Marcel Ophuls's *The Sorrow and the Pity* three years earlier. Often credited with almost single-handedly shattering the Gaullist myth of Resistance, *The Sorrow and the Pity* recorded in film a thoroughgoing counterhistory to the narrative proposed by the Gaullist myth.[1] This counterhistory embraced the defeatism of France's leaders in 1940 (evident in the comments of Anthony Eden about the actions and attitudes of French officials during the government's retreat to Bordeaux); the disturbing idealism and dignity of some pro-Nazi fanatics (in the person of Christian de la Mazière); the passivity and occasional opportunistic anti-Semitism of "the man in the street" (the merchant Klein, who during the war advertised the fact that he was not Jewish in order to keep his business functioning); and, finally, the horrors of official

Vichy anti-Semitism (evident especially in the show trial of the Jewish filmmaker Bernard Nathan) and the Final Solution (presented through Claude Lévy's discussion of the Vél d'Hiv roundups). To balance this negative portrait of France during the Dark Years, Ophuls also included moving portraits of some *résistants*, above all the Grave brothers, farmers whose quiet courage contrasts sharply in the film with the self-disculpatory remarks of many of the collaborators and *attentistes*. Notably absent from the film are the Gaullists and de Gaulle himself, whose invisibility, in Rousso's view, is "so glaring that the credibility of the film suffers" (but then, one of the targets of *The Sorrow and the Pity* is Gaullism).[2] Also almost entirely absent from the film are women.[3]

Like *Lacombe Lucien*, *The Sorrow and the Pity* elicited a wide range of critical commentary on both the right and the left. The extreme right-wing paper *Rivarol* delighted not only in the film's postwar portrait of one former *résistant* driving a Mercedes and selling televisions to former *collabos*, but also in images of the German veterans that did not cater to stereotypes of "dull-witted brutes." (Apparently the *Rivarol* reviewer did not notice the irony of the portrayal of the arrogant and self-satisfied Wermacht officer Tausend that opens the film.) In the newspaper *L'Humanité*, the Communists praised the film as a "political act" that was "not depressing but purifying." They were also delighted with the deflation of their wartime allies and current rivals, the Gaullists.

Not all those who commented on *The Sorrow and the Pity* were pleased with the film, however. Alfred Fabre-Luce, a former collaborationist and author, during the war, of *Mesure de la France*, a book heaping praise on Hitler's New Europe and Pétain's National Revolution, blasted the film in the pages of *Le Monde* for its use of "gimmicks, omissions, and deliberate falsifications" as well as for its criticisms of Pétain, especially those made by Jews.[4] According to Fabre-Luce, the latter owed the Marshall their lives. Fabre-Luce's absurdities were denounced by the former *résistante* Germaine Tillon, who nevertheless condemned the film for offering a "profile of a hideous country." Jean-Paul Sartre also criticized *The Sorrow and the Pity* as a film that "speaks neither political truth nor life in the concrete. It thus fails of both its goals, the only goals it could have set for itself. This is a film that makes you smile constantly, but the Occupation was by no means all laughs. Hence it is an inaccurate representation, deliberately so."[5]

Despite *The Sorrow and the Pity*'s remarkable success and its current status as a *lieu de mémoire* in its own right, it is interesting to note that in many interviews given since the release of the film, Marcel Ophuls seems to have taken to heart criticisms of his documentary rather than rest on the praise heaped upon it. In an interview with Melinda Camber Porter given in the mid-1980s, Ophuls appears, in effect, to be firing back at some of his erstwhile critics, especially those who come from the ranks of the Parisian intellectuals. He applauds the fact that many have now "come to recognize the central importance of the collaboration" as "a symbol of their [the Parisian intellectuals'] behavior in crisis." Ophuls singles out Sartre, stressing what he describes as Sartre's " '*Lord Jim*' attitude towards life" that accounts for the fact that, as Ophuls bluntly asserts, "Sartre did not resist."[6]

In a subsequent interview appearing in *American Film* given around the time of the release of *Hotel Terminus*, Ophuls expresses his displeasure with others among the French who appear critical of or even hostile toward *The Sorrow and the Pity* and to what it sought to accomplish. Ophuls admits in fact that he has become defensive in the face of a widespread presumption that it is his "self-assigned mission in life" to be a muckraker of the French past, or a "specialist in French guilt trips," as the interviewer would have it. According to Ophuls, "There's always that suspicion now: 'Watch out! Here comes the *Sorrow-and-Pity* man!' " Ophuls notes that even with friends like Claude Lanzmann, the suspicion surfaces. Learning of Ophuls's intention to make *Hotel Terminus*, Ophuls reports Lanzmann as saying: "Ah! You're going to do for Lyons what you did for Clermont-Ferrand [the town where most of *The Sorrow and the Pity* was shot]!" Ophuls also expresses his resentment at a comment made by Serge Klarsfeld while being interviewed by Ophuls in *Hotel Terminus*. At one point during the interview, Klarsfeld, as Ophuls notes, "suddenly draws himself up in front of my camera and declares: 'I have nothing against the French.' "

For Ophuls, this is clearly a shot at *The Sorrow and the Pity* and the supposed anti-French attitude of its maker. For his part, Ophuls considers *The Sorrow and the Pity* "a patriotic act."[7]

In the interview Ophuls makes clear that on a personal level he is sensitive on this point because he is "a naturalized Frenchman and the American son of a German Jewish refugee." Lanzmann, by contrast, is a "French Jew" (as is Klarsfeld). But the more interesting question is what impact, if any, did Ophuls's sensitivity to being implicitly labeled anti-French or even unpatriotic for having made *The Sorrow and the Pity* have on his subsequent work, especially his return to the French context in *Hotel Terminus*, his film dealing with the Barbie Affair? In the *American Film* interview Ophuls stresses the fact that something very important to be gleaned from the Barbie trial itself is the "decency" of the French people. The trial, he continues, can give one a "sense of what human justice should be about," and the French are to be praised for an "act of collective courage." It is, Ophuls concludes, "to their great honor" that the French tried Barbie, because the entire undertaking was "not easy."[8]

The proximity in the *American Film* interview of Ophuls's remarks concerning his sensitivity to implicit and occasionally explicit charges of pursuing an anti-French agenda in *The Sorrow and the Pity* to his statements concerning French courage and decency in relation to the Barbie trial is, I believe, not at all coincidental. In fact, I will argue here that these two attitudes reinforced each other in the making of *Hotel Terminus*. The result is a film that, in its structure and composition as well as in interviewing techniques employed by Ophuls, generally emphasizes French courage, decency, and heroism almost to the point of completely obscuring the widespread French complicity and passivity in the face of the Nazi victory that Ophuls had foregrounded in *The Sorrow and the Pity*. In this sense, *Hotel Terminus* offers nothing less than a counterhistory to the version of the Vichy years presented in Ophuls's earlier masterpiece. Moreover, as part of his strategy to articulate a positive narrative of French courage and decency, Ophuls sketches, by way of contrast, a very negative portrait of German amnesia and complacency, American stupidity and complicity with

Nazi criminals in the postwar years, and Latin American corruption. In this sense, a film that purports to get to the heart of the Dark Years and their legacy in postwar France in dealing with France's first trial for crimes against humanity gets sidetracked into writing *other* histories that divert attention from the central issue at stake: Klaus Barbie, his wartime crimes in Lyons, and France's efforts to come to terms with these crimes as a way of dealing with a troubled past. The result is that *Hotel Terminus* is, in many ways, less a coldly objective documentary representation of the past than "a monstrous postmodern detective novel in which there is a detective [Ophuls], but from which the crime, the criminal, and even the trial are missing."[9]

These remarks are not intended to suggest that *Hotel Terminus* is entirely Manichean in its presentation of "The Life and Times of Klaus Barbie" (the film's subtitle) or that its favorable portrait of the French and negative portraits of other peoples (especially the Germans, past and present) exclude the treatment of larger moral and ethical issues that transcend national boundaries and cultures. Naomi Greene points out that there are at least two episodes in the film in which the French *are* cast in a very bad light. In the first instance, in exploring the circumstances surrounding Barbie's arrest and deportation of the Jewish children of Izieu in the film, Ophuls includes testimony confirming that "the children's hiding place had been revealed to the Germans by a *French* informer." This left no doubt that "Barbie and the Nazis were not the only ones responsible for their deaths." The second instance occurs during the course of the interview with the laborer Julien Favet, when it becomes clear that despite the fact that he knew the children and the French informer, he was never called to testify at Barbie's trial. When the state prosecutor is questioned about this surprising omission, he is unable—unwilling?—to explain precisely why the laborer was never called to the stand. We are left to assume that the state did not want his disquieting version of events to be made public.[10]

As for the larger moral and ethical issues the film addresses, Ophuls himself notes in the *American Film* interview that the real enemy— "bigger than Barbie"—he wishes to engage is "moral relativism: the refusal to see what is specific about the Holocaust, the stupid idea that prosecutors are necessarily bad people and that criminals are always the underdog. These are things I find more and more disgusting."[11] Despite the views of Barbie's lawyer, Jacques Vergès, for example, who carps constantly in the film about the inhuman treatment of his client and compares Nazi atrocities to French abuses during the Algerian War, Ophuls in no way wishes the horror or uniqueness of the Holocaust to be obscured by the misguided humanitarian or relativist impulses occasionally voiced on screen. As the film amply demonstrates, such attitudes, in fact, frequently serve as smoke screens for unspoken sympathies for Barbie and his racist and xenophobic views. In this sense, *Hotel Terminus* is but one film in a "succession . . . of relentless documentaries" made by Ophuls, whose principal aim is to expose the stages "in an epic scandal that threatens to include an ever-increasing number of participants in the spiraling taint of Nazism."[12]

The fact remains, however, that despite these considerations, *Hotel Terminus* is fundamentally "pro-French" in outlook and that this emerges in the basic conception and structure of the film as well as in the four hours of interviews it includes. In *The Holocaust in French Film*, Pierre-André Colombat argues that what he describes as "the real center" of *Hotel Terminus* is the "necessary remembrance of Barbie's victims," but he adds that these victims noticeably do not include the Amsterdam Jews Barbie persecuted before arriving in Lyons.[13] Thus the emphasis falls virtually exclusively on Barbie's *French* victims, whether they were members of the Resistance arrested, tortured, and in some instances murdered by Barbie, or those he deported in carrying out the Final Solution. I will return to these individuals shortly.

As noted, one of the more obvious ways in which *Hotel Terminus* presents the French in a positive light is by casting them in relief against the "backdrop" of the blatant failings or vices of other nationals and nationalities in the film. In an essay in *Premiere* published in November 1988, Ophuls speaks of the technique of "investigative sarcasm" used in the film, a technique appropriately and effectively employed especially in interviews with Germans, Americans, and South Americans who either knew or worked with Barbie or who offer comments on the whole affair.[14] At best, these witnesses come across as ignorant, indifferent, or misguided in their sympathies and affections. At worst, their testimonies reveal deception, hatred, or the "orchestrated amnesia of the perpetrators."[15]

All of these attitudes are evident in the interviews conducted in Germany. Former neighbors speak affectionately of young "Sonny" Barbie and praise his vitality and courage in growing up in a troubled family. They refer to his brutal, alcoholic father, his strict Catholic upbringing, and his feeble-minded brother, who, as one neighbor innocently suggests, was "better off to have died young." A former classmate and later an officer in the German army speaks admiringly of Barbie's leadership qualities and of his having made the Nazi Party acceptable to his classmates by becoming a member himself. Another former officer expresses no regret for his own role in the war, since, as he argues, despite their defeat, the Nazis did "save the west" from communism.

More troubling are the interviews and exchanges with those who did not know Barbie and who are, for the most part, from subsequent generations. The "spiraling taint of Nazism," as Higgins refers to it, extends not only laterally and geographically but chronologically as well. Ophuls visits the Catholic school Barbie attended as a boy and interviews a student who finds it impossible to believe Barbie was ever enrolled there. An instructor intervenes and, when told of Barbie's status as a former student, professes ignorance. The whole episode speaks of an older generation that wishes to remain willfully ignorant of the Nazi past and tries to shield the next generation from that memory.

In seeking to interview former ss members, especially Barbie's subordinates at Lyons now living in retirement in Germany, Ophuls encounters open hostility not only from these men but also from neighbors who are frequently not even of their generation. In one segment Ophuls is shown climbing the stairs to the apartment of a certain Muller, former ss chief in Toulouse. When Muller answers the door, Ophuls, looking slyly innocent, asks the man what harm a two-year-old girl could do to Hitler's Reich. The question is apparently in reference to a girl Muller had sent to her death during the war. Muller begins to explain, then exclaims, "What's the use!" and closes the door in Ophuls's face. The filmmaker then mugs for the camera and sarcastically wishes Muller "Merry Christmas!" through the door. Clearly wishing to establish complicity with the spectator here, Ophuls moves dangerously close to violating one of his own cardinal rules for documentary making, which is never to turn those one is interviewing into "instruments of [one's] own propaganda."[16] In this scene, Ophuls is caught between the exigencies of his art and his personal need to express, albeit rather light-heartedly in this instance, outrage at the acts of former Nazis.

In his efforts to interview Barbie's former subordinates, Ophuls often encounters and films some of their neighbors. These individuals openly express their indifference to the Nazi pasts of those with whom they live and, on occasion, accuse Ophuls of sensationalism and greed. Other neighbors argue that these aging Nazis should be allowed to live out their days in peace. And when Ophuls actually manages to catch up to one of Barbie's former henchmen, the latter attempts to flee while yelling at Ophuls, "Whatever happened to human rights?"

In many of these interviews, Ophuls remains largely detached and objective, and the subtle compromising of the witnesses occurs either as a function of what they say or as a result of the natural hierarchy, which, according to Bill Nichols, obtains between interviewer and interviewee in the interactive mode of documentary film. As Nichols explains, the interviewer is "initiator and arbiter of legitimacy," and the ensuing dialogue is really a "pseudo-dialogue," since the interview format "prohibits full reciprocity or equity between participants."[17] Ophuls does, however, openly take advantage of his superior position on occasion when, for example, he asks the neighbors of Barbie's former cohorts if they care about the pasts of these men. It is already clear from their previous remarks that they do not, or that they wish to forget them, and Ophuls's disingenuous questions only serve to make them look worse.

In several segments shot in Germany—such as the Muller episode described above—Ophuls abandons any real pretense of objectivity. His anger and especially his sarcasm boil to the surface, affecting not only his interviewing techniques but his editing of the film itself. In approaching the residence of Barbie's former subordinate in charge of Jewish affairs in Lyons, Erich Bartelmus, Ophuls mockingly calls out "Herr Bartelmus" and pretends to look for him under objects lying about in the garden. Bartelmus, of course, fails to materialize, and a young neighbor appears and informs Ophuls that, among other things, he is trespassing. Of all the scenes in *Hotel Terminus*, this one best sums up and encapsulates German indifference and amnesia *past and present*. It also exposes Ophuls's *personal* frustration and illustrates his use of the technique of investigative sarcasm at its most biting. The only other scene comparable to this one in foregrounding the film-maker's frustration and sarcasm occurs when Ophuls stages a phone conversation with the imaginary wife of a former German officer. Ophuls plays the role of the wife, who shows a great deal of interest in the film he is making until she is told that it deals with Barbie. The woman suddenly develops amnesia, and the conversation is ter-minated. Here Ophuls steps beyond the bounds generally imposed by the documentary form itself—to use real and not imaginary wit-nesses—to drive home his point.

In a final segment worth noting in this context in which Ophuls also resorts to heavy-handed techniques to make his case, he films a magistrate announcing the German court's decision not to try Barbie due to "lack of evidence." Pretending then to turn off the camera, Ophuls pushes for further disclosures from the official, who becomes very flustered when he realizes the camera is still rolling and that he is being caught giving out more than the official story. Adding a further layer of ironic meaning to the scene, Ophuls adds shots of people in the streets with painted faces and wearing costumes to celebrate Car-nival. In such a festive atmosphere, Barbie and the Nazi past seem an unnecessary and unwelcome intrusion.

Some of the most damning evidence against Germany past and

present is provided by two German nationals. Through their mere presence on camera, however, they serve to alleviate, if only momentarily, the monotonous litany of German amnesia and bad faith. Ophuls includes in *Hotel Terminus* a film clip of a speech by the writer Günther Grass in which Grass speaks of the almost total lack of resistance within Germany throughout Hitler's rule. In another segment, Dany Cohn-Bendit, the former leader of the Paris student uprisings of May 1968 and now a Green Party politician, comments wryly on his countrymen by observing: "It is easier to get 200,000 Germans to protest the killing of 6,000,000 trees than 6,000,000 Jews."[18]

The Americans in the film fare no better than their German counterparts. Those interviewed consist primarily of former American intelligence operatives who hired Barbie following the Nazi defeat to work as a counterintelligence agent against the Communists. These men betray a remarkable gullibility and at the same time a certain deviousness that hardly disguises their basic indifference to Barbie's crimes. Some confess to not having cared about the political background of the agents they hired. As to Barbie himself, one states that he did not feel Barbie was particularly anti-Semitic, a comment that appears particularly disingenuous in the face of all the evidence to the contrary Ophuls has marshaled thus far in the film. The American agent doubts as well that Barbie ever resorted to torturing his captives. Barbie would not need to, the agent asserts, because he was "a damned skillful interrogator" who could get the information he wanted by other means. This testimony is juxtaposed in *Hotel Terminus* with that of French witnesses who describe precisely Barbie's torture techniques and the pleasure he took in abusing his victims. Another former agent, seated next to his German wife to whom he defers on a number of questions, admits that Barbie was allowed to recruit his own operatives, many of whom were black marketeers. When asked why Barbie was not turned over to the French, the excuses given are either lame or shocking in their ideological narrow-mindedness and paranoia. One agent, Erhard Dabringhaus, claims the French were not insistent enough in their demands for Barbie, while another, Eugene Polk, asserts that French intelligence at the time was infiltrated by Communists and that any information Barbie might have had about the Americans would eventually end up in the hands of the Russians.

The interviews with the American agents are carefully staged against comfortable backdrops that suggest a profound psychological and emotional distance from the brutal realities of the Occupation and cold war years. Dabringhaus sits by his swimming pool and Polk next to his Christmas tree. As Ophuls notes in the interview in *American Film*, most of the American interviews were conducted at Christmastime, and he had at one point considered calling the film "Joy to the World" (hence the title of the interview) referring, ironically of course, to the traditional Christmas carol. (The carol is in fact played on the soundtrack during some of the segments in Germany.) One American is interviewed sitting at the dinner table and sipping wine as he talks, although in this instance, the individual in question is responsible for the American apology for the U.S. role in helping Barbie, and Ophuls's staging of the interview in all likelihood carries no sarcastic or ironic intent. With the exception of this one instance, the comfort and ease of the situations of the American witnesses seem almost obscene when Ophuls juxtaposes them with the graphic descriptions of torture undergone by Barbie's French victims, especially the Jewish woman Madame Lagrange and the *résistante* Lise Lesèvre.

In the interview in *American Film* Ophuls expresses doubt concerning the reliability of the American intelligence agents, stating: "If you ask me, those former American agents . . . are carrying out some mysterious assignments—perhaps self-imposed, but more likely not—of preventing media attention from expanding sideways, and more particularly upwards."[19] The implied link between the Nazis and those at the highest level of American government in the postwar is suggested by footage of Ronald Reagan's visit to Bitburg Cemetery and long shots of presidential wreaths on the graves of ss members.[20]

When Ophuls and his crew arrive in South America, the combined weight of German and American denials, forgetfulness, and misplaced sympathy and admiration for Barbie make the expression of similar attitudes and sentiments by Barbie's South American apologists seem all the more ludicrous and distasteful, even when they are the product of political naïveté. For example, when one of Barbie's former business associates praises him for having done his duty during the Second World War, or when a local Indian who worked for Barbie—a man obviously completely ignorant of European political realities, past and present—praises him as a "good man," the viewer is forced to wonder how anyone, no matter how naive, could entertain such sentiments. Other witnesses confirm Barbie's close links with former governments in Bolivia as well as his ties to Nazi and neo-Nazi paramilitary groups thriving in South America. One is hardly surprised, then, when Ophuls and his crew are physically attacked by one of Barbie's former neighbors while attempting to shoot footage of the building in which Barbie lived before his extradition.

The final sequences of *Hotel Terminus* are shot in France and deal with events leading up to and following Barbie's trial. These are not, of course, the first scenes shot in France. Earlier, Ophuls had interviewed former members of the Resistance, several of Barbie's Jewish victims, and a few small-time collaborators, like Madame Hemmerle, a friend of Barbie's French henchmen who was arrested and accused of wartime profiteering following the Liberation. Ophuls also speaks with Albert Rosset, the leader in Lyons of the National Front, and, in the sequences dealing with the trial, Barbie's lawyer, Jacques Vergès.

As opposed to the interviews conducted in Germany, the United States, and South America, the majority of those conducted in France are characterized by the dignity, courage, and honesty of Ophuls's interlocutors. The *résistants* Raymond Aubrac and Lise Lesèvre speak of their imprisonment and torture at the hands of Barbie. In Lesèvre's case, her testimony is especially moving not only because of her dignity and honesty in recounting her own suffering, but because it becomes clear that her husband and son had died as a result of her refusal to talk. The courage and self-sacrifice evident in Lesèvre's case certainly outstrip those of any of the German or American witnesses. Lucie Aubrac describes her own courageous bluff to free her husband, a scene dramatized in Claude Berri's film *Lucie Aubrac*. Daniel Cordier, Jean Moulin's secretary in the Resistance, speaks reverently of his

Revising The Sorrow and the Pity

former boss, stating that even forty years after Moulin's death and all that Cordier had done for Moulin's memory, it would be presumptuous for him to claim Moulin as his friend.

The setting and tone of these interviews also stands in sharp contrast to those of the American and German interviews. No investigative sarcasm is evident on the part of the filmmaker, who effaces himself almost completely as he converses with his French interlocutors, very much unlike his approach in the German segments. Moreover, the surroundings themselves tend to underscore and reinforce the decency and modesty of those being interviewed. The Aubracs, for example, are interviewed in the quiet, discreet comfort of their living room, which serves as an appropriate backdrop for conversations revealing their calm heroism during the war. Lingering shots of Christmas trees and swimming pools that serve to ironize and ultimately discredit the American witnesses are completely absent.

When Ophuls interviews unsympathetic witnesses, including former collaborators, the FN (Front National) spokesman Rosset, and Jacques Vergès, his investigative sarcasm occasionally returns in the form of probing and repeated questions and deliberate misquoting of earlier remarks made by his interlocutors. For the most part, however, the witnesses discredit themselves either in word and gesture or, in the case of Vergès, simply in the choice of personal surroundings. Rosset's rigid and arrogant bearing and his dismissal of the Barbie trial as a "vieille histoire" (old news), a clearly ludicrous remark at this stage in the film, alienate viewers and make them all the more sympathetic to the *résistants*. Vergès's opulent office, his elegant, oily manner, his refusal to discuss his mysterious past, and his denial of any knowledge of François Genoud, the Swiss Nazi who financed Barbie's defense, all serve to compromise him and make Ophuls's hostile presence almost unnecessary.[21] As for Madame Hemmerle, her unpleasant appearance, her gleeful announcement that she brings bad luck ("je porte malheur") to those who cross her, and her links to extraordinarily unsavory and even repulsive collaborators like "Rubberface" (stills of whose deformed face are flashed more than once on screen), make her appear more witch-like than human.

It is clear in each of these cases that, as opposed to many of the Germans and Americans interviewed by Ophuls, the French deserving of condemnation are not ordinary "men and women on the street" but marginal iconoclasts like Vergès, political fanatics like Rosset, or malicious but rather pathetic "small fry" like Madame Hemmerle. Moreover, the comments made by these individuals ultimately make any defense of Barbie seem not only implausible but grotesque. They discredit the efforts of Barbie's defenders to lessen the magnitude of his crimes by pointing to those of others, often in an effort to challenge the uniqueness of the Holocaust.

But what of the role of the *French themselves* in the Holocaust, especially that of Frenchmen like René Bousquet, Paul Touvier, and Maurice Papon, who would be accused and, in the case of Touvier and Papon, tried for crimes against humanity in the 1990s for their participation in the Final Solution (as Bouquet would have been had he not been murdered)? One could argue that it is unfair as well as anachronistic to criticize *Hotel Terminus* for failing to deal with events that had not yet occurred, but this would be to ignore the fact that Touvier's crimes during the war as well as René Bousquet's role in implementing the Final Solution in France had been widely known since the late 1970s, and that Papon's role in the deportations of Jews from Bordeaux had been made public in a bombshell article published in the newspaper *Canard Enchaîné* in 1981. Moreover, at the time that *Hotel Terminus* was released in 1988, French courts were investigating charges of crimes against humanity against Bousquet's subordinate, Jean Leguay. The investigation concluded in 1989 at the moment of Leguay's death with the very unusual postmortem announcement that Leguay had in fact been guilty of crimes against humanity. It is unlikely that Ophuls was unaware of these cases.

It seems especially ironic that no comparison is made in *Hotel Terminus* between Barbie and Paul Touvier, the "French Barbie," whose case will be discussed in detail in the next chapter. An officer in Vichy's Militia in Lyons, Touvier bears a striking resemblance to Barbie in his background and career. Both men were raised in right-wing nationalistic Catholic families, both were anti-Semitic, antidemocratic zealots, both were to all appearances good fathers and husbands, both were crooks following the war, and both were helped after the war by right-wing elements within the Catholic Church. And the two apparently knew each other in Lyons.[22]

Although some comparison of Barbie and Touvier in the film would have been compelling and informative, it is ultimately the specter of a figure like Bousquet that casts the largest shadow over the beacon of French "decency," whose light is intended to illuminate *Hotel Terminus*. And it is perhaps for this reason that his presence can be felt, if only obliquely, in the film. Bousquet is present in the discussion of Meyer Bulka, one of the children of Izieu mentioned in the film, whose parents had already been taken to the Vélodrome d'Hiver in the roundup ordered by Bousquet and carried out by French police. He is also present—in person—in a wartime newsreel in which he is shown welcoming Reinhard Heydrich and other ss officials to Paris, footage already included in *The Sorrow and the Pity*, but whose resonance is much greater in the earlier film. These signs of Bousquet's presence are, I believe, doors that Ophuls opens in *Hotel Terminus* but beyond which he does not explore, and so he fails to exhaust the final ramifications of the Barbie Affair in France. Unlike *The Sorrow and the Pity*, *Hotel Terminus* offers a reassuring and ultimately misleading portrait of the French, and the juxtaposition of the two films thus recounts two different histories of the Dark Years that fail to mesh in their efforts to represent the Occupation. In this sense at least, Marcel Ophuls's efforts to come to terms with Vichy and its afterlife lead, ultimately, to an impasse.

5 : The Trial of Paul Touvier

The Law Revises History

On 17 June 1996, Paul Touvier, a former officer in Vichy's Militia during the Second World War and the first Frenchman convicted of crimes against humanity, died of cancer in the prison hospital at Fresnes on the outskirts of Paris. The subject of newspaper headlines and lead-off segments on evening news programs, Touvier's death prompted numerous rehearsals of what had been, in spite of the mediocrity and insignificance of the man himself, a remarkable life. A railway clerk turned officer for Vichy's brutal paramilitary police force, Touvier had spent the latter part of the Occupation hunting down the Militia's sworn enemies, primarily Jews and members of the Resistance, many of whom he subjected to torture and death. As head of the Militia's Second Service, or intelligence branch, first in his native Chambéry and later in the Lyons region, Touvier also became— at least temporarily—a wealthy man. He confiscated clothes, cars, and even apartments from his victims, sharing these on occasion with his fellow Militiamen as well as members of his family and his mistress at the time, a prostitute by the name of Marie-Louise Charroin.[1]

At the Liberation and with the help of friends in the priesthood, Touvier went into hiding, living under assumed names in towns in southern France before traveling to Paris to begin a life of petty crime. Arrested on suspicion of participating in a right-wing terrorist plot known as the "Blue Plan," Touvier managed to escape with the help of the arresting officers, to whom he had been happy to give the names of many of his coconspirators.[2] In the meantime, he had been condemned to death in absentia for the crime of intelligence with the enemy by courts in Chambéry and Lyons in 1946 and 1947.

On the lam within France once again, Touvier married secretly, had two children, and survived by ingratiating himself with an odd assortment of celebrities and powerful members of the Catholic clergy. The former Militiaman numbered among his sponsors the singer Jacques Brel, who, according to Brel's wife, was taken in by Touvier's tales of woe (Brel also wrote a song about his plight), as well as the actor Pierre Frenay, the star of such classic films as *La Grande illusion* and *Le Corbeau*, whose own reputation had not survived the Occupation untarnished. Touvier's most valuable supporters, however, were Catholic clergymen who, after years of sustained effort, secured his pardon from President Georges Pompidou in 1971. Although Pompidou's pardon was only for ancillary penalties associated with the 1946 and 1947 death penalties—the statute of limitations had run out on the convictions themselves—news of the pardon provoked a storm of public protest and Touvier was forced once again into hiding. He holed up for the most part in a series of *intégriste* and other right-wing monasteries and received support money from the ultrareactionary Chevaliers de Notre Dame.[3] Finally in May 1989, Touvier was arrested by gendarmes at the Saint-François priory in Nice. After protracted procedural debates and a series of spectacularly misguided court decisions, one of which is the primary focus of this chapter, Touvier was tried in the spring of 1994 by the Versailles assizes court.[4] He was convicted of crimes against humanity for ordering the murder of seven Jewish hostages on the morning of 29 June 1944 at the cemetery of Rillieux-la-Pape near Lyons. Touvier was condemned to life in prison and died shortly after his incarceration. At his funeral were members of his family, some Benedictine monks, his lawyer, Jacques Trémolet de Villers, and a few marginal politicians. For the Parisian newspaper *Libération*, the composition of the assembled group and the praise heaped on the deceased were disturbing evidence that Vichy and Pétainisme still flourished. But in a summer in which the Holocaust deniers in France had recruited a new and famous apologist, Father Pierre (see chapter 7), neo-Nazis were arrested for the 1990 desecration of the Jewish cemetery at Carpentras, and the National Front was purging public libraries in towns it controlled, this was, to put it bluntly, not news. It is not surprising, therefore, that within a week of the aging Militiaman's death, the twenty-five-year-old affair associated with his name faded once again from public view.

So what remains of the Touvier Affair, what role has it played in Vichy's afterlife, and what, ultimately, is its legacy? The various obituaries devoted to Touvier hardly do justice to the judicial and historical controversies and moral quandaries to which his case gave rise. These dilemmas, moreover, have still not been resolved several years after the trial itself. For example, for reasons to be explained shortly, Touvier could only be convicted in 1994 if it could be proven that he had acted on behalf of the Nazi Reich, and *not*, in effect, as a French agent, which he was. If he had acted for Vichy in ordering the murder of the Rillieux hostages, according to French law he could not be found guilty of crimes against humanity. In turning history on its head in this instance and in an earlier decision that created this situation in the first place, the French courts, as we shall see, engaged in the writing of counterhistories both of the Vichy years and of the facts of the Touvier case. Initially this was done to exonerate the former Militiaman in 1992, and secondly, to allow for his conviction in 1994. Referring to the resulting legal situation that obtained at Touvier's trial, Éric Conan and Henry Rousso have remarked that it is a strange law which in essence punishes complicity rather than the crime itself.[5]

By way of adding to the legal and historical ironies surrounding the entire case, Jean-Marc Varaut, who has recently served as Maurice Papon's defense counsel, noted that while French justice pursued Frenchmen like Touvier for crimes fifty years old, Nazi officers responsible for implementing the Final Solution in France have long since been pardoned by the likes of René Coty and Charles de Gaulle.[6] Moreover, before the trial of Klaus Barbie in the mid-1980s, Jacques Vergès, Barbie's defense counsel, cited another irony that applied at the time only to the charges against his client but in due course became applicable to the cases of both Paul Touvier and Maurice Papon. Vergès asserted that, apart from the crimes against humanity statutes, the other notable, recent example of French law being applied retroactively occurred under Vichy.[7] Beginning in 1941, the infamous "Special Sections" applied new measures aimed at Communists and so-called anarchists to cases already under review.[8] Thus, Vergès's comparison suggested, in seeking to punish the worst excesses of the Nazis and French complicity in these crimes, Fifth Republican France was resorting to Vichy's own tactics. As a final historical and legal irony (or worse), during Touvier's trial, defense counsel Jacques Trémolet de Villers called the court's attention to the murder of several thousands of Polish officers at Katyn in 1940. As long as these murders were thought to be the work of the Nazis, Trémolet noted, they were considered to be crimes against humanity. However, once Soviet culpability was brought to light, they ceased to be considered as such. Nothing had changed, of course, but the identity of the perpetrators. Trémolet was primarily intent on scoring ideological and legal points for the defense, but Tzvetan Todorov argues that such inequality before the law violates the most basic republican principles.[9]

The legal quandaries and disquieting historical echoes and ironies were not the only difficulties raised by the Touvier trial. The nation's "duty to memory"—one of the strongest motivating forces driving the proceedings—also became the object of sharp criticism for a variety of reasons. In a 1992 denunciation of European and specifically French indifference to the horrors being perpetrated daily in the former Yugoslavia, Alain Finkielkraut denounced the nation's cult of memory and specifically its obsessive fascination with the Touvier Affair. France's concern with fascism's past, he insisted, blinded it to fascism's present.[10] In a 1994 essay Bernard-Henri Lévy went one step further, arguing in hyperbolic prose that the reason for the nation's "mania" and "hysteria" concerning Vichy and Touvier in particular was the fact that memory was France's last source of social cohesiveness, its only "civic religion." Implicit in the cult of memory, Lévy concluded, was a disavowal of the present.[11]

But for many, the greatest inherent flaw in this line of reasoning had to do with the apparent disparity between the memory in question and the insignificance of the defendant and the role he played during the Occupation. As the symbolic whipping boy for Vichy anti-Semitism and complicity in the Final Solution (at least until the trial of Maurice Papon began three years later in Bordeaux), Touvier hardly appeared up to the task. Dismissed as "political rabble" by François Mitterrand, Touvier as a defendant was no substitute for the likes of the recently murdered René Bousquet, the former head of Vichy police responsible for the Vél d'Hiv roundups.[12] Unlike Touvier, Bousquet had served the Third Republic as well as Vichy and had been a highly successful businessman and friend of powerful politicians (including Mitterrand) in the postwar years. As such, Bousquet represented a certain continuity of the French state and French political and economic power from the prewar through the postwar years and including Vichy itself. This was at least equally true of Papon. To the degree that the trial of Touvier avoided dealing with this continuity, the defendant was merely a stand-in, a ludicrous substitute, and perhaps even a scapegoat.

This perspective is misleading to the extent that, as the examining magistrate Jean-Pierre Getti's 1991 indictment makes clear, Touvier was not in fact "political rabble" but a well-connected and fairly powerful operative within the hierarchy of the Militia.[13] As a ranking officer in the Second Service, Touvier was responsible for security within the organization and surveillance of its other branches. In this capacity, he exercised authority over many higher-ranking members of the Militia and reported not to superior officers at Lyons but directly to the highest echelons of the organization at Vichy. Acquainted with Joseph Darnand, the head of the Militia, Touvier had attended the elite officers' training school at Uriage.[14] Six months before the Liberation he was named a National Inspector of the

Militia. Thus, although Touvier may have appeared insignificant in the box of the accused in 1994, his role during the Occupation was hardly completely inconsequential; neither certainly was that of the Militia, whose own roots were in several ways sunk deeply in prewar French right-wing culture.[15]

But the real issue at stake, which the polemics concerning the duty to memory and the stature of the defendant in some ways obscured, was the role of law and the court in dealing with historical matters that had become burning issues in the present. The frustrated expectations of historians like Conan and Rousso are, I believe, attributable in part to an overestimation of the court's prerogatives in these matters. Following the trials in the early 1980s of the Holocaust denier Robert Faurisson (see chapter 7) and the Israeli historian Zeev Sternhell (sued by Bertrand de Jouvenel for implying that he, Jouvenel, had collaborated with the Nazis), the review *Le Débat* invited the distinguished legal experts Jean-Denis Bredin and Georges Kiejman to offer their thoughts on the topic of history and the law.[16] In their discussions, both men deal at length with the function of the court and the judge and the relation of both to historical truth and the craft of the historian. Examining the role of the judge, Kiejman argues that since history itself is a kind of tribunal and since many of the historian's methods are inspired by judicial procedure, judges are often wrongly viewed as possessing extraordinary powers of historical insight and judgment. They are therefore expected to function in the court as a kind of "super-historian" who rectifies the errors of the real historian. The attribution of this role to the judge is absurd, Kiejman argues, because, among other things, in reaching his decision the judge considers in principle only the material included in the criminal dossier. Unlike the historian, at least in principle, he cannot buttress or refine his views through recourse to historical archives.[17]

For Bredin, the crucial issue concerns the function the court actually plays in society. It is not the function of the court—or, for that matter, of the law—to discover definitive historical truths. Rather, both seek to transform moral values into norms of behavior and to organize social relations. The law watches over the peaceful maintenance of familial relations, the tranquillity of individuals, and the equality of interests.[18]

Court decisions, to cite Kiejman again, are in the realm of "the approximate, the living, the social." They are not "scientific" in their precision or their aim. Rather, they arise from a desire to find an equilibrium between individuals or groups comprising a social body at a given moment.[19] As such, they are not geared to satisfy the exigencies of the historian.

In light of the views of Kiejman and Bredin, what can the legal system and the courts be held accountable for in a case like Touvier's? They should not be expected to fulfill the nation's "duty to memory," they should not pass judgment on an entire political regime in the person of one aging defendant, and they should not be expected to resolve historical issues and debates that the historians themselves have failed to settle.

On the other hand, the legal system and the courts should be expected to treat all those involved in the case as equitably and dispassionately as possible. They should also recognize and act within the limits of their own jurisdiction and remain faithful, as much as possible, to their own traditions and precedents.

In at least one spectacular instance, this is precisely what the French justice system failed to do in the Touvier case. I am referring to the April 1992 decision by the criminal chamber of the Paris court of appeals to dismiss charges against Touvier, a decision that shocked government officials—indeed brought the government to a temporary standstill—and produced a vociferous but short-lived revolt among members of the legal profession.[20]

It is perhaps a dangerous exaggeration to compare the court of appeals' decision to Vichy's own anti-Semitic laws. But like the latter, the decision constituted what one legal expert has labeled a juridical "normalization of monsters" in at least two ways.[21] Vichy anti-Semitic law perverted French juridical concepts by deploying them to deny rather than protect the individual rights of members of a particular group, the Jews. Although the 1992 decision did not target a group, it did systematically discredit and dismiss the testimony of a specific

The Trial of Paul Touvier

category of witnesses: all those who testified or brought charges against Touvier. Of the eleven crimes attributed to Touvier, only one, the executions at Rillieux, was retained by the court, and this because the accused himself admitted to his role in the crime. Summing up the egregious manner in which the court proceeded in its evaluation of the evidence, Leila Wexler affirms that it "systematically discredited every single prosecution witness, but not once did it criticize Touvier. Yet the record is replete with examples in which Touvier contradicts himself."[22] Stated simply, the court of appeals proceeded, as Jean-Denis Bredin has asserted, "in order to exonerate."[23]

If the court of appeals was guilty of a breach of justice in its treatment of the testimony against Touvier, its most serious offense was the whitewashing of the Pétain regime itself. In effect, the court of appeals wrote nothing less than a counterhistory to the history of the Vichy past French historians had been carefully assembling at least since the publication of Robert Paxton's *La France de Vichy* in the early 1970s. Having determined that Touvier could be held accountable for the murders at Rillieux, the court then argued that these murders could not be considered crimes against humanity because they had been committed in the name of a régime, Pétain's Vichy, which, the court affirmed, did not practice a politics of "ideological hegemony." "At no time," the court argued, "did the Vichy regime have the vocation or the occasion to install any form of domination whatsoever or to impose a conquering ideology."[24] As a result of a 1985 court of appeals' decision taken in the context of the Barbie Affair, crimes against humanity could only be committed in the service of a regime fulfilling this definition. If Vichy was not "ideologically hegemonic" in its politics, Touvier was guilty only of war crimes, and the statute of limitations had run out on these crimes in the mid-1960s.

Much has been written about the April 1992 court of appeals' decision regarding Touvier, and it is to the credit of the French legal system that the decision was partially overturned by the criminal chamber of the high court of appeals in November of the same year. But what the higher court *failed to do* was to challenge the court of appeals' revisionist reading of Vichy or, more significant perhaps, chastise it for overstepping its bounds in rewriting the history of Vichy in the first place. The result was that Touvier had to stand trial on another false version of events, another counterhistory, this one concerning the particulars of his case, in being subject to conviction *only* if it could be proven he acted essentially as a German and not a French agent.

The interpretation of Vichy contained in the 1992 decision is in fact tendentious in the extreme. It constitutes, moreover, a "normalization of monsters" to the degree that it falsifies history by stripping the regime of its most sinister features. It denies any racist and persecutorial intent on the part of Vichy's leaders in stressing that none of Pétain's speeches contain anti-Semitic pronouncements.[25] Downplaying almost to the point of effacing the 1940 and 1941 anti-Jewish Statutes (which "certain figures at the controls of power . . . succeeded in [making the state] adopt") as well as other measures, the court also affirms that, as opposed to Nazi Germany, no official proclamation ever declared the Jew the enemy of the French state. Seeking to attenuate any possible "philosophical" links between Vichy and Nazism, the court asserts that the leaders of the État Français functioned throughout in a state of "complete ignorance where National-Socialist ideology was concerned."[26] The mere existence of agreements such as the July 1943 Bousquet-Oberg Accords ratifying ideological as well as practical links between the French and German police prove that the opposite was the case.

As to what in fact comprised Vichy ideology, in the court's view it consisted of a heterogeneous mix, or "constellation," of "good intentions" and "political animosities." Vichy's "political universe," the court affirmed, was "composite" in nature, its "political actions" were "variable, complex, empirical, inspired by circumstances, and its leaders had less and less control of events."[27] Vichy's politics did not, therefore, constitute a coherent ideology, which, the court argued, would only have been the case if it brooked no opposition to its own authority and was dominated by a single party. That the Militia in the later stages of the war supposedly attempted to impose such a single-party rule by "colonizing" Vichy, but failed in its efforts, was proof to the court that no politics of ideological hegemony had ever consolidated power under Pétain. The court completely ignored Vichy's very real and often murderous suppression of all opposition.

As the historian François Bédarida has argued, the errors in historical interpretation in the court's decision are nothing short of mind-boggling. Its conclusions and reasoning are so ill-founded that, as Éric Conan and Henry Rousso note, any French university student would have failed a history exam for making similar claims.[28] In the first place, Bédarida asserts, Vichy *did* possess a coherent ideology, constructed on a triple foundation of authority, hierarchy, and exclusion, all features of the regime and its ideology alluded to in the court of appeals' decision. Second, the court's statement explicitly compares Vichy's ideological incoherence to a supposedly consistent Nazi ideology, but as Bédarida also notes, the latter was no more coherent than Vichy's National Revolution when all its eclectic sources of inspiration and their influence are taken into account. But for Bédarida, perhaps the most serious flaw in the court of appeals' revision of the history of Vichy is that it completely ignores the evolution of the regime itself, which Bédarida characterizes in the following fashion: "In the beginning at Vichy, it was Leviathan who dominated, trying to impose a pitiless order . . . founded on authority and hierarchy as well as a total submission to the leader, a disciplinary power imposed on hearts, minds, and bodies. Then came the monster Behemoth, huge and terrible, the image of chaos, who gradually subdued Leviathan in a Vichy become more and more cruel and bloody, caught up in a civil war and [succumbing] to anarchic violence."[29] That Bédarida should choose biblical monsters to characterize the historical and political stages of Vichy's development completely elided by the court is, it would seem, entirely apropos.

Evidence of the court of appeals' lack of legal wisdom and judgment, not to mention objectivity, can be found in its tacit rejection of the Definitive Indictment submitted by the examining magistrate, Jean-Pierre Getti. The court was of course not obliged to accept Getti's indictment, but the evidently cavalier manner in which it dismissed the examining magistrate's carefully reasoned and meticulously developed arguments is confirmed by the egregiousness of its own legal and historical conclusions. In his indictment, Getti thoroughly dismantles Touvier's defense strategies, among them, the claim that the murders at Rillieux had already been covered in his 1946 and 1947 convictions and therefore Touvier could not be tried again for the same crimes. Getti also squares the retroactive application of France's 1964 statute on crimes against humanity with both French constitutional restraints and European human rights conventions. He also answers Touvier's claim that he could not be guilty of crimes against humanity because the Militia was not declared a criminal organization by the Nuremberg tribunal. As Getti notes, in 1964 French law incorporated Article 6C of the International Military Tribunal, which defines crimes against humanity, but *did not* incorporate Article 9, which defined criminal organizations. Therefore the latter article has no bearing on Touvier's case.

As opposed to the court of appeals judges, the examining magistrate also carefully evaluates the testimony of *all* witnesses, dismissing accusations where accounts of events do not plausibly coincide and where the crimes committed cannot be shown to fit the specificities of the statutes themselves. Next to the precision of Getti's elaboration and explanation of the charges, the court of appeals' dismissals are all the more glaringly inadequate.

But it is from the standpoint of the larger historical and legal considerations that the Definitive Indictment proves so damning to the court of appeals' subsequent decision in the Touvier case. In a carefully developed exposition marshaling testimony and evidence in the case, legal precedents, and a solid historical understanding, Getti confirms not only the extent of Vichy's historical and ideological complicity with the Germans but the interdependence of the Militia and Nazi intelligence in Lyons during Touvier's service. More significant, from a legal standpoint, Getti directly addresses the issue of whether Vichy practiced a politics of ideological hegemony and concludes emphatically that it did on the basis of its persecution of Jews. Acknowledging two stages in the development of Vichy anti-Semitism as well as historical and legal realities the court of appeals

The Trial of Paul Touvier

chose to ignore, Getti argues in favor of a progression from the anti-Jewish Statutes to Vichy complicity in the Final Solution beginning in the spring of 1942.[30] He concludes, moreover, that the Militia was "an essential instrument in the implementation of the politics of ideological hegemony embraced by the Vichy Regime."

Given the extent to which the criminal chamber of the Paris court of appeals "abused history and justice," in the words of Jean-Denis Bredin, in its dismissal of charges against Touvier in April 1992, there are certainly good reasons to take heart from Touvier's conviction two years later.[31] From a historical perspective, one could argue, for example, that the testimony and evidence presented in the Versailles courtroom proved beyond any reasonable doubt that Touvier was no "French Schindler," as his defense contended. He had not "saved" some twenty-three Jews by reducing the number of hostages to be executed from thirty to seven, as he had so often claimed. And for those who maintained that the defendant must have changed in the fifty years since the murders at Rillieux and should accordingly not be tried for crimes committed so long ago, Touvier proved them wrong as well. As many of those who witnessed the trial observed, Touvier remained as if frozen in the past. He was still an ardent defender of Vichy and the Militia, and, as the courtroom reading of the secret "green notebook" he kept during the 1980s revealed, he was still a vicious and unrepentant anti-Semite. Touvier still denounced politicians and movie stars as "kikes" (*youpins*) and spoke of Jewish conspiracies and cabals.

But given the symbolic weight placed on the Touvier trial, these considerations seem secondary. In order to make the trial "measure up" to the expectations placed on it, one could argue with Bédarida that since Touvier proudly assumed the excesses of Vichy collaborationism, he could and did serve as a sort of personification of the regime itself.[32] If this perspective seems a little too pat, it is possible to be encouraged by a comparison suggested by Pierre Vidal-Naquet. If one is disappointed that the trial of Touvier did not entirely satisfy the exigencies of history, memory, and justice, one need only imagine what the Vichy courts would have done with the Dreyfus case some fifty years after the fact.[33] If history could be rewritten at the Riom trials so that Vichy could blame Third Republican leaders for the war and France's defeat in 1940, it is not hard to imagine what liberties could and would have been taken with the Dreyfus case.

But it is as a legal event and precedent in French and international law that the Touvier trial must finally be evaluated, and here reactions are decidedly mixed. On the positive side of the ledger, legal experts have argued that the trial was exemplary to the degree that it "illustrated the important maxim that the heart of the criminal case lies in the details of proof."[34] Touvier's conviction was secured not through "rhetoric, prosecutional excess, [or] through judicial overreaching" but "through the quiet force of facts."[35] Although this may well be the case, it is also true that during the proceedings themselves, several key witnesses were forced to change their testimony on one crucial point or another to secure Touvier's conviction. For example, Jacques Delarue, who had written a report to Pompidou recommending against Touvier's pardon in 1970, reversed earlier statements claiming that Touvier had acted on behalf of Vichy to argue that he had in fact served the Germans.[36] This had of course become a crucial distinction if Touvier was to be convicted of crimes against humanity. Thus, as to the reliability of the witnesses, and not just Delarue, the 1994 trial could hardly be considered exemplary.

On a more positive note, the verdict did prove, along with the Barbie conviction, that "Nuremberg was not just a precedent of the moment."[37] Moreover, according to the legal expert Claire Finkielstein, the Touvier verdict also confirmed that the actions of an official of one state could be imputed to a second sovereign state. As a consequence, Finkielstein argues, "juridical thinking about the relation between individual actors and international states" has evolved, and perpetrators of crimes such as the murders at Rillieux can be convicted of crimes against humanity even if they acted in a more autonomous fashion than did Nazis similarly accused. Thus the Nuremberg precedent has not only been confirmed but surpassed.[38]

Optimistic conclusions such as these should, however, be tempered by other, more troubling concerns. In an effective counterargument to Finkielstein, Leila Wexler asserts that in the long history of the French courts' efforts to deal with crimes against humanity in the case of both Touvier and Barbie, they have "failed to construct a legal regime that would permit them to articulate both the substantive norms and procedural rules necessary to a stable and nonarbitrary basis on which future cases could be based. In so doing," Wexler continues, "even in convicting Touvier, the courts have weakened the effectiveness of their decisions as well as their value as [international] legal precedent."[39] Indeed, as the French magistrate Christian Guéry has argued, in their efforts to correct and adapt crimes against humanity law according to the exigencies of the moment, the French courts have created a definition of these crimes that is at once "narrow and volatile" and may ultimately have no real juridical meaning at all.[40] Similar views concerning the meaning and definition of crimes against humanity were in fact expressed by French jurists many years ago during the Nuremberg trials.[41] There is, then, a sad irony in the fact that in a country which has struggled so long and hard with the problem, very little optimism emerges.

So what is left of the Touvier case? In France, first of all, there is a recognition prompted also by events in Bosnia, Rwanda, and elsewhere that crimes against humanity need to be reconceptualized in legal, historical, and psychological terms, even down to the definition of "humanity" itself.[42] (Unfortunately, as we shall see, the Papon trial did not help to elucidate these matters further.) More specifically, for those who do not condemn the Touvier trial for the distorted version of history it was obliged to assume and perpetuate, or for the legal imbroglio it failed to resolve, another perspective is somewhat more reassuring. If the recent reemergence of the Holocaust denial in France, or *le négationnisme* as the French call it, proves anything, it is that discredited revisions of history are never definitively put to rest and must be challenged each time they recur. In the months following the Touvier verdict, alongside more objective accounts of the trial and of the events leading up to it appeared a hagiographic account of Touvier's persecution by his lawyer Jacques Trémolet de Villers. In Trémolet's book, the myth of Paul Touvier as a martyred innocent was relaunched. At the same time, revisionist accounts of the trial of Philippe Pétain painting him as a martyr and a national hero appeared on bookstore shelves. One of the books was penned by Papon's lawyer, Jean-Marc Varaut. In helping to make the Papon trial possible, the Touvier verdict at least set the stage for one more struggle against efforts to rewrite the history of the Dark Years and France's collaboration with Nazi Germany. Given the troubled memory of Vichy in what Alain Finkielkraut has labeled this "century of negations," this is perhaps the best one could hope for.

6 : Mitterrand's Dark Years

A President's "French Youth"

Few books published in France in recent memory have enjoyed the success, or to be more accurate, the succès de scandale of
Pierre Péan's *Une Jeunesse française: François Mitterrand 1934–1949*. Released in early fall 1994 and dealing in detail with Mitterrand's extreme
right-wing *engagement* in the interwar years, his service to Vichy, his
involvement in the Resistance, and, finally, his early postwar political
maneuverings, *Une Jeunesse française* immediately provoked a storm of
controversy in France and abroad.[1] In an effort to put an end to the
controversy, Mitterrand decided to go on national television on the
night of 12 September 1994 to discuss candidly his past and his attitudes toward Vichy and its leaders. He also spoke of his knowledge—
or lack thereof—of Vichy's anti-Semitic policies and his postwar
friendship with René Bousquet. Mitterrand's comments only exacerbated the situation and intensified debate in the media.

Following Mitterrand's television appearance, fellow politicians
and political allies, historians, political scientists, and others, invited to
discuss their views on the affair in the pages of *Le Monde*, *Esprit*, and

other publications, waded into the controversy. They offered their assessments of the impact of the revelations on Mitterrand's image and the legacy of his presidency, as well as their effect on the memory of Vichy. Several commentators, especially Mitterrand's fellow Socialists, speculated on how the revelations would affect the future of the Socialist Party and the fate of the left in France in general.

The resulting commentaries were fascinating both for the diversity of opinions expressed and the range of issues addressed. As to the scandal's impact on the image of Mitterrand the man, the commentary was almost uniformly negative, not to say devastating. Those who defended Mitterrand included longtime political cronies like Minister of Culture Jack Lang, who praised Mitterrand's courage for helping to bring to light troubling episodes in his past. (Mitterrand not only discussed his past on television but granted numerous interviews to Péan during the writing of *Une Jeunesse française,* the texts of which are sprinkled throughout the book.) They also included many on the extreme right, who took pleasure in noting, as did *National-Hebdo*, that this was "no scoop," since Mitterrand's Vichy past had been reported much earlier in *Crapouillot* and other neofascist reviews.[2] Hubert Massol, a National Front leader, praised Mitterrand's courage and loyalty for standing by old (right-wing) friends as well as his "sense of History." Massol also denounced "the politico-media plot which exploits and maintains Franco-French hatred for electoral purposes on the eve of a presidential election."[3]

In the chorus of denunciations by those who considered Mitterrand blameworthy, many attacked the president for his cynicism and opportunism, his overwhelming egotism, his inability to distinguish between his person and the office of the president of the republic, and, perhaps what is most interesting, his distorted and indeed dangerously misguided sense of history. Finally, precisely Mitterrand's sense of loyalty to individuals, regardless of *their* pasts, was called into question.

In one of the most scathing and thoroughgoing attacks on Mitterrand published in the wake of the scandal, titled, appropriately enough, *L'Homme au-dessus des lois* (The man above the law), Paul

Thibaud denounced Mitterrand's lack of principles and beliefs and his cynical exploitation of politics and the political process solely for the purpose of self-aggrandizement. For Thibaud, such an attitude denoted a monstrous egotism and an almost godlike self-sufficiency that placed him beyond the meager judgments of those who elected him: "It is not out of modesty that Mitterrand pretends to downplay politics, it is rather out of self-glorification. Politics are trifles, a question of simply giving shape to a series of pre-existing givens requiring only a little political skill. And political skill, he of course has plenty of that, you can be sure! But as for judging him on the basis of that skill, absolutely not! He's worth more than that. He cannot be reduced to his political accomplishments! The best of him lies elsewhere, where we can neither see nor judge him, but from whence he governs us."[4] Despite claims to the contrary by Mitterrand, Péan, and other biographers of the president, Thibaud insisted that the only cause Mitterrand learned to espouse during the war was his own.[5] The standard bearer of the postwar left in France was nothing but an opportunist.

Other commentators were equally harsh, denouncing an egotism that prevented Mitterrand from understanding history and led to an almost criminal conflation of his person and the office of the presidency itself. In his contribution to a special section of the November 1994 edition of *Esprit* titled "Le Président, Vichy, la France, et la mort," Olivier Mongin described Mitterrand as a bourgeois "nothing" who, by virtue of attaching himself to increasingly just political and social causes (presumably in moving from Vichy to the Resistance and the extreme right to Socialism), came to believe in his own moral superiority. But this did not, according to Mongin, give him a richer comprehension of the movement of history: "He remains mute in the face of History, because all he knows are the peripeteia of his own personal history."[6]

Other commentators focused less on Mitterrand's general lack of historical understanding than on specific blind spots suggestive of a willful disavowal of the realities of Vichy and an indifference to the most troubling aspect of its legacy in contemporary France: the regime's persecution of Jews and its complicity in the Final Solution.

During his televised interview, Mitterrand claimed that Vichy's 1940 and 1941 anti-Jewish Statutes were directed only at "foreign Jews."[7] He also stated that he had not paid particular attention to these statutes nor been attentive to French roundups of Jews beginning in the spring of 1942, when he was comfortably ensconced at Vichy. Moreover, during the television interview, Mitterrand went on to describe René Bousquet, his friend and the man responsible for implementing the Final Solution in France, as a man of "exceptional stature." Considered together, these assertions are two crucial building blocks in the construction of a veritable counterhistory of Vichy. First, they falsely limit Vichy's crimes by arguing that only foreign Jews were discriminated against (thus relaunching the old "shield" thesis, according to which Vichy protected all the French, including the Jews). Second, and perhaps even more surprising, they reverse moral notions of right and wrong learned so painfully from the Vichy experience and the Holocaust in characterizing Bousquet as essentially a "good man."

The implications of Mitterrand's statements here are disturbing and far-reaching in other ways as well. As Tony Judt noted in his review in the *New York Review of Books* of Péan's book and the scandal it provoked, Mitterrand's evident indifference to Vichy's anti-Semitic persecutions and the beginnings of the Final Solution in France make it hard to believe that he was, as he claimed to Péan, repulsed by the anti-Semitic character of right-wing demonstrations in the Latin Quarter in the late 1930s. Judt went on to note that an even more troubling attitude lay at the heart of Mitterrand's confusion as to who was targeted by Vichy's anti-Semitic laws: "[L]ike his friend Bousquet and many others at the time, Mitterrand instinctively and unthinkingly distinguishes foreign Jews from French ones and finds it somehow comforting to believe that Vichy only persecuted the former. . . . His statement simply and tellingly confirms that François Mitterrand was no different from the men of Vichy and that in fundamental respects he has not changed. That is why he cannot condemn the regime root and branch, because he would be condemning himself."[8]

Mitterrand's implicit defense of Vichy and its policies in his televised comments was, of course, not simply his affair alone, since he was, after all, president of the republic and therefore the spokesperson for the nation. Moreover, according to the historian Claire Andrieu, Mitterrand's self-indulgence on this score was more troubling still, since his office required him to defend the principles on which the French republic was founded, and "a president of the Republic who does not adhere to a republican discourse concerning France's past, who does not whole-heartedly condemn the Vichy régime, is failing in his function as guardian of the Constitution."[9] But if the affair proved anything, according to many commentators, it was precisely that Mitterrand did not and would not put the French republic and its laws before his own interests because, in a very real sense, he had long since confused the two to the detriment of the former. Thus, in speaking in his capacity as president before a nationally televised audience, Mitterrand apparently felt no compunction about praising Bousquet's "exceptional stature," even though Bousquet had come to symbolize the most inhumane and antidemocratic excesses of the Vichy regime. Bousquet's defense was, moreover, apparently undertaken for no other reason than the fact that he had been Mitterrand's friend and a long-standing political ally. Indeed, as noted earlier, Mitterrand had discreetly supported Bousquet during his 1949 trial for treason and in the early 1990s had tried to intervene in the judicial process to delay indefinitely Bousquet's trial on charges of crimes against humanity. Such a troubling willingness to privilege his interests and those of his friends over those of the nation, regardless of the moral and ethical, not to mention legal, implications, suggested a dangerous inability on Mitterrand's part to distinguish between "the private man and the public functionary."[10] Even Mitterrand's "familiar, conversational tone" in his public pronouncements confirmed the conflation of the public figure with the private individual.[11]

If the scandal surrounding Mitterrand's past severely damaged his reputation and in a number of ways compromised the office of the president of the republic in the process, for many it also did irrevocable damage to the nation's already profoundly troubled sense of its own past where the Dark Years were concerned. Claire Andrieu noted that whereas the Gaullist myth of Resistance had perpetrated a number of false illusions, at least it had the merit of helping raise the nation's morale and self-esteem in the wake of the devastation and humiliation of the Occupation. By contrast, Mitterrand's more recent comments on the period served only to confuse. His soft-pedaling of Vichy's excesses and the trajectory and timing of his political itinerary between 1941 and 1945 tended to blur the very real distinctions between collaboration and resistance. Having suffered through the demise of the reassuring and idealistic Gaullist myth in the early 1970s, the nation was now invited to share in the opportunistic and glibly postmodern epic of Mitterrand's wartime careerism.

If the revelations contained in *Une Jeunesse française* and the president's televised comments tended to trouble the waters of the nation's past, in the view of a number of commentators they also adversely affected France's political future, specifically that of the left. Most agreed that in the wake of the affair, the left, and the Socialists in particular, could no longer assume the attitude of moral superiority that had characterized them in recent years. Instead, it was their obligation to recognize "[l]'affairisme" and self-interest of *mitterrandisme* and to acknowledge that even if "everybody hadn't sinned . . . everybody was at least more or less aware that the sleaze factor had won out and that singing the praises of the Rights of Man was the best means of protecting oneself from being implicated."[12] Others, including Charles Fiterman of the French Communist Party, simply lamented the fact that Mitterrand had anointed himself—and was generally acknowledged to be—"the great organizer of the left."[13] The left's reputation and its future prospects could only suffer. Those to be blamed, according to Fiterman, included the president himself and those he duped—the French electorate and especially the Socialist Party.

Among Mitterrand's fellow Socialists, many expressed continued support and respect for their embattled leader, but others voiced the concern that the party itself should not go down with the sinking ship of *mitterrandisme*. Julian Dray stated in *Le Monde* that "we are not forced to shoulder responsibility for the comportment or the life of

François Mitterrand." Echoing these sentiments, Jean-Christophe Cambadélis affirmed: "[I]f the Socialist Party doesn't take a clear position, this will only continue. It is important to know from this moment on if the Party is independent—even vis-à-vis the President of the Republic." Other Socialist leaders commenting on the affair did not offer pronouncements on the party's future because they simply could not get beyond the shock of the revelations concerning Mitterrand's past. Specifically, the president's friendship with Bousquet left many dumbfounded or outraged. Jean Le Garrec expressed his dismay in stating: "As for me, I simply do not understand the president's comments about René Bousquet. What he says is extremely painful to us and it is a pain with which we will be forced to live." Pierre Moscovici was more blunt: "For me, to be a Socialist is to be anti-fascist and anti-fascist always! Never keep council with anti-Semitism! Never! What shocks me are Mitterrand's declarations concerning Bousquet, this zealous accomplice of the Final Solution. I've said that I am troubled because I *am* troubled."[14] It is worth noting, finally, that even several years after the scandal broke in 1994, the feeling of betrayal among the Socialists over Mitterrand's friendship with Bousquet still lingered. In an interview with Jean Lacouture on 15 April 1998, Lionel Jospin, now prime minister under Jacques Chirac, observed: "Whatever the moment that he [Mitterrand] met [Bousquet], he [Mitterrand] certainly knew enough about the history of the period [the Occupation] to refuse to have any personal relations with the man."[15]

In retrospect, the controversy surrounding the publication of Péan's *Une Jeunesse française* and Mitterrand's September 1994 television appearance is somewhat surprising for several reasons. First, Mitterrand's right-wing past, his service to Vichy, and his friendship with Bousquet had been widely known for many years and had been dredged up periodically by his enemies to damage his political career. Among the more recent "eruptions," in its July–August 1991 issue featuring a dossier provocatively titled "Mitterrand et la Cagoule," the neofascist magazine *Le Choc du mois* displayed on its cover and in the dossier itself photos of the young Mitterrand in right-wing, xenophobic demonstrations in the Latin Quarter during the 1930s. The dossier also reported Mitterrand's friendship while at Vichy and in the postwar years with former members of the right-wing terrorist Cagoule organization including André Bettencourt, François Dalle, and Eugène Shueller, who gave Mitterrand his first postwar job, and mentioned his long-standing friendship with Bousquet. The dossier and the photos created hardly a ripple at the time, presumably because *Le Choc*'s unsavory reputation cast long shadows on its credibility. The same photos and "revelations," of course, provoked a much greater outcry following the publication of the Péan biography. Similarly, in *Le Noir et le rouge* (*The Black and the Red* [1987]), a biography of Mitterrand published in the mid-1980s, Catherine Nay noted Mitterrand's prewar right-wing politics, including his stint as a writer for *L'Écho de Paris*, a profascist, pro-Franco newspaper, as well as his service to Vichy.[16] Mitterrand's friendship with and support of Bousquet were also widely known, but this information was not widely disseminated in the press, despite the allegations of *Le Choc*, because little concrete evidence of the links between the two men was available. (Indeed, a journalist at a major Parisian daily informed me in the summer of 1992 that Bousquet was known to be dining at the Elysée Palace, but the story went unreported because no one could provide proof.)

So the question remains, why the uproar surrounding the publication of *Une Jeunesse française*? The most obvious answer is that Mitterrand himself assisted in the project, providing documentation as well as commentary on the information Péan unearthed. Presumably, he agreed to work with Péan to set the record straight, to put his past to rest once and for all and, not coincidentally, to polish up his image for posterity. This was especially important to Mitterrand, since his health was failing and his tenure as president was nearing its end. But if these were Mitterrand's intentions, the desired ends were certainly not achieved—indeed, it is hard to imagine what could have been *more* damaging to Mitterrand and his reputation at that moment than the airing of his past in this fashion.

Other factors beyond Mitterrand's participation in *Une Jeunesse française* played a significant role in creating the controversy as well.

Another investigation into Mitterrand's (more recent) past appeared at almost the same time as Péan's book, this one by three young journalists titled *La Main droite de Dieu* (The right hand of God).[17] The title is, of course, a play on Mitterrand's nickname: Dieu. Harsher in its assessment of Mitterrand than Péan's book (the three authors acknowledged being disillusioned Mitterrand supporters), *La Main droite* provided further insights into Mitterrand's links with Bousquet and carefully explored the ways in which Mitterrand, through his associates, forwarded the cause of the National Front (hence God's "right hand") in the early 1980s by providing Jean-Marie Le Pen with the opportunity to appear on national television for the first time.[18] The book also discussed Mitterrand's leniency toward the former right-wing military leaders of the Algerian *putsch*, as well as his well-established tradition of annually placing a bouquet on Pétain's tomb, despite repeated public protests. In short, *La Main droite de Dieu* brought Mitterrand's right-wing "connection" up to date, thereby linking his Vichy past to his current actions as president. Following closely on the highly publicized trial of Paul Touvier for crimes against humanity, the Mitterrand scandal served as one more reminder of *l'actualité*, or timeliness, of Vichy in French public life.

As already noted, it is one of the ironies of the scandal surrounding Mitterand's past that just before *Une Jeunesse française* appeared, Éric Conan and Henry Rousso published their polemical text, *Vichy: Un passé qui ne passe pas* (*Vichy: An Everpresent Past*), in which they in effect called for an end to the nation's obsessive focus on the Vichy period and its thirst for a new "revelation" or skeleton from the closet of a famous politician, historical figure, or intellectual every few months.[19] Apart from the evident morbidity of this obsession with the Dark Years, Conan and Rousso argued that false "revelations" and glaring headlines did little to satisfy the nation's "duty to memory" and, instead, risked distorting the history of the period itself.[20]

The Mitterrand scandal proved, nevertheless, that Conan and Rousso's advice went largely unheeded, and that when it came to the Dark Years, the "acceptance" or integration of the period's troubled history called for by Conan and Rousso had not yet taken hold. It was clear, as Robert Paxton put it so provocatively, that "Vichy stirs the French public more than either money or sex" and that dispassionate closure on the period was not at hand.[21]

It would be a mistake, however, to ascribe the succès de scandale of *Une Jeunesse française* exclusively to the nation's obsession with Vichy or Mitterrand's willingness to talk about his past with Péan. At the time of the book's publication the French had been suffering through an extended period of political and social malaise characterized by the continuing problems of unemployment and strongly divided opinion on the issue of immigration, as well as the spectacle of political corruption and scandal on a large scale. Mitterrand's name, of course, figured significantly, especially in discussions of the last category, given his relationship with the disgraced Bernard Tapie and the former prime minister, Pierre Bérégovoy. Having been appointed in 1992 to clean up corruption in the Socialist ranks and having himself been implicated in financial misdealings, Bérégovoy committed suicide on 1 May 1993. Less than a year later, Mitterrand's former confidant, François de Grossouvre, who still maintained an office in the Elysée Palace, also apparently committed suicide, distraught over disagreements with Mitterrand over Grossouvre's criticisms of corruption among Mitterrand's cronies and friends.[22] In light of these events, the title of a study of the Mitterrand years published in Great Britain in 1994, *The Death of Politics*, seems disturbingly apropros.[23]

Given the extent of the controversy surrounding the publication of *Une Jeunesse française* and its impact on Mitterrand's legacy as well as discussions of the history and especially the memory of Vichy, it is important to look closely at the "revelations" the book supposedly contains. According to Robert Paxton, there are three *faits nouveaux* (to use the French judicial term) that can be gleaned from the book and Mitterrand's subsequent comments about its contents:

One is how deeply Mitterrand believed in a certain Vichy—the Vichy of moral renewal, national unity, and social solidarity—and may do so still. Secondly, that attractive program has made Vichy's exclusionary side invisible to him. It still seems difficult for him to focus on the Jewish Statutes (which he must have had to explain to returning Jewish prisoners of war in 1942–1943). How else can one fathom this normally precise speaker's famous lapse about their affecting only foreign Jews? Third is the perduration of Mitterrand's association with René Bousquet, whose role in the deportation of the Jews was made public not by Darquier de Pellepoix in the 1978 *Express* interview, as the President averred [in the television interview], but by Joseph Billig's *Commissariat général des questions juives* in 1955.[24]

Paxton concludes by noting that the book and the affair as a whole provide an important frame of reference for understanding some of Mitterrand's attitudes and actions as president: "Cumulatively, deeper knowledge of President Mitterrand's long-known Vichy past suggests that although his Social Catholicism could be reworked to fit a Socialist vocabulary, the president never really shared the sensibilities of his *'peuple de gauche.'* Now once baffling presidential decisions can fall into place: the wreath on Pétain's grave, the appeals for national reconciliation, the refusal to apologize for France's role in the deportations."[25]

While Paxton may be giving Péan too much credit in revealing the length of Mitterrand's relationship with Bousquet (the relationship is discussed more thoroughly, or at least more provocatively, in *La Main droite de Dieu*, and was disclosed earlier, as noted, in *Le Choc du mois*), his comments as to the extent and effects of Mitterrand's commitment to Vichy ideology are altogether apposite. Mitterrand's espousal of Pétainisme, as well as his imprisonment in Germany and successful career at Vichy, are in fact thoroughly, if sympathetically, documented in *Une Jeunesse française.*

After fighting apparently reluctantly in May–June 1940 for republican "values (nonvalues) in which I did not believe," Mitterrand was captured and sent to prison camps in Germany.[26] During some eighteen months in captivity, he distinguished himself through intellectual activities, such as lecturing fellow inmates on various topics and writing editorials for camp newspapers. Although a good deal of Mitterrandian mythology has it that it was in experiencing solidarity with his fellow prisoners that Mitterrand began to move to the left, Péan calls this view into question by noting that while in the prison camps, Mitterrand was firmly committed to Pétainisme and shared the marshal's *revanchiste* attitudes toward the Third Republic and its leaders. Nevertheless, the image Mitterrand projected to his fellow prisoners was highly ambiguous, both politically and personally. In recounting his interviews with many of these former fellow prisoners, Péan notes that some took Mitterrand to be somewhat leftist, while others were convinced he was royalist or on the extreme right. Virtually all recognized in him "an ambitious and proud individual. He already thought of himself as being above the masses."[27]

Perhaps the most accurate portrayal of Mitterrand at the time was provided in the camp newspaper, where he was likened to Balzac's Vautrin in *Old Goriot*, a man "of multiple incarnations." (Later, François Mauriac would also liken Mitterrand to a "character out of a novel," and, indeed, of the same novel, comparing him more flatteringly to the young Eugène de Rastignac, noted obviously for his social ambition.)

Another component of the Mitterrand myth debunked by Péan concerns his persistence in attempting to escape. Mitterrand did indeed attempt three escapes, succeeding on the third try, but he was motivated less by a spirit of resistance in undertaking these endeavors than by a desire to save his engagement to his prewar sweetheart, who, during Mitterrand's captivity, had fallen for someone else.

Upon his arrival back in France in December 1941, Mitterrand did not, of course, pass more or less unproblematically into the Resistance as he maintained in *My Part of the Truth* ("upon re-entering France, I entered the Resistance, without any real crisis of conscience"), but instead went to work almost immediately at Vichy as an ardent young Pétainiste.[28] But even before his arrival at Vichy, Mitterrand had already thoroughly absorbed a number of the essential tenets of what would become the ideology of the National Revolution. Among these was a return to the soil, a hearkening back to France's ancient, natural roots and the sturdy "race" of men that inhabited the land. In an article published in the April 1943 issue of Vichyite *Métier du chef,*

Mitterrand noted that, upon returning from Germany: "Henceforth, attentive to the fragrances and colors, the changes in the sky, the movements of animals, the cycles of the seasons, and the customs of men subject to the rhythm of life in this corner of the earth, . . . I would be able to lend the regular cadence of my breathing to the omnipotence of the original breezes."[29] His generation, Mitterrand concluded, "will have made a hundred detours before understanding that France is a *person*," and that all men were joined to this "person" by "a mystical link."[30]

This sort of integral nationalism, so reminiscent of the likes of Péguy and Barrès, among others, served Mitterrand well at Vichy. There, he quickly joined the Légion Française des Combattants, the organization that also welcomed Paul Touvier and would eventually evolve into the Militia. As Péan puts it discreetly, the "ideological program advertised" by the Légion did not "repel" the young veteran, but instead appealed to his hatred of the Third Republic and its "decadent" values and his penchant for what can only be described as the more fascistic virtues of force for its own sake and a deep-seated anti-intellectualism. Péan concedes that Mitterrand's stint in the Légion marks the "high water mark of his *pétainisme*." In a letter dated 22 April 1942, Mitterrand calls for the creation of stronger militias to create a more powerful France and notes in an earlier letter dated 26 March, "I am more and more horrified by ideas."[31] In other correspondence, Mitterrand also laments a "lack of fanaticism" among Vichy officials, who, he believed, did not demonstrate enough fervor in pursuing the ideals of the National Revolution.

During this period Mitterrand also frequented friends who were former members of the Cagoule and now occupied powerful positions at Vichy. Among these were Gabriel Jeantet, for whose Pétainist review, *France: Revue de l'état nouveau*, Mitterrand penned his now infamous article, "Pèlerinage en Thuringie" (Pilgrimage to Thuringia), in which he describes the history of postrevolutionary (and republican) France as "one hundred and fifty years of errors."[32]

Even in taking his first step toward resistance in attending a secret meeting of ex-prisoners at Montmaur in late 1942 (the group would soon come to be known as La Chaîne), Mitterrand's outlook was still highly elitist and authoritarian. It had nothing in common with the egalitarian spirit Mitterrand supposedly embraced for good in the stalags. In a letter written before attending the meeting, Mitterrand outlined what he considered to be the principles that should inspire and animate the group. The principles speak for themselves, and in no way mark a break with the spirit of Pétainisme:

1. A group can only be led by a few men,
2. Who in no way must be accountable to this group,
3. Who must lead it according to their pleasure which, for *us* [my emphasis: note the change in person] must be our conscience and our will to succeed.[33]

Indeed, the disdain for the masses implicit in these principles is reiterated even more crudely in subsequent remarks in Mitterrand's correspondence following a visit to a friend in a tiny village in the heart of Auvergne. Here, Mitterrand even appears to renounce the Pétainiste return to the soil and its idealization of rustic virtues of the noble "race of men" of the countryside. He describes the local residents as "crude individuals, little working people, ugly," and their language as a "dialect laced with French." In a passage striking for its condescension, Mitterrand wonders how to "inspire" these people: "How does one give a spark back to these people? What separates them from pigs, except what they screw up? I think of these words of my friend from Montmaur: 'We are the ones, with our blood and our heroism, who will pay for everyone. It is necessary, there must be sacrifices made for masses.'"[34] Although for Mitterrand it is now the heroic elite who must pay, the Pétainiste theme of remorse and repentance for past sins is all too evident.[35]

If Mitterrand's deep-seated elitism and disdain for "the people" changed during the course of his career as a *résistant* and even in the political maneuverings in the immediate postwar period, these changes are not evident in *Une Jeunesse française*. In fact, the image that emerges of Mitterrand or "Morland," the head of the veterans' Resistance movement, is, as many commentators have noted, that of an overly ambitious careerist intent on exploiting all available avenues to achieve power. Mitterrand's courage and cunning are beyond doubt but so, too, is a lingering and still strong Pétainisme, which resulted, during the Purge trials, in Mitterrand's affirming during the trial of the marshal that those truly responsible for the Occupation were the Third Republican leaders who got France into war in the first place. One wonders what the Resistance hero thought of the Riom trials, when these Third Republican leaders—Léon Blum and Edouard Daladier among them—were tried by Vichy as those responsible for causing the war. The spectacular failure of the trials as a public relations fiasco was made glaringly evident when Hitler himself told the Vichy authorities to put an end to them.

Mitterrand's animosity toward the likes of Blum and Daladier did not, however, prevent him from casting his lot with them when he considered it expedient. In 1946, he ran on the Rassemblement des Gauches Républicaines ticket, a party headed by the former Radical Edouard Daladier. In explaining this and other wholly opportunistic political moves, Péan writes: "[I]t is clear that Mitterrand's primary objective was to get himself elected: the political party was secondary."[36] Indeed, the same expedient attitude seems to have informed more personal decisions as well. In order to provide himself with a more comfortable living and firm financial base from which to launch his forays into politics, Mitterrand accepted a sinecure arranged by friends and relations as editor of *Votre Beauté*, whose funding came from the L'Oréal group, many of whose executives had previously played important roles in the Cagoule. In fact, to the degree that Mitterrand displayed real constancy during this period, it was in the context of loyalty to former right-wing friends. The two most notable examples were Gabriel Jeantet (mentioned above) and Jean Bouvyer, both imprisoned and largely unrepentant former Cagoulards. Apart from playing a role in the Cagoule's murder of the antifascist Rosselli brothers in the 1930s, Bouvyer also worked for the CGQJ during the Occupation.

If Mitterrand's career during and immediately after the Occupation is reminiscent of a character out of a novel, as François Mauriac suggests, it appears to be less that of the *engagé* political figure created by leftist writers including Nizan or the Malraux of *La Condition humaine* and *L'Espoir* than of the supremely egocentric and often politically and ideologically distasteful heroes of Montherlant and Drieu la Rochelle. Indeed, Mitterrand's admiration for these and other reactionary writers, including Robert Brasillach and Charles Maurras, became clear in Péan's biography. In a statement as remarkable in its way for its political insensitivity as his statements on television concerning Vichy's anti-Jewish Statutes, Mitterrand describes Maurras to Péan as a "intransigent patriot," and this despite Maurras's description of the French defeat of 1940 as a "divine surprise," a statement with which Mitterrand must surely have been familiar.

Of Mitterrand's literary predilections and affinities, perhaps none is more interesting than what might be described as the "Montherlant connection." In his comments on the scandal over Mitterrand's Vichy past, Stanley Hoffmann discusses Mitterrand both as literary character and as *littérateur* and notes that the most decisive influence on Mitterrand's style was Montherlant.[37] Péan, for his part, remarks on Mitterrand's interest in Montherlant in the 1930s, discussing at length Mitterrand's favorable review of *Service inutile* in the *Revue Montalembert* in December 1935. In his review, the young Mitterrand is particularly struck by a phrase that in many ways captures Mitterrand's own trajectory and expresses the sterile egotism shared with Montherlant: "I have only the idea I create of myself to keep me afloat on the seas of nothingness." But the affinities do not stop here. In a 1938 letter Mitterrand affirmed, "My great regret is to be incapable of plunging myself into everything. I would be delighted if the destiny of all those I encounter would be to be my prey, into which, according to my whim, I could immerse myself. How could God have created the world without me being at the source?"[38] This "ferocious desire to dominate, to vampirize others," is highly reminiscent of attitudes expressed in Montherlant's interwar essays like "Aux fontaines du désir" and "Syncrétisme et alternance."[39] In these texts, for example, Montherlant speaks of "this anguish of not being able to embrace all things, both through one's intelligence and one's senses" as well as of his "nostalgia to be ubiquitous."[40]

Two final points of comparison between Mitterrand and Montherlant are worth underscoring. Like his young admirer, Montherlant was also obsessed with French decadence in the 1930s, and, like Mitterrand, he witnessed firsthand the annihilation of the French army in the face of superior German forces in 1940. Impressed by the health, vitality, and indeed virility of France's conquerors, Montherlant described the sheer physical presence of these men in glowing terms in *Le Solstice de juin*, a collection of essays first serialized in the arch-collaborationist periodical *La Gerbe* and then published in book form. Montherlant contrasts the Nazi troops—which he characterizes as "big schoolboys" with "naked legs" from the "Kingdom of Clovis," playing harmonicas as they marched—with the skinny, "bespectacled" French troops "lost beneath their helmets."[41] The book was so offensive to some that when it was displayed in the window of the Rive Gauche bookshop in November 1941, the bookstore was bombed. In his wartime journal, Jean Guéhenno noted disdainfully that in its praise of the German victory, *Le Solstice* was "the lyrical chant of a Chateaubriand gone to seed."[42]

Mitterrand, of course, penned no praise of the German soldiers during the war, and he certainly never compromised himself in the Parisian collaborationist milieus, as did Montherlant. But in 1986, he gave an interview to the journalists Pierre Jouve and Ali Magoudi in which he described the German soldiers he witnessed in 1940 in terms strikingly similar to those used in *Le Solstice de juin*: "[O]ne could see the Germans arriving, magnificent, in shorts, singing, machine guns on their arms."[43]

What should one make of these affinities between the two men? Perhaps very little, but a more judicious response might suggest that Montherlant and Mitterrand's shared distaste for republican "decadence," as well as their admiration, expressed many years apart, for the vitality and indeed virility of the German soldiers form part of a broader nexus of ideas and attitudes associated with the French cultural and intellectual fascism of the interwar years.[44] It was certainly these shared perspectives that led both men to enthusiastically endorse Vichy at the outset and eventually led Montherlant to collaborate with the Nazis in Paris.

Mitterrand's prewar reactionary outlook, however, led to explicit forms of *engagement* in the 1930s. His actions in this context constitute not only some of the most interesting "revelations" in the Péan biography, but they go a long way toward explaining Mitterrand's Vichy commitments. Not only did Mitterrand participate in right-wing student demonstrations against foreigners *and Jews* in the mid-1930s, but he was a fervent admirer of Colonel de la Roque, the demagogic leader of the fascistic Croix de Feu.[45] As Péan reports, Mitterrand joined the youth auxiliary of the Croix de Feu, the Volontaires Nationaux, whose lapel pin he proudly wore, even though this once resulted in a beating at the hands of leftist students. Mitterrand also wrote for the reactionary newspaper *L'Écho de Paris*, which, through its editor, Henri de Kerillis, led the charge against French support for republican Spain after the outbreak of civil war in 1936. According to Péan, in its editorials *L'Écho* also characterized de la Roque and Jacques Doriot, the former Communist leader-turned-fascist, as martyrs of the "Reds." While writing for *L'Écho*, Mitterrand penned articles of support for right-wing student demonstrations and laments concerning the invasion of the Latin Quarter by *métèques* (swarthy foreigners), laments which, to contemporary audiences, must certainly recall the rhetoric of the Le Pen and National Front: "[H]enceforth, the Latin Quarter is this complex of colors and sounds so cacophonous that one has the impression of rediscovering this Tower of Babel, something we did not want to believe possible."[46] While working at *L'Écho,* Mitterrand also contributed five hundred francs to a campaign to oust Léon Blum and his Popular Front government, and, while doing charitable works for the poor, nevertheless expressed his disdain for them publicly on at least one occasion. In a June 1937 speech, Mitterrand stated: "Without a doubt, it would be easy to prove that there is nothing more different from a stereotypical poor person than the real thing—that the hypothetical saintliness of

Mitterrand's Dark Years

poverty doesn't jive with these badly-mannered, often dirty individuals who don't hesitate to spend anything they have, as long as it is to satisfy their pleasures of the moment. There is in reality no greater scandal for the well-intentioned than to be confronted with the luxuries in which indigence clothes itself, with the demands of the hungry, and the self-indulgence demonstrated by the poor."[47] Statements such as these certainly cast a different and more troubling light on the sincerity of Mitterrand's "populist" sympathies in his role as leader of the French left in the postwar years.

In attempting to explain his reactionary sympathies and political commitments in the interwar period, Mitterrand informed Péan during one of their interviews that in the 1930s he acted "more through instinct than reason," and that it was not until his captivity in Germany that he developed "an original manner of thinking." Like so many other statements in *Une Jeunesse française*, Mitterrand's comments here are intended to reassure and to clarify, but in fact they only serve to muddy the waters. If the young Mitterrand learned to think for himself for the first time as a prisoner of war, then the intellectual maturation brought on in captivity resulted not in a break with his past and its values but in a *reaffirmation* of the beliefs and principles that guided it through a commitment to Pétain and his National Revolution. The more mature and independent-minded Mitterrand returned from captivity not to join the Resistance but to go directly to Vichy. Unwilling to disavow *that* past, Mitterrand has ultimately proven incapable of disavowing what led up to it as well.

So what lessons can one draw from *Une Jeunesse française*, both as concerns its subject and the nation he governed for so long? As for Mitterrand himself, the "portrait of the adventurer" elaborated in such detail offers no hard and fast conclusions concerning the man, other than the fact that although they share a certain shrewd political opportunism, Mitterrand was no real-life Lacombe Lucien, as some have suggested. In fact, the former's career through the late 1930s and early 1940s was remarkably consistent and sprang unquestionably from deeply held political beliefs. To the degree that Mitterrand acted opportunistically, it was, unfortunately, in his move into the Resistance and to the left in the immediate postwar years. It was then that he proved himself something of the Montherlantian *condotierre*, defined by his gift for political about-faces and his ability to "change ideals . . . like perfumes."[48]

And what of France itself? The trajectory of one man, even if that man has served as president of the republic for fourteen years, cannot be said to define the nation's trajectory. Nevertheless, Mitterrand's destiny and that of the nation itself can be said to overlap in at least two significant ways. First, like Mitterrand's Pétainisme, France's Vichy period was not an aberration, a break with what had gone before, as historians had long maintained, but the continuation, indeed the fulfillment of reactionary, authoritarian, and xenophobic attitudes that had been there all along. Moreover, Mitterrand's selective memory and understanding of Vichy and his thinly disguised efforts to somehow exonerate it recall the nation's belabored and lengthy efforts to deal with Vichy's afterlife. But in keeping with the psychoanalytical metaphor proposed by Rousso in *The Vichy Syndrome*, the past can never be completely or permanently repressed, and it came as no surprise that Mitterrand's Vichy past resurfaced once again several months later, this time in conversations with Elie Wiesel. For those who might have hoped that the presence of an interlocutor who had survived the Holocaust would give Mitterrand pause before articulating the same revisionist, counterhistorical views that outraged many the previous September, these hopes were dashed in a most jarring fashion. Mitterrand reiterated his strongly favorable opinion of Bousquet, describing him as "direct, intelligent, and even brilliant." He praised Bousquet's physical courage for his role in saving individuals during the floods in southwest France in the 1930s and reiterated the misleading assertion that Bousquet had already been tried for his crimes in 1949. Once again, Mitterrand ignored the issue of crimes against humanity in Bousquet's case and stated that he, Mitterrand, impeded the wheels of justice as they concerned Bousquet in the 1980s and 1990s because his role as president was to pacify internal divisions (shades of Pompidou!). As a new and final twist, Mitterrand even suggested to Wiesel possible reasons why Bousquet might have allowed himself to become involved in the implementation of the Final Solution in France. Perhaps, Mitterrand suggested, Bousquet overestimated his own intelligence. In any case, these speculations only served to humanize Bousquet and make him less antipathetic. In short, they sought once again to exonerate him, or at least lessen his culpability. Summing up his attitude vis-à-vis his friendship with Bousquet and his own Vichy past taken as a whole, Mitterrand affirmed: "I am at peace with myself."[49]

On 16 July 1995, at the site of the monument dedicated to the victims of the Vél d'Hiv roundup of Jews during the Occupation, Jacques Chirac, Mitterrand's successor as president of the French republic, publicly recognized the role of Vichy—*l'état français*—in "seconding" the "criminal madness" of the Nazis in carrying out the Final Solution. Chirac also spoke of a "collective sin" on the part of the French. As Conan and Rousso assert, Chirac's words marked a "sharp break with his predecessors' tradition" and were greeted "with satisfaction by the great majority of the public."[50] Indeed, one could argue—and many did—that Chirac deserved praise for the courage he demonstrated in making the speech. Although this is certainly the case, it is also possible that from Chirac's perspective, given his predecessor's misrepresentations of his own past and the distorting mirror he held up to Vichy, he, Chirac, simply had no choice.

7 : Denying the Holocaust in France
The Past and Present of an Illusion

In late June 1996, publicity posters appeared in bookshop windows and newsstand displays throughout France, announcing the upcoming issue of the popular French weekly magazine, *L'Événement du jeudi (L'ÉDJ)*. Frequently used by *L'ÉDJ* and other French magazines to attract readership, these posters regularly announce provocative cover stories and include striking photographs. The poster for the 27 June–3 July issue was no exception. In bold red, black, and white letters, the poster announced: "The Holocaust: The Victory of the Revisionists." The headline was superimposed on a crisp color photograph of the familiar, bearded face of an aging priest known throughout France as "Father Pierre." When the issue of *L'ÉDJ* appeared on the newsstands, it sold out within hours.

Although the headline alone was certainly shocking enough to attract a large readership, it was the juxtaposition of the announcement of the victory of the "revisionists" with the photo of Father Pierre that brought into sharp focus the latest episode of what has come to be known in France as "negationism," or the denial of the Holocaust—in many ways the ultimate counterhistory of the Dark Years.[1] In November 1995[2], Pierre Guillaume, director of the ultraleftist La Vieille Taupe (The old mole) publishing house and a veteran "negationist"[3] himself, announced the forthcoming publication of a new book by Roger Garaudy titled *Les Mythes fondateurs de la politique israélienne* (The founding myths of Israeli politics).[4] Despite its grandiose title, the book is on close inspection little more than a rehash of earlier "scientific proofs" that the Nazi plan to exterminate the Jews was a myth, that the gas chambers, where they had actually functioned, were used for delousing, and that the Allies were at least as intent on exterminating the Germans as the Germans were of ridding themselves of the Jews. Like many of its predecessors, Garaudy's book also denounces the Nuremberg trials as "show trials" where the "victors' justice" unjustly blamed the war on the vanquished while papering over the Allies' responsibilities. As Garaudy bitterly remarks, "Neither Churchill, nor Stalin, nor Truman was ever in the dock for war crimes."[5] The only relatively new twists to Garaudy's negationism are the extent, nature, and vehemence of his attacks on Israeli and Euro-American racism.[6] Comparing Menachem Begin's racism to Hitler's and insisting that there is no real difference between the two, Garaudy goes on to argue that the "myth" of the Holocaust is essential to Israel in order to justify its own form of aggression—"Zionist colonialism"—and its oppression of the Palestinians. Israeli power, in turn, serves the global ambitions of the United States, which seeks to subjugate the Third World and appropriate and control the flow of all Middle Eastern oil. Broadening his attacks on Euro-American racism, Garaudy also asserts that what Hitler did to "whites" was no different than what European and American colonialists did to people of color for centuries. He argues, in fact, that the American "genocide" of black Africans during the period of slave trading dwarfs Hitler's supposed genocide of the Jews. Using a "scientific" logic and statistical "evidence" that would make his fellow negationists proud, Garaudy argues that since ten to twenty million Africans were "deported" into slavery, and for each deportee ten were killed in their efforts to elude capture and deportation, the real figure for the American "genocide" of black Africans is one hundred to two hundred million.[7]

Guillaume's announcement of the forthcoming publication of *Les Mythes fondateurs de la politique israélienne* was not simply intended to inform fellow negationists of a new book to their taste or to attract a few new converts. His strategy, according to Pierre-André Taguieff, was more complex.[8] First, Guillaume counted on some members of the press to publicize Garaudy's book by denouncing it. This, in turn, would inevitably result in lawsuits against Garaudy, because it is illegal in France, since the passage in May 1990 of the Gayssot Law, to "contest the existence of one or more crimes against humanity as they are defined by Article Six of the Statute of the International Military Tribunal annexed to the London Accords of 8 August 1945." Named after a Communist deputy involved in drafting the legislation, the Gayssot Law has been roundly criticized by historians, intellectuals, and government officials who, like Simone Veil, believe that "one cannot impose a historical truth by law."[9] Being charged under such an unpopular and misguided law, the negationists—in this instance, Garaudy—could cast themselves in a more favorable light, even to the extent of assuming the role of victim in a legal controversy they themselves had set in motion.

The strategy worked to perfection, and at a press conference held on 18 April 1996 to discuss Garaudy's book and the legal controversy surrounding it, the author of *Les Mythes fondateurs* dropped another bomb. He removed from his hat a lengthy letter of support from his old friend Father Pierre.

In order to understand Father Pierre's role in the controversy and the impact of his involvement, it is necessary to know something of the backgrounds of both Father Pierre and Roger Garaudy and the history of their relationship. Of the two men, Garaudy is less interesting and certainly less significant. In many ways a perfect example of Eric Fromm's "true believer," Garaudy has gone from one commitment or faith to another. At one time a militant Stalinist who denied the existence of the gulag, Garaudy became disaffected with commu-

Denying the Holocaust in France

nism, converted to Christianity, and more recently converted again, this time to Islam.[10] As part of this most recent conversion, Garaudy became a passionate advocate of the Palestinian cause—hence his hatred of Israel and his challenge to its "founding myth," the Holocaust. A prolific writer whose works were once published by distinguished publishers including Gallimard and Presses Universitaires de France, Garaudy through his supporters has laid claim to a certain intellectual legitimacy in order to lend support to his recent revisionist claims. It is thus Roger Garaudy, the respected "philosopher," who presented the latest evidence of the Holocaust "hoax" to the French public.

A loyal friend to Garaudy through all his metamorphoses, Father Pierre is an altogether different sort of figure, both in terms of his past and his stature in contemporary France. Raised in a devoutly religious household in Lyons, the young Henry Grouès (to use his real name) accompanied his father each Sunday to minister to the poor in hospices around the city.[11] On his own initiative he also frequented orphanages where, legend has it, he gave away his favorite toys. Sensing within himself a deeply religious vocation, Grouès joined the Capuchin order, but medical problems forced him to give up convent life and join the priesthood. A vicar in Grenoble when the Second World War broke out, Grouès quickly joined the Resistance, taking as his *nom de guerre* "Father Pierre." During the war, Grouès protected Jews, fought in the Vercors region, and at one point saved the life of Charles de Gaulle's younger brother. A true war hero, Grouès received the War Cross and the Cross of the Resistance for his efforts.

In the postwar years, having permanently adopted his *nom de guerre,* Father Pierre entered politics. Joining the MRP (Mouvement Républicain Populaire) he was elected deputy to the National Assembly.[12] It was there that he met and befriended Roger Garaudy, who was serving as a Communist deputy at the time.[13] Abandoning the MRP, Father Pierre joined the independent left and was defeated in the 1951 elections. A longtime defender of the poor and homeless, Father Pierre founded Emmaüs (an international organization to help the homeless help themselves) in 1949 and continued to militate on behalf of the downtrodden in a variety of circumstances for the next five decades. Public opinion polls indicated he was France's national conscience and the most popular Frenchman alive.

For years before his scandalous support of Garaudy and his negationist theses, however, Father Pierre had shown signs of poor judgment and prejudice bordering on racism. Having allowed into his inner circle of confidants and advisors individuals formerly involved with the Italian Red Brigades and closely linked to the Palestinian cause (one of these, Françoise Salvoni, informed Father Pierre that Garaudy's book was "not anti-Semitic"—a view Pierre accepted, since he had not read the book), Father Pierre on occasion spoke out on behalf of a former Red Brigader arrested in Italy for gun trafficking with Palestinians and criticized French police for investigating a language school in Paris supposedly harboring former Red Brigade members. In a different context, during the war in Bosnia, Father Pierre also denounced the massacre of Bosnians "even if they are Muslims." He later retracted this statement.

But Father Pierre's most troubling assertions, at least in light of his subsequent support of Garaudy, were statements made in the early 1990s concerning the Bible, specifically the book of Joshua. To the shock and amazement of his interlocutors at the time, Father Pierre argued that the first crime against humanity, the first "Shoah," had been committed by the Jews themselves in their "genocide" of the Canaanites.[14] In his view, this crime would compromise the Jews' claim to the Promised Land. Moreover, Father Pierre argued in another context that the "Zionist" excesses of today's Israelis made of them not victims but "executioners" in their own right. Assertions such as these, along with a call for a new debate on the existence of the Holocaust, were included in Father Pierre's letter of support to Garaudy distributed at the latter's press conference.

Called upon by outraged supporters and enemies alike to renounce his support of Garaudy, Father Pierre, already known for his stubbornness, not only held firm but upped the stakes of his commitment. In an interview in *Libération*, he ignored demands that he distance himself from Garaudy's negationist views and reiterated his call for a new debate on the historical reality of the Holocaust. In comments quoted in the National Front daily *Présent* on 21 June 1996, Father Pierre denounced what he called "a world wide Zionist plot" and claimed that Zionists had adopted "attitudes identical to Hitler's on the issue of racism" and used the same murderous means in achieving their ends.[15]

Under pressure from LICRA (Ligue Internationale Contre le Racisme et l'Antsémitisme), Father Pierre finally backed away from his support of Garaudy, but the damage had already been done.[16] In lending his prestige even if only briefly to Garaudy, France's "saintliest man" had given a new legitimacy to negationism in the public view. In late spring and early summer 1996, signs asking, "And what if Father Pierre were right?" appeared on the sides of overpasses crossing the *périphérique* beltway around Paris. Despite shock and disappointment in many quarters, polls indicated that Father Pierre's popularity had not diminished significantly, and among his fervent admirers, new doubts about the Holocaust were raised.[17] Why would a man who had devoted his life to fighting against human suffering lie about Auschwitz? In recruiting the individual who had for many come to personify postwar French humanitarianism, the negationists had in effect succeeded in finding the perfect weapon in their struggle to efface the most inhuman of crimes. For the leftist activist Gilles Perrault, Father Pierre was nothing less than the "Pétain of the nineties." Like the marshal in 1940, he brought his enormous prestige to an evil cause and through the sheer weight of his own celebrity made it plausible to significant portions of the French public.[18]

As a number of commentators have noted, the implications of Father Pierre's support for Garaudy and his book in the spring of 1996 extend well beyond questions concerning the historical reality of the Holocaust and the existence of the gas chambers. The aims and ambitions of negationism, as well as the ideological motives driving it are, especially in France, much more complex and indeed dangerous than the stated desires of the negationists to "set the record straight" would allow. Negationism constitutes, first of all, an expression of and an effort to "banalize" or legitimize anti-Semitism and, through attacks on "Zionism," reintroduce it as a "threat" to be debated in the public forum.[19] In denouncing "Zionist"—read Israeli—racism, and comparing it in theory and practice to Hitlerian racism, Father Pierre contributed not only to what Taguieff labels a "conspirationalist judeophobia" but, through his person, linked a traditional French Catholic anti-Semitism to a more current hatred of Israel.[20] The results, according to figures including Pierre Vidal-Naquet and Bernard-Henri Lévy, were devastating. The negationists, in Vidal-Naquet's words, "had won." They were "in the process of inventing the anti-Semitism of the twenty-first century."[21] And although Father Pierre could certainly not be accused of recognizing or promoting negationism's most sinister design, that design remains, according to Robert Redeker, the continuation of the Holocaust in the present through its erasure in the past.[22] Or as Jean Baudrillard would have it: "Forgetting the extermination is part of the extermination itself."[23]

Negationism is, of course, also intent on rewriting history and, as the example of Garaudy's book suggests, not just the details of the Holocaust itself. Garaudy's distortions embrace German and Allied motives during the Second World War, the Nuremberg trials, the American "genocide" of black Africans, and so on. Father Pierre's historical revisionism is perhaps even more egregious, since as Alain Finkielkraut notes, it conflates contemporary Israeli politics with the biblical massacres of the Canaanites.[24] Moreover, it implicitly compares the latter with the Nazi genocide of the Jews by describing the destruction of the Canaanites as the first "Shoah." The dangers of such comparisons are all too evident, since as the Historian's Debate in Germany revealed, they serve to relativize or "banalize" the Final Solution.[25]

If the Roger Garaudy–Father Pierre affair disturbed the French and especially French historians and intellectuals as much as it did, that malaise was attributable in part to a strong sense of déjà vu where the Holocaust denial is concerned. Negationism has erupted in French public life at regular intervals since the late 1940s, when the fascist Maurice Bardèche published *Nuremberg ou la terre promise* (1948). In his book, Bardèche articulated a number of theses that Garaudy, among other subsequent negationists, has reiterated. These included the claim that the Allies were as culpable of war crimes as the Germans; that the gas chambers were used for disinfection purposes, not killing Jews; that deaths in the concentration camps were due to food shortages and epidemics; and that the "'solution to the Jewish problem' simply referred to the establishment of ghettos in the East."[26]

But Bardèche was a self-professed fascist with strong links to wartime collaborationism (he was Robert Brasillach's brother-in-law) and hence not the most reliable source for an objective discussion of Nazi crimes. It required the intervention of a former Socialist, Paul Rassinier, to launch negationism along the path it has followed in France ever since.

Beginning his career as a member of the Communist Party in the 1920s, Raul Rassinier was excluded from the party in 1932 and quickly became a functionary in the Socialist Party. Resolutely pacifist even when other Socialists had changed their views as a result of the Nazi threat, Rassinier was an ardent supporter of the Munich Accords. When war came, Rassinier, unlike many of his fellow pacifist Socialists, joined the Resistance. Arrested by the Gestapo in November 1943, Rassinier was tortured and deported to Buchenwald and then to the underground factory at Dora, where working conditions were reputedly among the worst. After the Liberation, Rassinier returned to France and served briefly as a Socialist deputy before veering to the right.[27]

As Pierre Vidal-Naquet explains in his preface to Florent Brayard's excellent study of Rassinier, two things are particularly striking about Rassinier's writings on the camps and on the Holocaust itself. The first is that the horrors of the concentration camps were, according to Rassinier, not fundamentally attributable to the ss members who ran them (and with whom Rassinier maintained good relations) but to the nefarious prisoners who insinuated themselves into positions of authority within the system. Second, Rassinier's negationism emerged only gradually over several years and through the publication of a series of books. In *Le Mensonge d'Ulysse* (1950), for example, Rassinier admits the existence of the gas chambers but argues they were run by

a few crazed ss members and those at the top of the prisoners' hierarchy. But by the time of the publication of *Le Véritable procès Eichmann*
(1962), Rassinier had, as Vidal-Naquet remarks, "gone to the limits of
negationism," citing as primary evidence for these views his own
experience of the camps.[28]

In his writings, Rassinier, like other negationists, revealed himself
to be an obsessive anti-Semite. The Jews, he argued, not the Nazis,
were responsible for starting the war, and during the cold war years
during which he wrote, Rassinier argued that they would soon be responsible for another war as well. Now on the extreme right, Rassinier
contributed to postwar reactionary reviews like *Rivarol* and published
his books with presses like Maurice Bardèche's Les Sept Couleurs,
named after Brasillach's profascist novel by that name published in
the 1930s. A vehement opponent of Israel at the end of his life,
Rassinier died just after the Six Day War in 1967.

Although the reasons for Rassinier's turn to negationism, especially given his Socialist and *résistant* past, are of psychological interest
(Brayard, for one, attributes it to his profound sense of guilt over
having survived, and indeed thrived, while interned in the concentration camps), it is precisely his left-wing origins that make him a figure
of particular interest in the long and sordid history of French negationism. For in the next scandalous eruption of negationism in
France, which followed the publication in *Le Monde* in December
1978 of negationist articles by Robert Faurisson, what surprised and
shocked many was that Faurisson's most vociferous supporters came
not from the extreme right but the extreme left, specifically the disaffected Trotskyists of La Vieille Taupe. Moreover, when Faurisson's
book defending his negationist claims was published in 1980 by La
Vieille Taupe, it was prefaced by none other than the distinguished
American linguist and leftist activist, Noam Chomsky.[29] I shall return
to Chomsky's role in the affair shortly.

Unlike Paul Rassinier or, later, Roger Garaudy, Faurisson was neither a concentration camp survivor nor a political activist. He was
instead a professor of French literature, first in a girls' high school in

Denying the Holocaust in France

Vichy (where, perhaps appropriately, he resides) and later at the University of Lyons II, where he served as a lecturer in twentieth-century French literature. In statements made in the hagiographic account of his life written by François Brigneau (a former arch-collaborator and postwar extreme right-wing activist linked to *Le Choc du mois*, among other publications), Faurisson also claims not to be, or ever to have been, pro-Nazi or an anti-Semite.[30] In fact, in his youth during the Occupation, Faurisson states that he was staunchly *résistant* and anti-German. Teased by his classmates for being pro-English (Faurisson's mother was British), the young Robert was punished for carving "Death to Laval" on his desk, and he claims as well to have been in favor of the harshest punishments for collaborators.

But it was also during the war, or at least at the Liberation, that Faurisson supposedly developed sympathy for the sufferings of France's erstwhile enemies, the Germans, and became suspicious of Allied justice and the "myths" the Allies generated concerning the conflict. Attending in person the trial of a Militia member after the war, Faurisson claims to have witnessed firsthand the inequities of the "victor's justice." Henceforth the "justice of Nuremberg" would make him "nauseous."

According to his own account, Faurisson did not become interested in the Holocaust or begin to entertain doubts about its occurrence until he read Rassinier in 1960. This was followed by years of reflection and arduous research, culminating in the "good news to humanity"—that the Holocaust was a hoax—which he announced in the pages of *Le Monde* in 1978.

In his book on Rassinier, Florent Brayard carefully dismantles what he describes as Faurisson's "novel of origins," that is, his claims concerning his early political views and the chronology of his "enlightenment" where the Holocaust is concerned. Brayard notes that Faurisson happened to attend high school in Paris in the late 1940s with Pierre Vidal-Naquet and others, and that the latters' testimony confirms that Faurisson was already avowedly pro-Nazi and an anti-Semite. Brayard also cites evidence, drawn from Faurisson's own version of events, that he was well aware of Rassinier and his negationist theses, as well as those in the work of Maurice Bardèche, long before 1960.

If Faurisson's fallacious account of his past and his conversion to negationism calls his credibility into question, it is his approach as a literary critic that accurately foreshadows key features of his later "methodology" as a negationist. Indeed, Faurisson achieved his first notoriety not in revealing "the truth" where the Holocaust was concerned but in disclosing the "real meaning" of Arthur Rimbaud's famous poem, "Voyelles" (Vowels). In an essay published anonymously in 1961 in the literary review *Bizarre*, Faurisson offered his analysis under the provocative title, "A-t-on lu Rimbaud?" (Have we really read Rimbaud?). Faurisson claimed that several generations of literary critics had completely misinterpreted the poem. In reality, Rimbaud's famous poem was little more than a disguised erotic fantasy of an adolescent schoolboy dreaming of women. According to Faurisson's analysis, the letters "A" and "U," for example, were inverted figures of the female sex and hair, respectively, while the letter "E" figured woman's breasts, tilted upright. As one critic commenting on Faurisson's reading explained, it was precisely because of the erotic nature of his analysis that he wished to keep his identity a secret. He did not wish his students back at the girls' high school at Vichy grinning knowingly at him while he delivered his lectures.

Remarkably, the publication of "A-t-on lu Rimbaud?" created quite a stir in Parisian literary circles. In the pages of leading reviews, including *Les Temps modernes*, the *Nouvelle revue française, Combat, L'Express*, and many others, prominent literary critics responded to Faurisson, often favorably. Luminaries including André Breton and Antoine Adam praised "A-t-on lu Rimbaud?" for its originality.[31]

Encouraged by his success, Faurisson followed his study of "Voyelles" with similar, "definitive" readings of Gérard de Nerval's *Chimères* (Pipe dreams) and Lautréamont's *Les Chants de Maldoror*. In both cases, he claimed to overturn generations of faulty interpretations to get at "the truth" of the works in question, and, as was the case with his reading of Rimbaud's poem, provocatively titled his reading of

Lautréamont "A-t-on lu Lautréamont?" As these titles imply, all previous interpretations of the literary works in question are, according to Faurisson, no more than "mystifications," a term that would recur with a much more ominous meaning in the author's subsequent writings on the Holocaust. It is Faurisson's intention, as Brayard suggests, not just to challenge previous interpretations but to bury them, since, as Faurisson affirms, "Every text has only one meaning or it has no meaning at all."[32] Moreover, the method is "totalitarian," Brayard continues, in the sense that where Faurisson chooses to apply it, there is no meaning possible other than the one that he imposes. Faurisson's disdain for all previous readings and interpretations and all "external" considerations is evident in the description in "A-t-on lu Lautréamont?" of his own "radical" methodology:

> The method that we constrain ourselves to adhere to is of an austere simplicity. This method will appear forbidding to more than one reader. It consists in taking the attitude of a profaner who considers it his obligation to understand everything about a work concerning which he knows nothing, beginning with the name of the author and the historical period during which the work was written. The method consists in finding the meaning of the word in the sentence, the meaning of the sentence in the page, the page in the book or poem, without recourse to biography, bibliography, or "sources," without reference to historical considerations, without concerning oneself with the author's declarations concerning his own work, without the assistance of other works, without any support other than dictionaries of the French language—and these to be consulted with suspicion. Whether the work in question is poetry or prose, it must be considered by itself, for itself, naked, raw, and . . . only at the exact level of the text itself.[33]

As his lengthy discourse on his methodology suggests, there is ultimately for Faurisson no authority, no *cogito,* other than himself and no frame of reference or epistemological principles to which he ultimately holds himself accountable. Moreover, as "profaner," it is his job to strip the work of its sacred meaning just as one scours a dirty pot or pan. It is not surprising that Faurisson's students referred to his approach as the "Ajax method."[34]

The arbitrariness of Faurisson's "method" and his willingness to violate his own principles when it suits his purposes become abundantly clear when the "method" is applied to reading the Holocaust. In *Assassins of Memory,* Vidal-Naquet implicitly debunks many of Faurisson's "purist" pretensions in his discussion of the tactics of French negationists, Faurisson in particular. The negationist strategy is in fact riddled with prejudicial presuppositions, the arbitrary inclusion or dismissal of evidence, deliberately faulty historical contextualization, and so on. As summarized by Vidal-Naquet, the "analytic principles" followed by the negationists are as follows:

1. Any direct testimony by a Jew is a lie or a fantasy by definition.
2. Any document dating from before the Liberation is to be treated as a forgery or a rumor.
3. Any document containing firsthand information on Nazi methods—for example, those testimonies concerning the Warsaw ghetto—are either forgeries or they have been tampered with.
4. Any Nazi "coded" document—i.e., using euphemisms for practices associated with the extermination of Jews—is to be interpreted in its strictly literal meaning, whereas any document speaking plainly of the genocide is to be ignored or "underinterpreted."
5. Any Nazi testimony dating from after the war is to be considered as obtained under torture or other forms of coercion.
6. An enormous amount of pseudotechnical evidence is to be marshaled to confirm the impossibility of the existence and functioning of the gas chambers.
7. Any complementary evidence that would make the Holocaust more plausible in historical and evolutionary terms—such as the Nazi euthanasia of the mentally ill or the activities of the Einsatzgruppen—is either "unacknowledged or falsified."[35]

The result can nevertheless be effective. As one critic describes it, negationist writing is "an amalgam" that "skillfully mixes truth and falsehood" and maintains "a kind of confusion of genres to such a point that the reader experiences a kind of vertigo reading" the text.[36]

As noted earlier, when the scandal erupted following the publication of Faurisson's negationist claims, public consternation and shock were less attributable to doubts about the Holocaust Faurisson may have sown than to the support he garnered on the far left. Noam Chomsky's preface to Faurisson's *Mémoire en défense* was preceded by his signature on a 1979 petition describing Faurisson as a "respected professor of twentieth century French literature and document criticism" and called for an end to the "vicious campaign of harassment, intimidation, slander and physical violence" to which he had been subjected following his pronouncements concerning the Holocaust.[37] The petition also called on university and government officials to guarantee Faurisson's right to "academic freedom" and free access to "public libraries and archives."[38] What the petition did not explain was that the archives in question were the Centre de Documentation Juive in Paris. Set up to preserve the memory and document the history of the Holocaust, the Centre de Documentation Juive had allowed Faurisson free access to its archives until his purpose in carrying out his research had become all too clear.

Chomsky's preface to *Mémoire en défense* follows much the same line of reasoning, defending Faurisson's right to "free speech" and attacking many members of the French intelligentsia for their lack of respect for the "facts" and for "reason," both in their desire to gag Faurisson and in their misrepresentation and denunciation of the petition Chomsky had signed. Chomsky goes on to assert that no such violation of civil rights in this context would occur in the United States, and he concludes by noting that the evidence he has seen suggests that Faurisson is not a rabid anti-Semite or pro-Nazi zealot but "a sort of apolitical liberal." It was this statement, perhaps more than his attacks on French intellectuals in general, which genuinely outraged many.[39]

Before turning to French extreme left-wing support for Faurisson's negationism, which brings us full circle to the Roger Garaudy–

Father Pierre affair in the 1990s, it is important to consider the denouement of the Faurisson Affair and one final issue it foregrounded.

In May–June 1981, Faurisson stood trial in Paris on three separate charges. The first was a slander charge, brought by the distinguished historian Léon Poliakov, whom Faurisson had accused of falsifying his sources vis-à-vis evidence of the gassing of the Jews. The second charge concerned the responsibility of the historian. Faurisson was accused of willfully distorting history in violation of Article 382 of the civil code. The final charge was that of incitement to racial hatred, a charge brought against Faurisson for anti-Semitic comments made on French radio in which he claimed that the lie of the Holocaust had been exploited by the State of Israel to "swindle" money from Germany and victimize the German and Palestinian people.[40]

Of the three charges, the most troubling from a legal, historical, and indeed historiographical point of view is the second charge. From a legal perspective, the court was asked to pass judgment on a version of history, a procedure fraught with danger, as amply demonstrated in the discussion of the April 1992 Paris court of appeals decision in the Touvier case (see chapter 5). From an historical and historiographical perspective, the problem is that in refuting negationist arguments and interpretations of the evidence, the historian engages with them, thereby giving their claims an aura of respectability as well a legitimacy that they do not merit. As Vidal-Naquet observes: "A dialogue between two parties, even if they are adversaries, presupposes a common ground, a common respect—in this case for truth. But with the 'revisionists,' such ground does not exist." To underscore the absurdity of this type of exchange, Vidal-Naquet wonders if one could "conceive of an astrophysicist entering into a dialogue with a 'researcher' claiming that the moon is made of Rocquefort cheese."[41] For his part, Charles Korman has suggested recently in the context of the Roger Garaudy–Father Pierre affair that the best way to deal with negationism is to confront it on its real turf, racism: "Jurists and historians make a mistake in playing along with the negationists. One should not speak of History with them, nor condemn them in the name of history, but speak instead of racism and condemn them for that. A negationist is simply someone who incites to racism."[42]

If racism and a visceral anti-Semitism account for extreme right-wing support for the negationists—and young neofascists showed up at Faurisson's trial to, among other things, snicker at the gruesome details of the gassings—what, finally, explains the support Faurisson received from Pierre Guillaume, Serge Thion, and other radical left-ists associated with La Vieille Taupe?[43] As the Roger Garaudy–Father Pierre affair confirms, that support continues today, so much so that, according to Pierre-André Taguieff, the distinctive trait of French negationism as opposed to that of other countries is its "anchorage" on the extreme left among "anarcho-communists" of the "Trotskyist tendency."[44] It is this seemingly paradoxical phenomenon that Alain Finkielkraut set out to explain in 1982 with the publication of *L'Avenir d'une négation* (*The Future of a Negation* [1998]).

Finkielkraut was, first of all, no stranger to anti-Semitism or anti-Zionism, nor for that matter was he unfamiliar with the excesses of post-"sixty-eight" radical left-wing thinking in France. The son of Polish Jews (his father had been deported to Auschwitz and survived), Finkielkraut had already meditated on Jewish identity and the implications of the Holocaust in *Le Juif imaginaire* (1980). A short while after the publication of *L'Avenir d'une négation*, he would write on anti-Zionist and anti-Israeli sentiment in *La Réprobation d'Israël* (1983). Initially a committed "sixty-eight" activist, Finkielkraut abandoned his studies as the student movement gained momentum and participated actively in the political upheavals. He renounced his radical stance after a year and returned to school to finish his studies.[45]

In accounting for left-wing support for Faurisson in *L'Avenir d'une négation*, Finkielkraut focuses his attention initially not on the views of figures like Guillaume and Thion in the 1970s and 1980s but on the attitudes of many prominent Socialists at the time of the Dreyfus Affair. These attitudes, he believes, set the stage for the negationism to come. Finkielkraut notes that at the time of the affair, the renowned German Socialist leader Wilhelm Liebknecht went on record, first in Germany and then in the pages of *Action Française*, denouncing the Dreyfusards and proclaiming Dreyfus's guilt. Moreover, the possibility that Dreyfus might be innocent was, for Liebknecht, logically impossible. As Finkielkraut explains, in Liebknecht's view the ruling class had only one enemy, the proletariat, and if the former wished to punish one of its own, the wealthy bourgeois officer Dreyfus, it had to be for a good reason—he had to be guilty. Although the logic employed by Liebknecht is not overtly anti-Semitic, it is implicitly so to the extent that Jews were associated with capital and thereby implicated with the abuses of the latter in their suppression of the working class.

So how does this fin-de-siècle leftist anti-Dreyfusard logic come to permeate the thinking of Guillaume and his colleagues at La Vieille Taupe? The intervening eighty years and the momentous events that transpired during that time must certainly have influenced the thinking even of a group of disaffected and isolated radicals. Finkielkraut's answer is that they did and did not. The great events and ideological struggles are taken into account, but they are subsumed in the same paranoid logic that informed Liebknecht's critique of the Dreyfus Affair. For the "anarcho-communists" of La Vieille Taupe, capital embodied in the Western democracies is still the archenemy in the class struggle, to be joined in this century by the corrupt Stalinism of the Soviet Bloc. But where does that leave fascism, and Nazism in particular? Following the traditional Marxist analysis, Nazism was simply a hypertrophied form of capitalism that evolved as a bulwark against the threat posed by the proletariat. According to this line of thinking, then, in reality very little separates the three systems in question, since all were ultimately geared to suppress the revolution of the workers and the downtrodden to the benefit of capital.

But in a particularly diabolical manipulation designed to dupe the workers as to who their real enemies were, the West, with the support of the Soviets, sought to demonize the Nazis, to make *them* the embodiment of all evil. And the best way to accomplish this aim was to point to the Holocaust, that quintessentially evil event, which set the Nazis completely apart from those who had struggled against them.

So the Holocaust, as Finkielkraut explains, was the sticking point in the logic of history espoused by La Vieille Taupe: it was quite simply a stumbling block that had to be removed at all costs. In effect, in order to rewrite the history of this century on the grandest scale by insisting on a massive conspiracy between the West and the Soviets, it was necessary to rewrite it on a "lesser" scale by erasing the Holocaust. One counterhistory, by necessity, had to include the other. So when Faurisson appeared with his voluminous "evidence," he provided the Vieille Taupe group not only with a means of removing the obstacle they had not previously been able to overcome but also with a cause that has served as their rallying cry ever since.

In the wake of the Roger Garaudy–Father Pierre affair, Finkielkraut was asked to comment on the implications of this latest episode of negationism in the pages of *L'Événement du jeudi*. Situating the French version of the Holocaust denial in a broader historical context, Finkielkraut asserted that our century is "the century of negation" and explained: "History has become the theatre of Reason. No distance should remain between the real and the 'rational.' But what does one do with facts which do not coincide with the supposed logic of History? The simplest thing is to deny them."[46] Although the Roger Garaudy–Father Pierre affair is for all intents and purposes over, the same cannot be said of the ongoing efforts of the negationists in France, including those of Garaudy himself. Ever true to his commitment, in 1998 Garaudy published yet another book in which the Holocaust is relativized and ultimately erased through bewildering and specious comparisons with the crimes of the Soviets, the Allies, and others. On the book's back cover, Garaudy is praised for his refusal to back down in the face of a "media lynching."[47]

And what of Father Pierre? In a special issue of the journal *Panoramiques* titled, appropriately enough, "Le Lynchage médiatique," Jean-Pierre Denis argues that during the Roger Garaudy–Father Pierre affair Father Pierre served as an innocent scapegoat whose function was to bind the community together in the Girardian sense. Moreover, what the media sought to do in reality was to compromise Pierre's charitable Christian efforts—and thereby to silence him—by yoking these efforts to the scandal of his support of Garaudy.[48]

Whatever Denis's intent in offering his analysis, the net effect, sadly, is to minimize Father Pierre's very real involvement in Garaudy's effort to deny the Holocaust and thereby to minimize the scandal of negationism itself. In the debates over Vichy's afterlife, the "duty to memory" has often been criticized and misapplied, but where negationism is concerned, it is very necessary indeed.

8 : From Vichy to Sarajevo

French Intellectuals and the Balkan Conflict

In an article appearing in 1996 assessing the impact of the war in the former Yugoslavia on France's intellectual community, Emmanuel Wallon states that not since the Dreyfus Affair has a single event so profoundly affected traditional political allegiances and alignments as well as prevailing notions of civic responsibility. Wallon adds that the nature and intensity of the commitments of any number of intellectuals confirmed that, for these individuals, the issues raised by the conflict greatly surpassed strictly political concerns.[1] Indeed, in his detailed account of his own *engagement* on behalf of Bosnia, *Le Lys et la cendre*, Bernard-Henri Lévy describes the manner in which his involvement affected his worldview, his emotions, his friendships, and even his self-image. By the time the Dayton Peace Accords were signed, Bosnia had become for Lévy a "second homeland," and he describes his passionate involvement on behalf of the Bosnian people as a "love story."[2]

If political considerations of the moment do not suffice to explain the intensity and duration of the commitments of Lévy and many others including Alain Finkielkraut, Pascal Bruckner, Edgar Morin, André Glucksmann, and Jacques Julliard, what was it about the Balkan conflict or the manner in which it was perceived that made it such a cause célèbre among many of France's most visible intellectuals? Even Lévy, while describing the passion of his own commitment to Bosnia, notes that the country whose cause he espoused "was not my style."[3] Indeed, as Wallon observes, the Parisian sound and fury aroused first by the war in Croatia and especially by the brutal conflict in Bosnia were disproportionate both to a traditionally limited French interest in the area and the modest size of the countries involved.[4]

Tony Judt, for one, attributes the French intellectuals' *engagement* in part to their abiding concern for broader issues that were central to the Balkan conflict and especially to the Bosnian war. These include the defense of the rights of the individual and of ethnic minorities— above all the right to self-determination—and an outspoken faith in the ideal of "Europe," which, as Judt insinuates, remained nevertheless fairly vague and ill-defined in the writings Finkielkraut, Lévy, and others devoted to the conflict. Judt also asserts more cynically that the defense of the breakaway republics—and especially Finkielkraut's championing of Franjo Tudjman's Croatia—coupled with assaults on the Serbian cause put the French intellectuals in their favorite position: to oppose the stance of their own government.[5] If not overtly or systematically pro-Serb, François Mitterrand remained at best largely neutral throughout the conflict. As Bernard-Henri Lévy recounts in *Le Lys et la cendre*, Jacques Chirac, for his part, refused to intervene until late in the game.[6]

Judt cites other motives for the commitments of the intellectuals as well. These include the opportunistic urge to be where the spotlights are as well as a desire to make amends for the errors of an earlier generation of French intellectuals, the majority of whom wrongly championed the Communist East European dictatorships in the 1940s and 1950s despite the horrors perpetrated by these regimes. This particular line of reasoning is of course in keeping with Judt's own assessment of that earlier generation as described in *Past Imperfect*, but it also coincides with the view expressed by Finkielkraut in *Comment peut-*

on être croate? (*Dispatches from the Balkan War and Other Writings* [1999]).
According to Finkielkraut, Western Marxist intellectuals spared the
terror of the Eastern Bloc were nevertheless ideologically blinded to it,
even to the point of branding as reactionary bourgeois those dissidents
who sought asylum in France.[7] Finkielkraut's own *engagement* on behalf
of Croatia clearly derived in part from his acute awareness of his
predecessors' blindness. As he remarked in a 1994 essay in *Le Messager
européen*, for the sins of the fathers this generation of the French
intelligentsia "feels an irresistible need to be pardoned."[8]

The motives Judt offers to explain the commitments of French
intellectuals in the Balkan conflict are both comprehensive and generally accurate. Nevertheless, they do not include another, crucial di-
mension of these *engagements*: the legacy of the Second World War,
Nazism, and Vichy itself. In the writings of Lévy, Finkielkraut, Julliard, Bruckner, and others, the specter of the Second World War and
its troubled memory—summoned up by the events in the Balkans—
returns again and again to cast an apocalyptic pall over the future of
Europe and to recall past and present inadequacies of the French
nation itself. Indeed, in many instances, such are the frequency and
detail of these analogies to the Second World War and its legacy that
the specific nature and events of the war in the Balkans—exceedingly
complex in their own right—are all too often obscured in the process.

For example, despite the brutality of Slobodan Milosevic and the
Bosnian Serb leader Radovan Karadic and the horror of their methods, greater Serb ambitions and aims were not synonymous with
those of the Nazis fifty years earlier, as French intellectuals often
stated explicitly, or at least implied. Historically of course, the Serbs
thought of themselves as Nazism's enemies and justified their own aggression in the early 1990s in claiming to fight, in Croatia, Hitler's former allies. But while Serb propaganda regarding Croatia's fascist heri-
tage was deliberately excessive, it is also true that Franjo Tudjman's
rise to power in Croatia was based "squarely on the national question"
and that his campaign funding came, in many instances, from former
Ustacha members living abroad. Moreover, as Marcus Tanner asserts,
while Tudjman was on occasion critical of the Ustacha, he openly

praised its nationalism. Their members were "the malevolent manifestation of a benign impulse."[9]

To the extent that French intellectuals rightly wished to cast the Serbs in the role of brutal oppressors by comparing them to the Nazis, some, notably Alain Finkielkraut, became excessively caught up in the logic of these comparisons and consequently ended up stripping Croatia's drive for independence of its more sinister features. In this and other instances, the superimposition of the Second World War on the events in the Balkans in the early 1990s not only obscured events but distorted the reality of the situation as a whole.

Conversely, the spectacle of European passivity in the face of the Yugoslav catastrophe conjured up for French intellectuals disturbing reminders of the failures of France and the European democracies in the 1930s and 1940s and cast these failures in the harshest possible light. Ironically, what emerged—at least in the portrait of the French past—was another version of what Stanley Hoffmann, as noted earlier, described as the *Lacombe Lucien* myth. The image was that of a "weak and complicitous France" and of a regime that not only furthered the "desires and pressures of the occupier" but "could count on the support of a debased people." Thus, in prompting negative comparisons of France past and present, the Balkan war revived an old, but clearly not entirely discredited, myth or counterhistory of the Vichy years.

But it would be a mistake to assume that nothing positive or constructive emerged from the numerous analogies between the events in the Balkans and the Nazi and Vichy pasts. The spectacle of massive destruction and murderousness only a few hours from Paris by plane inspired in many of the intellectuals under discussion here a new sense of urgency, an overwhelming desire not to repeat the mistakes of the past. This, in turn, suggested to them the need for a new reformulation of the "duty to memory" that would imply constructive action in the present as opposed to a sterile and facilely moralizing judgment of the past.

Both the positive and negative features of these comparisons are underscored below.

The policy of ethnic cleansing carried out primarily by the Bosnian Serbs provoked cries of outrage and numerous comparisons internationally with the Nazi Final Solution. For French intellectuals, especially Jacques Julliard, Bernard-Henri Lévy, Alain Finkielkraut, and Pascal Bruckner, other comparisons between the history and practices of Nazi Germany and Slobodan Milosevic's Serbia and its Bosnian minions could also be drawn. In their writings, Julliard, Lévy, and Finkielkraut elaborate sweeping scenarios linking a European and, for Lévy, a global crisis, best exemplified in the Yugoslavian situation, with the social, cultural, and economic turmoil leading first to the collapse of Weimar and the rise of Nazism and then, several years later, to the catastrophe and moral bankruptcy of the Munich Accords.

In his 1994 polemic provocatively titled *Ce fascisme qui vient . . .* (This fascism that is coming . . .), Jacques Julliard examines three key ingredients crucial to what he labels *fachogénèse*, or "fascogenesis." These include a sense of loss over a diminished national grandeur, which is blamed on others; political chaos due to social instability and the fragility of the political system itself; and a lingering and deepseated economic crisis. All of these conditions, according to Julliard, prevailed in 1933 Weimar Germany, and he notes that the same conditions obtain in post-Communist Eastern Europe and, to a lesser degree, in Western Europe itself, a point to which I shall return later. The concrete form assumed by fascogenesis is, according to Julliard, the creation of extreme variants of nationalism and the genesis of a fascist Schelerian "man of resentment" who combines a violent hatred of the other with a sense of his own complete impotence. Julliard concludes that such individuals were prime candidates for Hitlerism. Moreover, a new generation is being bred and nurtured in Milosevic's greater Serbia. Hence the inspiration for Julliard's title.[10]

Julliard is not alone in linking the current European crisis and its most visible manifestation, the conflict in the Balkans, to the German crisis of 1933, although others who invoke the analogy, including Lévy and Edgar Morin, are not as thorough or systematic in their analyses.[11]

Morin mentions two of the ingredients described by Julliard—economic chaos and an exacerbated sense of national impotence and frustration—but in his view the crucial ingredient explaining Serb aggression is a new form of nationalism—"total nationalism"—born of a complex mix of the vestiges of a Stalinist conservatism, a renascent integral nationalism, the dislocations of a new market economy, and the remnants of still-powerful "economico-military sectors" left over from the Communist years.[12]

According to Morin, the threat posed by this new "total-nationalist" menace has been greeted by the Western democracies in the same way they greeted the Nazi threat some fifty years earlier, and hence the comparison with Munich. In both instances, the response of the democracies has been, in Morin's words, "shortsightedness, deafness, and chitchat."[13] For Alain Finkielkraut, however, the comparison with Munich leads to the disclosure of a more sinister attitude on the part of the democracies in both instances. Although the democracies are most often blamed for their cowardice at Munich, for Finkielkraut, what lay at the heart of their failure was their arrogance and what he describes as their "cultural disdain." The fate of the Czechs in 1938 and the Balkan peoples today are ultimately a matter of indifference to the French and to the Western democracies in general. Czechs then and Croats and Bosnians in the 1990s are certainly not worth fighting and dying for. As Finkielkraut concludes, the crisis in the Balkans in the 1990s not only recalls Munich but it allows us to see the earlier event in an even more damning light.[14]

If Julliard, Finkielkraut, and others often make reference to specific historical moments in comparing Serb nationalism and aggression to Nazism, in *La Tentation de l'innocence* Pascal Bruckner follows a different path. Bruckner explores parallels between Nazi and Serb psychology and propaganda techniques by linking both to the Girardian model of the victim-turned-victimizer. In each instance, aggression and genocide are rationalized and even justified in advance by a process that allows the aggressor to cast himself in the role of the innocent victim by blaming all past and present sufferings on a demonized other or scapegoat. (Though not as concerned as Bruckner with the theoretical niceties, Finkielkraut admirably sums up this part of the process in the case of Serbia by asserting, "The Nazis of this story have wanted to pass themselves off as the Jews."[15]) The persecution and annihilation of the scapegoat can then be accomplished both without remorse and in a fashion that serves to bind the persecuting community together. For the Serbs, the scapegoats par excellence are their historical enemies, the Croats and Muslim Bosnians. If the West has failed to recognize the logic of scapegoating for what it is, at least in the case of Serbia, it is because we are eternally deluded by what Bruckner labels "the blackmail of the victim's discourse."[16] Once we accept the notion that a particular people has been the victim in the past, we are incapable of grasping that that role is being exploited to perpetrate crimes in the present and that yesterday's innocent victim may be today's executioner. Schematic as Bruckner's analysis may appear, it does unfortunately help explain how many, including François Mitterrand, justified their tacit support for the Serbs by recalling Serb victimization at the hands of Croatia's fascist Ustacha regime during the Second World War.[17]

As noted earlier, ethnic cleansing and genocide in the former Yugoslavia have been compared repeatedly to the Nazi Final Solution in the international media, and the name of Auschwitz has been invoked in efforts to communicate the horrors of the massacres and concentration camps so much a part of the Balkan conflict. French intellectuals have of course also made these comparisons, their indignation heightened by the fact that this time the world and its political leaders were aware of the genocide.[18] In *Le Lys et la cendre*, Lévy even reiterates the charge made by the Bosnian leader Alija Izetbegovitch that he had informed Mitterrand of the existence of the Serb camps several weeks before they became public knowledge and that Mitterrand failed to publicize or act on the information.[19]

But for Lévy, Finkielkraut, Julliard, and others, of equal if not greater concern was the nature of the response that the Balkan genocide did in fact elicit—humanitarian efforts on behalf of the suffering carried out by the international community. While the humanitarian actions themselves are condoned, the principle underlying these actions is roundly condemned. By its very nature, humanitarianism, or at least the "new humanitarianism" evident in the 1990s, fails to distinguish victim from victimizer and, as a result, it exonerates the perpetrator. The net effect, according to Finkielkraut, is "the humanitarian exoneration of the crime against humanity."[20] In a particularly bitter critique of this "new humanitarianism," Finkielkraut writes: " 'Nothing that is human is foreign to me,' affirm the proponents of humanism. 'Nothing that is truly human interests me,' asserts, to the contrary, the new humanitarian sensibility, which, the better to pity the refugees, strips them of their identities, their being, and their raison d'être; that is to say, of all that which comprises their humanity."[21] Bruckner pushes this logic to greater extremes. In bringing about the "triumph of the principle of equivalency" by reducing victim and torturer alike to the status of barbarians, the new humanitarianism constitutes nothing less than "negationism carried live." If one were to judge the antagonists of the Second World War according to the same criteria, it would be impossible to separate the good from the bad, and the Shoah "would only have been the response to the Soviet menace, a thesis dear to the German revisionist school."[22]

While for Jean Baudrillard the "new humanitarianism" does not necessarily reiterate the logic of negationism, it is nonetheless the pathetic, sterile response of an intellectual, cultural, and political order that can no longer lay claim to any value other than commiseration. But for Baudrillard what was really at issue during the Balkan genocide was even more sinister. The reason Europe and the West generally failed to respond in any definitive fashion to Serbian ethnic cleansing was because the Serbs were accomplishing what Europe secretly wishes to accomplish itself, the "purification" of the continent through the eradication of ethnic and racial minorities. The Serb crime, modeled on Nazi excesses, is in reality the crime of the New Europe and beyond that, of the New World Order itself: "The fine point of the story is the following: in carrying out ethnic cleansing, the Serbs are Europe's cutting edge. The 'real' Europe in the making is a white Europe, a bleached Europe that is morally, economically, and ethnically integrated and cleansed. In Sarajevo, this Europe is victoriously in the making. In a sense, what is happening there is not at all an accidental occurrence along the way to a nonexistent, pious and democratic Europe, but a logical and ascending phase of the New European Order, whose global characteristic is white fundamentalism, protectionism, discrimination, and control."[23] Baudrillard's choice of the expression "New European Order," reminiscent as it is of the Nazis' "New Europe," is clearly not coincidental.

Vichy: The Wages of Guilt and the Price of Memory

Baudrillard's comments suggest a European and French complicity in Serbia's Nazi-like crimes that brings the conflict home, so to speak, in a particularly painful way. Similarly, numerous references to Vichy and its troubled memories in other texts dealing with the Balkan conflict are clearly intended to break down French apathy in the present—to inspire a new and more meaningful "duty to memory"— by projecting feelings of guilt associated with the nation's past onto a war that was very much a part of the present. In *Dispatches from the Balkan War and Other Writings,* Finkielkraut recalls that what typified Vichy was precisely its inaction, and that as opposed to many of their neighbors, during the Second World War, the French led lives that were relatively undisturbed. French inaction and apathy in the face of Serbian aggression prove that the French have not really rejected their Vichy past but are instead the inheritors of its legacy. Vichy lives on, and European and French indifference and appeasement suggest a new, revisionist interpretation of recent history: Chamberlain, Daladier, Bonnet, and the rest were right after all at Munich in September 1938, and two years later the majority of Frenchmen were justified in their support of the "maréchalist solution." According to this scenario, de Gaulle becomes not a national hero but "a fanatical and irresponsible nationalist."[24] Finkielkraut's ironic condemnation of de Gaulle in the passage just cited is in fact in keeping with a number of recent and more overt expressions of nostalgia for Gaullism on the part of French intellectuals in their condemnations of French apathy and inefficacy vis-à-vis the Balkan conflict. In *Le Lys et la cendre,* Lévy frequently finds himself speculating on what de Gaulle would have done faced with the war in Bosnia, and André Glucksmann roundly condemns French and international indifference in his 1995 essay appropriately titled *De Gaulle, où es-tu?*

For Lévy, Finkielkraut, and their compatriots, the duty to memory as generally conceived and practiced in relation to the Dark Years has played a far-from-benign role in conditioning French responses to the Balkan conflict. In *La Pureté dangereuse,* Lévy wonders why the need for justice evident in the successful effort to bring Paul Touvier to trial for crimes against humanity does not translate into a comparable effort to bring the Bosnian Serb general Radko Mladic to trial on similar charges, and why a widespread knowledge and understanding of historical fascism does not help the French grasp fascism's more contemporary manifestations. For Lévy at least, the answer lies in the fact that in the absence of other, more positive sources of social cohesiveness, the obsession with the ills of the past and of Vichy in particular serves to bind the community—the French nation—together. But to count on this version of the duty to memory, which, as noted earlier, Lévy describes as "the last civic religion," to accomplish something really positive in the present—and outside France—is to indulge in a groundless optimism. The cult of memory where Vichy's crimes are concerned leads, sadly, to a retreat from, a disavowal of, the real, pressing issues of the present, rather than the reverse.[25]

For Finkielkraut, the cult of memory where Vichy and the Dark Years are concerned, at least as it expresses itself in such events as the Touvier trial, is simply "the latest version of French navel contemplation."[26] The most obvious consequence of this narcissism is, for Finkielkraut as it is for Lévy, an indifference to injustice in the present brought on by an overriding concern with past iniquities. But of equal importance, according to Jacques Julliard, is a dangerous loss of historical perspective that will haunt the nation in the future and, not coincidentally, helped make the French defeat of 1940 and the advent of Vichy possible in the first place: "Historians will record that the big question that agitated the defenders of the rights of man in France during [an] entire year when Bosnia lived a nameless horror, was the placing of a bouquet on the tomb of Pétain, the treasonous former marshal, by the President of the Republic. In France, one doesn't stand for any nonsense when it comes to symbols. It is too bad the same isn't true when it comes to realities."[27]

As the preceding remarks suggest, comparisons of the war in the former Yugoslavia to the Nazi and Vichy pasts serve the polemical function of dramatizing the horrors of the Balkan conflict by linking them to darkest moments of France and Europe's recent past. But the deployment of such analogies also allows Finkielkraut, Lévy, Julliard, Bruckner, and the rest to evoke a broader European crisis and especially the acute form it has assumed in France itself. For example, in evoking a climate tailor-made for a new fascogenesis in *Ce fascisme qui vient* . . . , Julliard is not referring simply to the Balkan climate but to the European and French contexts as well. It is perhaps no accident that alongside his two recent books devoted to the Balkan crisis, Julliard has published a journal of a disastrous 1995 in France, cataloging many of the same ills he describes in the larger European context. Although Julliard, and for that matter Finkielkraut, Lévy, and their compatriots make very few specific references to the rise of the National Front, or, for that matter, to disturbing electoral successes in the early to mid-1990s of the far right in Austria and Italy in their evocations of a new Serbian fascism, these analogies are clearly implicit in their discussions. A new "dangerous purity," in Lévy's words, is clearly taking hold in Europe, and the danger of not acknowledging its impact in Bosnia entails, perhaps surprisingly, trouble down the road for France itself. In *Le Lys et la cendre*, Lévy speculates on the impact on France's own Islamic population if a cosmopolitan, laicized Muslim population of Bosnia is allowed to be suppressed or destroyed by Serb ethnic hatreds. Such a result can only encourage the growth of Islamic fundamentalism in France itself—and a concomitant growth of the National Front. The dangers are all too evident.[28]

But if the comparisons between the current situation in the Balkans and Europe in the 1990s on the one hand and the earlier European crisis of the 1930s and 1940s on the other are about political and ideological similarities, they are also about the respective roles of the intellectuals in facing these crises. After a period of relative silence and inaction in the 1980s, France's intellectuals in the 1990s are attempting more and more to assume an active role in domestic and international affairs. It is not coincidental that the writings on the Balkans by Finkielkraut, Lévy, Julliard, and their compatriots include meditations on their predecessors as role models to be imitated or as negative examples to be avoided. The exemplary presence of Malraux, for example, haunts the pages of *Le Lys et la cendre*, whereas for Finkielkraut Sartre's ideological blindness where Eastern Europe was concerned appears as something to be avoided at all costs. It provokes, in fact, a new "anxiety of influence."

But if the respective commitments of 1990s intellectuals vis-à-vis the Balkan conflict suggest similarities with an earlier generation of thinkers, they also suggest disheartening differences as well. The Dayton Peace Accords that brought the Balkan conflict to a close (at least temporarily) were not a source of rejoicing for Lévy, Finkielkraut, and their compatriots. In *Le Lys et la cendre*, Lévy asserts that the end of the conflict spelled the tragic defeat of Bosnia and the cosmopolitan ideal it represented. As such, it marked nothing less than a "European debacle."[29] Lévy, moreover, is not alone in sounding such apocalyptic notes. One of Finkielkraut's recent books, which among other things attempts to offer some definitive conclusions as to the meaning and final implications of the Balkan conflict, is titled, appropriately enough, *L'Humanité perdue* (Lost humanity).

And what of the role of Vichy's afterlife, and all that that entails, in the analysis of and polemics over the Balkan conflict? In proposing, implicitly or explicitly, a new, more ambitious, and in their eyes at least, a more constructive outlet for the duty to memory in fighting Serb expansionism, Finkielkraut, Lévy, and many of their colleagues sought to move beyond what they considered to be that duty's more sterile and narcissistic applications in events like the Touvier trial. In effect, what they proposed was to choose what Todorov labels "exemplary memory"—where the memory of past injustices inspires just actions in areas not directly linked to those past injustices—over "literal memory"—whose sole purpose is to punish the original malefactor as well as all those linked to or associated with the original injustice.[30]

Given their final assessments of the Dayton outcome, it is clear that for Finkielkraut and Lévy at least, Europe, and France in particular (their primary audience, after all), failed to take up the challenge of "exemplary memory" in the Balkans. Instead, during the fall of 1997 and the winter of 1998, the French nation was riveted by what, following Todorov's terminology, can accurately be characterized as the most spectacular example of the exercise of a duty to literal memory in the postwar years, the trial of Maurice Papon for crimes against humanity. One crucial stumbling block to the success of the exercise—Papon's postwar suppression of Algerian protesters while serving as prefect of Paris police in 1961—is the subject of the final chapter.

9 : Memory's Time Bombs

The Trial of Maurice Papon and the Algerian War

Near the outset of Didier Daeninckx's 1984 detective novel, *Meurtres pour mémoire*, the young historian Bernard Thiraud sets out with his girlfriend from Paris to drive to Morocco, where the two plan to vacation together. Along the way, the lovers stop for a layover in Toulouse. At dinner the night of their arrival, Thiraud announces that he needs to conduct a few days' research in the archives of the local prefecture, the nature of which he is, nevertheless, reluctant to discuss.

The next day, working among registers and other official documents in the administrative library, Thiraud pauses at lunch to telephone his girlfriend and announce excitedly that he is on to something big. But on leaving the prefecture at closing time, he is tailed by an old man. When the two men are alone on an isolated street, Thiraud's pursuer draws a pistol and guns him down for no apparent reason.

Assigned to the case, Toulouse Police Inspector Cadin begins an investigation that will take him into the past and, initially at least, to the Occupation period. A preliminary visit to the archivist at the prefecture reveals that Thiraud had been looking at the files whose headings begin with the letters "DE." Among these files is one for "Deportation," a file whose contents, despite the subject matter, convey the same bureaucratic tone as that of any other administrative dossier: "[T]he functionaries seemed to have filled out these forms with the same care they brought to coal credits or to the beginning of the school year. In this fashion they handled death in the same way they handled hope. Without asking themselves any questions."[1] Perhaps, the reader is led to believe, the young historical researcher has been murdered for a secret he had exhumed concerning the Final Solution.

But as is the case in any good detective story, the first lead uncovered does not directly produce a solution to the crime. In fact, as the novel progresses, the lead even appears to be a red herring. Pursuing his investigation in Paris and into the young historian's background, Cadin discovers that the victim's father, Roger Thiraud, also a historian, had been murdered, also under mysterious and apparently political circumstances. A witness to the massive demonstrations by Algerians on 17 October 1961 against a curfew imposed on them by the prefect of Paris police, Thiraud had been watching the brutal suppression of the protesters by police forces in front of the Rex theater near the Bonne-Nouvelle metro stop when he had been attacked from behind and shot through the head. Following a brief, telegraphic description of Thiraud's demise, the police report states: "European element probably linked to the Algerian terrorist movement."[2]

Pursuing his investigation despite warnings that to do so would be both politically unwise and dangerous, Cadin comes to appreciate the full horror of the events of October 1961 and the murderous brutality of his fellow officers. So bloody and unwarranted were the police attacks on the Algerian protesters that one of the witnesses Cadin encounters, a former police photographer, left the force after photographing the confrontations at close range. Referring to what he witnessed that night, the former *flic* tells Cadin, "I haven't spoken to anyone about it in twenty years. I promised myself to forget everything."[3]

Given the widespread culpability of *forces de l'ordre* on the night in question, it is not surprising that, through a brilliant piece of detective work, Cadin learns that Thiraud *père* had in reality been assassinated by a former member of a secret special force of the CRS (Compagnie Républicaine de Sécurité [French riot police]) charged with the elimination of France's political enemies, especially "terrorists." Confronting the elder Thiraud's killer—now living in retirement and dying of cancer—Cadin tells the assassin that Thiraud had in fact not been a "terrorist" or even a political activist of any sort. The retired policeman tells Thiraud in turn that, when assigned a killing, he was never told anything about the victim, nor was he aware of who ordered the execution.

So why was Roger Thiraud killed, and what does his death have to do with his son's death so many years later? In the novel's denouement, the reader is taken back to the Occupation wherein lies the key, ultimately, to both murders. It turns out that Thiraud *père* had at the time of his death been working on a history of the place of his birth, Drancy. The name, of course, carries an ominous connotation, because Drancy served initially as a concentration camp for Jews arrested by French police during the Dark Years and then as a staging area for the deportation of Jews rounded up throughout France who ultimately were sent to death camps to the east. Later, many would refer to Drancy as the "antichamber to Auschwitz."

Shortly before his murder, Roger Thiraud had gone to Toulouse to look into the reasons why a disproportionate number of Jewish children sent through Drancy to their deaths had been arrested in the Toulouse region. In the files under "deportation," he had discovered that the functionary responsible for organizing the deportations was now a powerful figure in the French police. The latter's accomplice, the archivist of the files of the Toulouse prefecture, had informed his superior of Thiraud's research, and the police official, using one of his special operatives, had ordered Thiraud's death on the pretext that he had been a pro-Algerian "terrorist." Informed twenty years later by the same archivist of Thiraud's son's digging around in the archives on the deportations, the police official, who turns out to be the director of criminal affairs of the prefecture of Paris police, drives to Toulouse himself and murders the younger man.

As the novel closes, Cadin decides to visit the Bonne-Nouvelle metro stop, which is under renovation. An Algerian worker is busily removing from the tile walls scraps of advertisement and other postings accumulated over many years. As he works, fragments of a message warning of police measures against domestic unrest and terrorism are gradually exposed. The message is signed the Militaerbefehlshaber Stülpnagel.

For anyone familiar with the case of Maurice Papon, former Vichy official, prefect of Paris police, and minister of budget under Valéry Giscard d'Estaing who was tried in 1997–98 for crimes against humanity in the assizes court of Bordeaux, it is not difficult to recognize in *Meurtres pour mémoire* a brilliantly crafted roman à clef, deserving of the Grand Prix de la Littérature Policière and the Prix Paul-Vaillant-Couturier, both of which it won in 1984. Change Toulouse to Bordeaux, and the pieces fall into place. Like the shadowy, police official villain in Didier Daeninckx's novel, Papon had successfully hidden his role in the deportations in order to make a successful career in the corridors of power in postwar France. After extended periods as a colonial administrator in Morocco and Algeria—career moves that Daeninckx's villain apparently does not share, but to which we shall return—Papon was appointed prefect of Paris police in March 1958 by the Socialist Félix Gaillard and maintained in that post in June of the same year by Charles de Gaulle. In his capacity as police prefect, it was Maurice Papon who organized and oversaw the brutal suppression of Algerian demonstrators on 17 October 1961. And twenty years later—when Thiraud *fils* visits the archives in Toulouse—Papon, then minister of budget under Raymond Barre, was exposed in the pages of *Le Canard enchaîné* on 6 May 1981 as having ordered the deportation of Jewish men, women, and children from Bordeaux during the Occupation. Although the 1981 revelations of Papon's role in the Final Solution were orchestrated in part to help seal François Mitterrand's presidential victory and were published, in fact, with

Mitterrand's approval (there is a certain irony in this, given the 1994 revelations of Mitterrand's own Vichy past, discussed earlier), the revelations did nevertheless eventually bring an end to Papon's high-profile career.[4] Papon's political demise is figured symbolically in *Meurtres pour mémoire* by the actual murder of the villain.

But if Didier Daeninckx's prize-winning detective novel became timely again due to the trial of Maurice Papon, what makes the novel even more eerily apropos is the fact that its structure prefigures in significant ways the first stages of the trial itself. *Meurtres pour mémoire* thereby establishes certain thematic and historical "parallels" that massively contributed to the controversy as well as the political, juridical, and moral malaise surrounding the trial, its conclusion, and aftermath.

Maurice Papon's trial for crimes against humanity opened on 8 October 1997 to a flurry of national and international media attention and in France, to renewed debates, stock-takings, and self-flagellations in virtually all sectors of public life over the Vichy past, especially its role in the Holocaust. Just before the trial opened, the Catholic Church in France, in an unprecedented move, apologized for its role vis-à-vis Vichy and the deportations and asked forgiveness of the Jews. The Church's act of contrition was followed in short order by similar apologies from the national organizations of France's doctors and police. In bookstores, numerous books on the Papon case were on display, as well as more general works such as Marc Olivier Baruch's massive, scholarly study of the French administration under Vichy, *Pour servir l'état français* and more popular eructations against the nation's continuing obsession with Vichy, such as Henri Amouroux's *Pour en finir avec Vichy.*[5]

On radio, television, and in the printed media, Vichy collaborationism and the actions of the accused were discussed and debated endlessly, and many of the same issues raised during the trial of Paul Touvier were raised again, as if the trial of the former Militia member had never occurred. Was it fair, for example, to try a man for crimes committed fifty years earlier? In trying Papon and through him, symbolically, the nation's Vichy past, were the French trying once again to avoid coming to grips with contemporary issues, as Alain Finkielkraut argued in *Le Monde*?[6] Did the French public, especially the younger generation, feel trials of this sort were necessary for pedagogical reasons?[7] Whatever the answers to these questions, Vichy's afterlife was once again all the news. President Jacques Chirac's summer 1995 effort to put the Vichy past to rest for good by avowing the nation's responsibility for Vichy and its excesses had apparently come to naught, and an exasperated Prime Minister Lionel Jospin called for an end to the national obsession with the Dark Years on the floor of the National Assembly shortly after Papon's trial began.[8]

But after an initial dispute over the president of the Bordeaux assizes court Jean-Louis Castagnède's controversial decision to free Papon from incarceration for medical reasons and after the official reading into the record of the indictment against the accused, the trial for crimes against humanity for acts committed during the Occupation got sidetracked onto a whole different part of the nation's past during the court's traditional examination of the curriculum vitae of the accused. As in *Meurtres pour mémoire*, the path leading back to Vichy ran directly through *another* past, one also partially obfuscated by myths and countermyths, guilty memories, and lingering animosities: *la guerre sans nom,* or the Algerian War. Among other things, the incorporation of this other past into the trial compromised from the outset any attempt to limit the proceedings in Bordeaux to an exercise to fulfill a duty to "literal memory," in this case, to identify and punish only those responsible for or linked to the original injustice, the implementation of the Final Solution in France. More important, as we shall see, the introduction of Papon's role in the struggles over decolonization served also to blur the specificity of his actions and the nature of his crimes during the Occupation by setting up a competing narrative of Papon's supposed criminality in the postwar years. The result was the distortion and conflation of the two distinct historical moments in question—each thus acted as a kind of counterhistory to the other—and in some quarters (see Vidal-Naquet's comments later in this chapter), a call for what amounted to a revision of the historical and legal bases of crimes against humanity in France. The ghost of Barbie's lawyer Jacques Vergès was clearly in evidence.[9]

During the assizes court audience of 15 October 1997, Papon's role as a government functionary in France's North African possessions in the 1940s and 1950s, especially in 1956–57 (in the Constantinois region of Algeria, where he worked under Robert Lacoste, then governor of Algeria), came under review. Asked about his activities and his attitudes at the time, Papon asserted that he had been a constant opponent of the use of torture, but that he had no control over the military.[10] But if this was a distortion, Papon's version of events became even more flagrantly misleading when the discussion turned to 17 October 1961. In reference to the *ratonnades*, the offensively colorful French term for the racial beatings of Algerians in particular (a *raton* is a young rat), Papon exculpated the police forces he commanded in their entirety, claiming that only "fifteen or twenty North Africans [had been] thrown into the Seine." These deaths, moreover, were attributable, according to Papon, not to police violence but to a "settling of scores" among rival Algerian factions, the FLN (Front de Libération Nationale) and MNA (Mouvement National Algérien). Papon scoffed at reports that at least two hundred protesters had died, and, when the question of police responsibility for the deaths was raised, Papon noted that a judicial investigation into the events resulted in no charges being filed.

The groundswell of indignation following Papon's blatant misrepresentation of the events of 17 October 1961 was immediate and widespread. Minister of the Interior Jean-Pierre Chevènement asserted on the same day of Papon's testimony that he "was completely ready to get at the truth" of the events out of respect for "the duty to memory." A commemoration of the victims was called for the night of 17 October, and survivors of the *ratonnades* were invited to speak. The commemoration was sponsored by more than thirty political and social organizations and held at the Saint-Michel Bridge, very near to where many of the worst brutalities occurred in 1961. One of the organizing committees for the rally also called on the government to

Memory's Time Bombs

open the state archives on the events to expedite the exposure of the full truth. On 16 October, Minister of Culture and Communication Catherine Trautmann announced that the archives would indeed be opened, affirming: "This decision is part of the government's effort to bring completely to light [the details] of the tragic repression of that day." What the archives actually contained—had they, for example, already been purged?—no one knew for sure, nor did many ask whether the opening of the archives was necessary to "bring everything to light" in the first place. For his part, the historian and specialist on the 1961 events, Jean-Luc Einaudi, was already aware of the extent to which Papon was lying, and in an interview in *Le Monde* of 17 October 1997 stated unequivocally that the former police prefect's responsibility for the events was "direct, personal, and overwhelming."

In fact, in 1991 Einaudi had already published a book, *La Bataille de Paris*, dealing with the night of 17 October 1961 as well as the events leading up to it and its aftermath. Making use of newspaper accounts, official reports, and especially the detailed testimonies of victims and witnesses to the events contained in the archives of the FLN in France, Einaudi had carefully exposed Maurice Papon's role. One had to wonder, therefore, why the courtroom debate, Papon's misrepresentations, and the correctives offered in the press caused such a stir. It appeared that the same sort of "pseudorevelations" that repeatedly provoked flare-ups of the Vichy Syndrome according to Éric Conan and Henry Rousso were now also provoking similar flare-ups where the Algerian War was concerned.[11]

But while Vichy collaborationism has been relentlessly examined in the media and thoroughly studied by historians, the majority of whom have reached a consensus as to its nature, the same cannot be said of the events of 17 October 1961, especially Papon's responsibility for their occurrence. Despite the general reliability of Einaudi's account—cited not only in the press but in the study of Papon's post-Vichy past published shortly before the trial by Gérard Boulanger, one of the lawyers for the civil parties at Papon's trial—other accounts offering different versions of the events and Papon's role (including Papon's memoirs, to which we shall return) circulated both in and out of court.[12] Indeed, Papon's lawyer, Jean-Marc Varaut, attempted to introduce the official report mentioned earlier and essentially exonerate Papon into the court record. Given these discrepancies, it is helpful to rehearse quickly Papon's colonial past (as far as it is known) and what is generally accepted concerning the events of 17 October 1961. It should then be possible to ascertain how and why Vichy and the Algerian conflict were conflated in the Papon trial and what the troubling consequences of this conflation are.

Papon served three administrative stints in North Africa between the Liberation and his assumption of duties as prefect of Paris police in 1958. In October 1949, he was named prefect of Constantine in charge of the Constantinois region, at the time the poorest department in French Algeria but also the largest in terms of land area. The Constantinois contained some three million inhabitants, among whom barely two hundred thousand were French of European origin.[13] During the two years he spent there, Papon was involved largely in the administrative reorganization of the region. He learned that he was to be transferred to the Paris prefecture of police in November 1951.

In June 1954, Papon was once again in North Africa, this time serving as secretary-general of the protectorate of Morocco. Arriving in a climate already charged with animosities between Europeans and native Arabs, Papon's stint in the protectorate was marked by anti-European riots, pillaging, and the murders of European nationals. The situation was complicated by French terrorism against Moroccan nationalists as well as those of European origin who supported them. At least initially, the response of the French authorities was a rigorous suppression of native "terrorists," involving roundups and detentions throughout the protectorate that were applauded by the European inhabitants. In charge of these police operations, Papon displayed his customary zeal, and before leaving Morocco, he was awarded the kingdom's highest honor. He was made an officer of the Ouissam Alaouite for "services rendered to Morocco in executing his exalted functions."[14]

Three months after being appointed in March 1956 as technical advisor on Algerian affairs in the cabinet of the new secretary of state for the interior, Marcel Champeix, Papon was once again sent to Algeria, this time as inspector-general of administration on a special mission to the Constantinois, where he had served several years before. The difference was that the region was now at war. Among other responsibilities, Papon was in charge of the police.

After a bomb explosion in Constantine in June 1956 that wounded some forty persons, Papon, already popular with the colonists, ordered a crackdown on the Muslim population. The crackdown involved roundups, interrogations, and searches in the Arab quarters of towns and cities throughout the Constantinois. Denounced back in Paris by the Communist *L'Humanité* for these measures, Papon brought charges of defamation against the newspaper while continuing his campaign of harsh repression of the native population in Algeria. In September 1956, after a meeting with the military generals he would later blame exclusively for acts of torture, Papon ordered a police crackdown on the population of the city of Bône. One individual, resisting a police search, was killed. Meanwhile, army forces working in concert with the police carried out acts of repression in the countryside against "rebels." In a statement to the populations of the Constantinois, Papon affirmed the success of these operations: "Whatever the impotent rage of the terrorist outbursts, the year that is now concluding is experiencing the righting of a situation that twelve months ago was dominated by anguish. Let one not forget this."[15] By the end of Papon's first year back in the Constantinois, the forces of order had exacted quite a toll on the native populations: 4,200 rebels killed, 226 wounded, 401 captured, and more than 1,000 weapons seized.[16]

The next year saw more of the same. Along with other repressive measures, and despite Papon's later disavowals, torture practiced by both the military *and* the police became, according to Jean-Luc Einaudi, "an habitual, normal means of gaining information."[17] Encouraging a state of siege mentality among the civilian European population at a press conference on 17 September 1957, Papon affirmed that the Constantinois was in a state of "total war" and demanded of all "civilians that they conduct themselves as soldiers." Henceforth, he continued, "There is no more distinction between military and civilian personnel. Now there can only be soldiers."[18] Firmly in the camp of the colonists, Papon would find his zeal praised and rewarded by his superiors. On 27 November 1957, Papon's direct superior, the governor-general of Algeria, praised his commitment and efficiency on the floor of the National Assembly. That same month, Félix Gaillard, the new premier, sent him to the United Nations to defend French policy in Algeria. But not all those among the nation's elected officials found Papon's actions during his final tenure in Algeria praiseworthy. In 1961, Claude Bourdet, then a municipal counselor in Paris, condemned Papon in the pages of *France-Observateur* as "one of the most ferocious artisans of the repressions."[19]

Following police demonstrations in Paris outside the National Assembly in March 1958—demonstrations provoked by the policemen's growing frustration at being targets of both sides in the colonial war now moved to the mainland—the prefect of Paris police was removed, and Maurice Papon was chosen to replace him. Leaving his Algerian stronghold, which many had now come to refer to as "la Paponie," Papon returned to the capital and immediately established himself as the "strongman" the government felt it needed. Turning down the opportunity to serve as minister for Algeria in Pflimlin's cabinet in May of the same year, Papon instead undertook measures to consolidate his position and authority in his role as prefect of Police.[20] These measures, in turn, set the tone as well as the stage for the events of October 1961.

Making a smooth transition to Gaullism in being confirmed in his position as police prefect by the general in June 1958, Papon quickly inaugurated repressive measures similar to those that had earned him his strongman reputation in Algeria. In August 1958, following the FLN's decision to launch an armed "offensive" on metropolitan France, Papon organized massive roundups of Algerians in the streets of Paris. Those arrested were taken to detention centers at the former Beaujon Hospital and the Japy gymnasium where, during the Occupation, on 14 May 1941, some 4,000 Eastern European Jews had been

Memory's Time Bombs

detained by French police before being sent to detention camps at Beaune-la-Rolande and later to the death camps to the east. Still others were interned at the infamous Vél d'Hiv. Rumors of Algerian deaths at the latter were dismissed as "false allegations" by the prefect of police, and calls for an investigation came to nothing.[21]

In September 1958, Papon announced a curfew for "North African workers" in Paris between the hours of 9:30 P.M. and 5:30 A.M., but this curfew, according to Einaudi, was not strictly enforced. In January 1959, an identification center was established at Vincennes for the detention of Algerians arrested by the police. Although the center was only authorized to detain individuals for a maximum of fifteen days, according to Boulanger these detentions often lasted much longer.[22] During the same period, Papon authorized police searches of hotels where immigrant North African workers lived in the eleventh, fifteenth, and twentieth arrondissements. Rallies protesting the mistreatment of Algerians organized by groups including the League of the Rights of Man were forbidden by the police prefect. Acting on orders from Michel Debré, the minister of the interior, Papon established special, auxiliary police forces consisting of European-born officers and *harkis*—pro-French Algerians known for their brutality— to deal with Algerians living in Paris. Interrogation centers where Algerians were tortured by these auxiliary French police were established first in the Rue Harvey and the Rue du Château-des-Rentiers in the thirteenth arrondissement, and then later in the eighteenth arrondissement, in the basements of buildings along the Rue de la Goutte-d'or. Torture techniques used included water torture, impaling on bottles, and electric shocking, all of which had been previously employed in Algeria. As Einaudi affirms: "Under the responsibility of Maurice Papon, torture installed itself in Paris." He continues, "Men disappeared. The Prefect of Paris police had the newspapers that denounced these exactions seized. He knows that one must always deny the use of torture."[23] Those who survived torture, or who were spared it, were detained for lengthy periods of time in Paris and then often sent to detention camps established for them in metropolitan France at Saint-Maurice-l'Ardoise, Thol, Vadenay, and Larzac.[24]

Although the massive protests by Algerians on the night of 17 October 1961 were called by the FLN to protest Papon's new curfew announced on 5 October, the tensions that exploded in the brutal and tragic suppression of the marchers had obviously been building for some time. Police morale was low as a result of attacks and threats from the OAS (Organization de l'Armée Secrète) and Algerian nationalists, although the FLN, for its part, had recently called off acts of violence in France itself. In statements to his charges, Papon left no doubt as to how the police were to deal with these attacks. In a speech at the 2 October funeral of a slain policeman, Papon told those present in the courtyard of the prefecture of police, "For every blow received, we will administer ten blows!"[25] But events suggested that the police had already taken this attitude to heart. During the month of September, the bodies of Algerians, many apparently killed by the police (although infighting among rival Algerian nationalist factions was in the air), were fished out of the Seine.

In essence, the 5 October curfew stipulated three things. First, "Muslim Algerian workers" were not to circulate in the streets of the capital or the suburbs between the hours of 8:30 P.M. and 5:30 A.M.. Second, those who were required by their jobs to be out during these hours were forbidden to circulate in groups, since "it has been confirmed that attacks [against the police] are, most of the time, the actions of groups of three or four men."[26] Finally, drinking establishments where these Algerian workers congregated were to be closed everyday at 7:00 P.M.

Because the law was ultimately to be enforced only according to the racial characteristics of the workers in question, by definition the curfew lent itself to a broader repression than was intended. Although Algerians were targeted, all other Arabs, as well as any others who resembled them, were, de facto, targeted as well. During the period the curfew was in effect, Moroccans were frequently accosted, and on the night of 17 October, a dark-complected young American tourist was attacked by police as well. Thus, the curfew was for all intents and purposes racist. Einaudi argues that it was unconstitutional as well. Article 2 of the Constitution of the Fifth Republic "guarantees the legality of all the citizens before the law."[27] After 17 October, some would compare it to racist measures against the Jews in Nazi Germany. In an editorial published in *Témoignage chrétien* on 27 October, Hervé Bourges wrote: "In 1936, in Hitler's Germany, Himmler explained to the Jews that the ghettos had been created to insure their protection. In 1961, Papon assures the muslims that the curfew measures have been put in place 'with their interests in mind.' We have known times when the Jews were required to wear the distinctive sign of the yellow star. So when will we see green stars on the chests of Algerians?"[28]

From its inception, the 17 October protest organized by the FLN was to be peaceful in nature. Orders went out that no weapons were to be carried by the marchers. The plan, as Benjamin Stora notes, was for the marchers to congregate at various points around the city and then march "toward public places like the [Place de la] Concorde, the Champs-Elysées, the grands Boulevards."[29] Some thirty thousand Algerians, directed by FLN militants, assembled within the city at various times, mostly at various metro stops, to begin their march.

The police, aware of the protest in advance, according to Einaudi, were fully prepared. Acting on orders from his superiors that the protesters were to be prevented from marching, Papon had placed at his disposal some seven thousand regular police and fourteen hundred CRS and mobile guards. Apart from police *paniers à salade* (paddy wagons), Papon also requisitioned Paris public transport buses to carry the arrested Algerians to detention centers. Later, many drivers and workers were horrified by the mission Papon had imposed on them. After the events, many of the buses had to be thoroughly cleaned to remove the blood of the protesters they had carried. The police, moreover, had been well prepared by their superior for the violence to come. In the days leading up to 17 October, Papon had circulated among his men, assuring them that whatever extreme measures they undertook, "You will be covered, I give you my word on that. Besides, when you advise headquarters that a North African is down, the officer in charge who will come to the crime scene will have everything necessary to make sure the North African has a weapon on him, because in the current state of affairs, there can be no mistakes."[30]

Once the 17 October protest got under way, police suppression of the demonstrators assumed a variety of forms. In some instances, Algerians were assaulted as they exited the metro stations. Policemen waiting for them beat them with nightsticks (some carried the newly designed *bidule*, an extra-long nightstick capable of doing more damage), punched them, or kicked them before loading them into waiting buses. Some of those loaded onto the buses were already dead.

In other areas, marchers quietly chanting slogans were assaulted, beaten, and then shot in front of onlookers. Among the latter, some were horrified, while others were happy to join in with the police. At the Neuilly Bridge, protesters attempting to enter Paris from the *bidonvilles* (slums) were shot and thrown into the river. Marchers on the Boulevard Saint-Michel were brutally attacked, as were others at the Boulevard Saint-Germain. A witness to the latter assault, Pierre Berger, a journalist for *Démocratie 61*, observed the violence from his office window:

> Our windows looked out on the Rue de Lille and the Boulevard Saint-Germain. It was in front of our windows that a squad of CRS and a group of police agents, night sticks in hand, blocked the Rue de Lille. Coming from the other direction, a group of Arabs advanced toward the Boulevard Saint-Germain. These men were walking quietly. They were chanting quietly the slogans that summed up their reasons for being in the streets. The charge that followed was brief. The forces of order pinned the protesters against the wall. Then they hit them with their fists, their sticks and they kicked them as well. The police agents had their revolvers ready. One fired his gun. The CRS agents told us to close our windows and turn out our lights. There was no question of turning out the lights as we had to finish the issue of our journal. We also left our windows open. Because we risked nothing in so doing. Because we had the good fortune not to be Arabs. To conclude my testimony on this scene of gratuitous and futile violence . . . I will add that all this took place in front of the Ministry of Algerian Affairs. For me, this was the hour of shame.[31]

Marchers moving along the Boulevard Bonne-Nouvelle going from the Place de la République toward the Opéra were attacked without warning by the CRS in front of the Rex theatre, whose proprietor quickly closed the grill in front of the theater when he saw trouble coming. This episode—witnessed by Thiraud *père* in *Meurtres pour mémoire*—was one of the bloodiest. Protesters were shot or beaten to death, and a Breton sailor who had come to see a movie at the Rex but was caught outside the grill had his skull shattered.[32] Other Algerian protesters, trapped or rounded up in the courtyard of the prefecture of police, were beaten and their bodies apparently thrown into the Seine nearby. (Some policemen, horrified by the violence in the courtyard, in which some of the Algerians were apparently strangled with bits of rope or brake cable, went to see Claude Bourdet and reported to him that the number killed and thrown in the river was fifty Algerians.[33]) Whether or not Papon witnessed this violence is subject to debate, but what is known is that he was installed most of the night in a command center in the prefecture and that all police radio broadcasts and messages from throughout the city passed through this center.[34] From all appearances, Papon did nothing to prevent the relaying of false rumors from one police post to another that policemen had been shot or otherwise killed by the protesters. These rumors, by all accounts, precipitated most of the lethal violence by the police against Algerians. Moreover, as the brutalities continued through the night, Papon issued a communiqué that stated unequivocally that during police "operations," "gunshots were fired at members of the forces of order, who responded."[35]

All told, some 11,730 Algerians were arrested and taken to detention centers around the city and on its outskirts. As they were hauled inside these facilities, which included the Palais des Sports, the Parc d'Expositions, as well as the aforementioned location, their wallets and watches were confiscated, and the beatings often continued. At the Palais des Sports, where up to 6,000 Algerians were detained, medical help for the wounded was scarce and sanitary conditions became unbearable. Toilet facilities overflowed, and the detainees were forced to live in their own filth. At the identification-detention center, witnesses reported that gas was used to put the detainees to sleep. All were forced to sleep on the floor. Military doctors, even one hardened by recent experiences in the war zone of Algeria itself, were horrified by what they saw when sent to care for the detainees.[36] On 6 November, members of a parliamentary commission established to ascertain conditions in internment facilities in France and Algeria showed up at the center and, despite Papon's efforts to prevent their entry, made their way inside. What they saw led them to conclude that conditions there betrayed a lack of respect for "human dignity."[37]

On 18 October, the official report on the events of the previous evening listed three protesters dead (two Algerians and one protester of European extraction) and sixty-four wounded. Among the police, thirteen were reported wounded, and Agence France-Presse reported that none of the latter had been wounded by gunshot. Unofficially, word went out that up to twenty Algerian protesters had in fact died. Following the regular Wednesday meeting of de Gaulle's council of ministers, a government spokesperson, who, as Einaudi remarks, seems to have been "ill-informed," reported that two of the injured policemen had gunshot wounds. He continued by noting that many of the protesters, whom he called "poor bastards," supposedly were driven against their will to protest by the FLN and were more than happy to be hauled off to the safety of police headquarters. The same night, at the National Assembly, Roger Frey of the ministry of the interior told the representatives that gunfire between the police and protesters was exchanged at several locations. At the same session, the police were praised for doing their duty, and accusations were hurled against members of the Communist Party for having helped to organize and participate in the demonstrations. A young deputy on the right, Jean-Marie Le Pen, called for their arrest.[38]

Initial reactions in the press the day after the events were generally supportive of the police. But on 19 October, the left-wing press began to raise questions concerning the accuracy of the official reports, based on their own investigations into events. Witnesses testified to the peaceful intentions of the demonstrators, thereby calling into question claims that police had been fired upon. Rumors of police

Memory's Time Bombs

brutality following the arrests were also beginning to circulate.[39] *L'Humanité* went so far as to assert that "the forces of repression in the capital have acted with a brutality without precedent."[40]

In the days that followed, a growing sense of outrage at what had actually occurred was expressed in the press and in other fora as well. By the end of the week, even the conservatives had begun to speak out against the police repression of both 17 October and of smaller demonstrations by the wives and children of the jailed demonstrators on the days that followed. On 21 October, a protest rally held in the courtyard of the Sorbonne attracted some two thousand students and professors. A petition was drawn up and signed by the likes of Michel Butor, Simone de Beauvoir, Pierre Vidal-Naquet, Louis Aragon, André Breton, and many others, which stated in part: "In remaining passive, the French would make themselves the accomplices of racist furors of which Paris is now the stage and that take us back to the darkest days of the Nazi Occupation. We refuse to draw a distinction between the Algerians stacked up at the Palais des Sports and Jews [earlier] parked at Drancy."[41] In *Les Temps modernes*, comparisons to an earlier, murderous European anti-Semitism were also made: "These unarmed men were massacred, left suffering in the gutters, and finished off in the triage centers. Pogrom: the word, thus far, has not been translated into French. By the grace of the Prefect Papon, under the Fifth Republic, the lacuna has been filled."[42] Maurice Papon reacted by having *Les Temps modernes* seized.

In the halls of government as well, Papon was equally relentless in stonewalling any effort to bring all that happened on 17 October to light. On 27 October, before the municipal council, he refused to answer Claude Bourdet's precise questions concerning the number of protesters killed. He simply affirmed: "The Parisian police simply did what it had to do."[43] Later, at the same meeting, the council expressed by vote its confidence in and gratitude to Papon.[44]

But not all protests were quelled as of yet. At a meeting of the National Assembly to go over the budget of the ministry of the interior, Eugène Claudius-Petit, vice president of the National Assembly and a former Resistance leader, spoke out against the police violence, which he labeled racist, and concluded: "Is it necessary that we witness soon, because this is the slippery slope we are on, the shame of the yellow crescent after the having known that of the yellow star?"[45] To suppress the creation of a commission by the National Assembly to look into the events of 17 October, Papon launched some twenty-seven judicial inquiries into the deaths of the bodies being found in the Seine. A maneuver totally out of keeping with normal practice, the pursuit of such inquiries prevented the launching of the commission since, according to French law, all such inquiries had to be completed before a commission could be created. Within two years, all the judicial inquiries were dropped. On 13 November, Papon could claim: "We have won the battle of Paris!"[46]

Having explored in some detail what the limited but most reliable accounts have to say about the "Battle of Paris," I find it fascinating—and most instructive—to consider briefly Papon's own version of events, recounted in his memoirs, *Les Chevaux du pouvoir*. Given that the memoirs cover more than five hundred pages, it is surprising at first glance that only ten pages are devoted to 17 October 1971, as well as the events immediately preceding it and its aftermath. But then, Papon's intention is clearly not simply to exonerate the police—and himself—but to paint them as heroes. Accordingly, the bloody details of the actual confrontations are elided, and the number of victims minimized—Papon asserts that only two protesters were killed. Moreover, only passing reference is made to the detention facilities where the protesters were held in horrific conditions in the days following the arrests. Where Papon waxes eloquent, as well as verbose, is in singing the virtues of his subordinates or in describing in detail statements made at the time in defense of the police actions either by himself or government officials, most of whom were on the right. He also takes pleasure in skewering those who denounced police brutality against the Arab protesters. Discussing the 27 October meeting of the municipal council, Papon gleefully notes that after Claude Bourdet's hard questions to the police prefect as to the number of Algerians killed, another member of the council reminded his fellows that Bourdet had earlier called on foreign powers to help the FLN while on a visit to Belgrade.[47] As for the well-known intellectuals like Sartre and de Beauvoir who had signed petitions denouncing police actions, Papon presents them as lacking the courage to face the perils of protests in the streets, preferring instead to make declarations and sign appeals from their "comfortable rooms."[48]

Papon's treatment of the major players and the events themselves read more like political melodrama than history, since it is clear that from his perspective, the police and the actions taken by the chiefs as well as the rank and file are almost without exception laudatory, while those who oppose them are unequivocally nefarious. Papon describes his subordinates as so many warriors from a chanson de geste. One is "crowned with white hair, with eyes of steel," while another is "efficient and subtle." All are "solid men, devoted to public service, faithful to their mission, used to discipline."[49] Their opponents, the FLN militants, are desperate men who have failed to achieve their ends militarily and are now seeking to win support through "a coup d'état of great psychological resonance."[50] In supposedly threatening the lives of the workers in order to get them to march—Papon offers no evidence to support this claim—the FLN militants employ tactics that "smell of totalitarian sulphur." It is not surprising, then, that many of the marchers greet their removal by police to "welcome centers"— Papon's expression for the detention centers—with "relief."[51]

As for the police rank and file, Papon allows that only a few acts of brutality against protesters occurred and that these were provoked by recent memories of violence against police and by the violence of some of the demonstrators themselves. In his memoirs, Papon reiterates the claim made in his communiqué issued the night of 17 October that police returned, rather than initiated, gunfire. In his view, police violence occurred because the officers had been pushed far beyond normal limits of tolerance. They were given little time to prepare to face a numerically superior opponent (Papon claims that the police knew of the protests only on the morning of 17 October and fails to mention the number of forces he had at his disposal), which invaded Paris like a hydra-headed "malevolent monster." Nonetheless, at the end of the day, the forces of order won out in their struggle to prevent the inundation of Paris by "by waves of Algerians," and the FLN's ambition to transform a "peaceful demonstration" into a "murderous riot" had failed.

What is most noteworthy in Papon's version of events, apart from its literary pretensions and its failure to coincide with reliable historical accounts, is that it belies Papon's own testimony in front of the Bordeaux assizes court in October 1997. Neither the number of victims on the night in question nor the circumstances of their deaths remain the same. In *Les Chevaux du pouvoir*, Papon does mention Algerian workers murdered by the FLN, but these murders occurred *before* the 17 October confrontations, and the murdered workers were not killed because of internal struggles between rival Algerian groups but because they had failed to follow FLN directives. So Papon either lied before the court, or he lied in his memoirs, or both. Although this may shock Anglo-American audiences, it is not new in the context of crimes against humanity cases in France. René Bousquet lied during his 1949 trial (although, as noted, he was not on trial for crimes against humanity then), and Paul Touvier repeatedly lied before and during his 1994 trial, even about the murders at Rillieux. And as court officials at the time acknowledged, ironically it would seem, "only the accused had the right to lie." As for Papon, who was not on trial for his actions of 17 October 1961, the point would appear to be that if he was willing to lie about these events, he was certainly capable of the same where the deportations of Jews during the Occupation were concerned.

But is this in fact the point? From legal and judicial as well as historical and cultural perspectives, the real issues at stake ultimately lay elsewhere. As Jean-Denis Bredin had already noted in an article published in *Le Débat* in 1984 (see chapter 5), those who expect the court to concern itself primarily with uncovering historical truth are inevitably sorely disappointed, because what Bredin described as "progress in the science of knowledge and intelligence" is not the court's concern.[52] The court's concern was to try Papon for crimes committed during the Occupation, and *only* those crimes, because they alone can be considered crimes against humanity under French law, and they alone are therefore imprescriptible. The furor raised during the trial concerning the events of 17 October 1961 demonstrated just how difficult adhering to the letter of the law could be, even in the courtroom itself. It also raised questions once again concerning the advisability of trying individuals for crimes committed fifty years earlier. In Papon's case, the crucial issue was not whether he had become a "different man" in the intervening years—the court was clearly dealing with the same wily and deceitful functionary committed to serving the powers that be, no matter what the price in moral terms—but whether it was possible to return to a precise point in the past and interpret and judge it without reference to subsequent events—subsequent *pasts*—in which the accused was involved. Was the examination of Papon's actions as prefect of Paris police under de Gaulle necessary to illuminate his role in Bordeaux during the Occupation? To ask the same question metaphorically, as does Didier Daeninckx in *Meurtres pour mémoire*, does it require an Algerian worker to peel away the layers of the past encrusted on the metro walls to put us in the presence, once again, of the horrors of Nazi hegemony?

What this perspective suggests, in many respects, is a dangerous *parallel* between the implementation of the Final Solution in France and the excesses of *la guerre sans nom*. At the time that the 1961 "Battle of Paris" was debated at Papon's trial, cartoons in the Parisian press made the parallel explicit, in some cases by showing buses used to carry Jews to the Vél d'Hiv in 1942 side by side with those used to haul Algerians protesters away in 1961, with Papon in between. On the front page of the 18 October issue of *Le Monde* another cartoon showed policemen throwing protesters off the Neuilly Bridge. Standing beneath the image, Papon states, "I remember: in 1961 I was also crying at Christmastime." The reference is to Papon's earlier statement before the court that he had cried at Christmas with his wife during the Occupation over the fate of the Jews he had deported.

In an interview in *Le Nouvel observateur*, Pierre Vidal-Naquet went a step further, insisting on a virtual legal *parity* between the crimes committed in both instances. Arguing that one should not relativize all crimes in relation to Auschwitz, Vidal-Naquet asserted that the

17 October 1961 racist suppression of Algerian marchers was a crime against humanity and should be judged as such.[53] As Vidal-Naquet was certainly aware, this would require revising years of carefully articulated French jurisprudence which, ill-advisedly or not, has explicitly set out to limit crimes against humanity to the Second World War and the excesses of Nazism, and those complicit with it in particular.

The conflation of the excesses of the Nazis and their Vichy minions with French crimes committed during the Algerian conflict is, of course, nothing new. In *The Vichy Syndrome*, Henry Rousso notes that the antagonists during the conflict itself cast their enemies in the role of Nazi or Vichy zealots and proudly claimed for themselves the mantle of the Resistance. And as the reactions at the time of the 17 October 1961 events confirm, the brutality of the Parisian police, as well as the concerted plan to halt the demonstrations, suggested almost immediately comparisons between the Nazis and Papon's police on the one hand and the Jewish and Algerian victims on the other.

Although the brutality and racism in both cases were (and are) certainly deserving of comparison and condemnation, the historical contexts were in reality different, and it is this difference that risks being overlooked. As Rousso has stated, "When viewed in hindsight, and with strict objectivity, the Algerian War has only a tenuous relation to the Occupation."[54] But this did not prevent renewed comparisons from being made during Papon's trial, and in the skewed equation that emerged, Gaullism equaled Vichy. From a historical perspective, this was both ironic and ludicrous.

Nevertheless, if Paul Thibaud is to be believed, this is the price that must be paid for the introduction of the notion of imprescriptibility into French law. Rather than rectify past injustices, imprescriptibility allows those living in the present to sit in judgment over past events they did not witness and thereby to assert their moral superiority over the past. Perhaps the lesson to be drawn from the controversy surrounding the events of 17 October 1961 during Papon's trial is that it really does not matter what that past is, as long as its inferiority vis-à-vis the present is established. At least in 1961, the conflation of Gaullism's treatment of Algerian protesters with the Nazi treatment of Jews was intended to stir indignation and bring a halt to an injustice *actually taking place*. To return to Todorov's distinction, memory in 1961 was paradigmatic, not literal. This was not true in 1997.

But to conclude on this note is perhaps too pessimistic. If there is a duty to memory where the Vichy past is concerned, then, as Jean-Pierre Chevènement argued in October 1997, there must also be a duty to the memory of the Algerian War as well. And if the controversy over Papon's role in the Paris police's suppression of Algerians on the night of 17 October 1961 serves to stimulate a responsible historical exploration and better understanding of all aspects of France's role in the Algerian War—and perhaps rescue that past from what Benjamin Stora calls "gangrene and forgetfulness"—then it served a valuable function.

But to date, the results are not encouraging. On 6 January 1998, Counselor of State Dieudonné Mandelkern submitted to the ministry of the interior a report he had been asked to write concerning what the archives revealed about the events of 17 October 1961. Chevènement decided to withhold the report from the public until after the conclusion of the Papon trial. Accordingly, Mandelkern's conclusions were released on 4 May 1998 in *Figaro* under the headline, "October 1961: The True Figures of a Savage Night." Dismissing the conclusions of Einaudi, among others, the report stated that the protesters killed numbered in the tens and not in the hundreds, and that the brutality of the police was due to their being overwhelmed by the sheer number of protesters and the lack of warning they had received. In arriving at its figures concerning the dead, the Mandelkern report relied exclusively on Paris police archives and those of the Department of the Seine, ignoring those of the Department of Seine-et-Oise, where bodies were also reportedly found. The report mentioned that the archives of the *brigade fluviale* (river brigade) had been destroyed recently and could therefore not be consulted. Given that it was this brigade that would have fished from the river bodies thrown into the Seine by the police, these archives, it would seem, would be crucial in establishing a reliable inventory of the dead. As if these lacunae were not enough, no mention is made in the Mandelkern report as to what happened in the courtyard of the prefecture of police, where some of the worst abuses apparently occurred. And, irony of ironies, the name "Papon" does not appear once in the report.

Commenting on the Mandelkern report in the 20 May 1998 edition of *Le Monde* in an article titled "October 1961: For the Truth, at Last," Jean-Luc Einaudi criticized the report's procedures as well as its conclusions. Addressing Mandelkern's readiness to ignore crucial sources while drawing important conclusions concerning the number of protesters killed (rather than simply inventory the police archives), Einaudi asserted: "In a democracy, it is not the role of high functionaries acting in that capacity to write History."[55] For those who recall the April 1992 Paris court of appeals decision in the Touvier case in which the court revised the history of Vichy, Einaudi's statement has a familiar ring. While both Papon and Touvier were finally convicted of crimes against humanity for crimes committed during the Occupation, the cost in both cases was an unsettling revision of history that, ultimately, called the duty to memory into doubt. The difference in the Papon case was that two memories, two pasts, were, ultimately at stake, and neither, it seems, had been put definitively to rest.

Conclusion

The End of the Affair?

It is appropriate to conclude a book dealing with Vichy's afterlife with the trial of Maurice Papon for several reasons. First, to return to the seemingly paradoxical definition of "afterlife" given in the introduction as signifying both "the life after death" and "the latter part of one's life," what the Bordeaux proceedings confirmed was that Vichy lived on long after its historical demise in the minds and hearts of those who remembered its victims as well as in the eyes of a nation, for whom the trial of Papon was perhaps the quintessential moment of a "past that would not pass." But in the very intensity of the experience it produced as well as the lack of closure evident in the issues it raised, the past(s) it explored, and the verdict it produced, the trial seemed to suggest that the memory of the Dark Years was not simply "the life after death" of Occupation but "the latter part of its life" as well.

At the same time, although the Papon trial was ultimately intended (despite the disclaimers of many) to set the record straight concerning the role of the Vichy administration in the Final Solution, at least in the case of the accused, the effort to write that historical narrative ran afoul of another history—that of the Algerian conflict—which ultimately undermined the specificity of Papon's crimes during the Occupation in historical and legal terms. As I hope to have shown in the chapters included here, the intrusion of counterhistories of this sort has made the memory of Vichy all the more difficult to comprehend and to reckon with and has only served thereby to prolong its afterlife.

However, it is curious that the Papon trial and *its* aftermath seem to have marked at least a transition in Vichy's afterlife, if not the announcement of its conclusion. The exhaustive length of the trial and the disappointment—for many—of its outcome seem to have quelled, at least temporarily, the obsessive concern with the Vichy past. Papon himself "moved on," so to speak, fleeing to Switzerland in October 1999 before his appeal was heard, thus guaranteeing its dismissal. He was arrested and is now, at last, serving his sentence outside Paris. Several months before his flight, however, Papon sued Jean-Luc Einaudi for defamation of character not, of course, for anything Einaudi said about Papon's *Vichy* past but for what he asserted about Papon's actions in Paris in 1961. Papon lost. Moreover, the government, dissatisfied with the Mandelkern report, has apparently organized a new commission to investigate what actually happened on the night of 17 October 1961. If there is a malady or syndrome attached to the memory of Vichy, these developments suggest that it has now infected the memory of the Algerian conflict. Or perhaps, as many argue, that memory has suffered from its own syndrome all along.

But it could be that Vichy's moment, and the weight of its legacy, are passing. In political terms, the National Front, many of whose leaders and ideological tenets were linked directly to Pétainisme, is currently undergoing a crisis in leadership that, while making the party no less reactionary, will certainly distance it from the legacy of the Vichy past. In the Balkans, war in Croatia and Bosnia, which, because of Europe's inaction at the time, prompted French intellectuals to recall Nazi aggression and Vichy cowardice and passivity, has now given way to the war in Kosovo. NATO's aggressive posture and France's participation in the war against Milosevic and Serbia do not seem to be prompting comparisons with Vichy. Rather, in some quarters they rekindled another traditional passion among French intellectuals: anti-Americanism.

In historical terms, a strong interest in and reexamination of the legacy of communism, especially its crimes, strikingly evident in the 1997 publication of *Le Livre noir du communisme* (*The Black Book of Communism*), have clearly focused attention away from the Occupation. It is true, however, that in Stéphane Courtois's introduction to *The Black Book of Communism*, the text most responsible for launching the debate, Courtois compares the crimes of communism to those of Nazism largely by qualifying both as crimes against humanity as defined in *French* law. Given that the *Black Book* appeared during the early stages of the Papon trial, the implicit comparison of the crimes of the Communists and the Nazis with those of Vichy could hardly be entirely coincidental. So here again, at least in Courtois's introduction, Vichy's afterlife was in evidence, inflecting an historical debate with which it had very little if any real connection, and vice versa. Courtois's introduction of French crimes against humanity statutes into the analysis and his comparison of Communist and Nazi crimes could hardly further the already complicated efforts to apply these statutes to French crimes, as the trials of Papon and Touvier clearly showed.

And in French fiction as well, where, as noted in the introduction, the Vichy past continues to sell novels, there are indications of change, or more precisely of a change in attitude, even toward the memory of the Shoah. In a novel by Pierre Assouline appearing in August 1998 titled *La Cliente*, the young Jewish narrator discovers that the woman who denounced many members of the family of his in-laws during the war—denunciations that led to their arrest and deportation to Auschwitz—is still a customer in their shop fifty years later. Determined to punish the woman and see justice done, the narrator haunts the woman and makes her only too well aware of her past. When the woman cracks under the pressure and eventually dies, the narrator learns from a neighbor that she had denounced members of his in-laws' family in the hope of saving her brother, *her* only relative, under arrest at the time, and whose release had been promised in exchange for the whereabouts of the Jewish family in hiding.

Although some (indeed many) may not agree with the "moral of the tale," that moral appears to be not necessarily one of forgiveness but of a recognition that even some of the worst crimes committed during the Dark Years had understandable, "human" motives, and that the distinction between good and evil is not always as clear as one might hope. For the novel's narrator, humanizing the Vichy past, removing it from the larger context of the historical forces at play, and personalizing its traumas allows him, as he says (quoting Eliot), to "see it for the first time"—and, to a degree, move beyond it. Although the narrator's path to overcoming the past in *La Cliente* may be unsatisfactory to some, his recognition that it is necessary, at last, to exit the impasse of Vichy's afterlife is certainly a sentiment that all of the French can share.

Notes

Introduction

1 Rousso, *The Vichy Syndrome*, p. 1.

2 Conan, "Enquête sur le retour d'une idéologie," p. 27. All translations are my own unless otherwise specified.

3 Among those most satisfied by the verdict were the lawyers and "memory militants" Serge and Arno Klarsfeld. Arno Klarsfeld represented some of the victims of the deportations in the Bordeaux assizes court and argued for a "graduated" sentence for Papon, which Klarsfeld felt was in keeping with the nature of Papon's crimes. Klarsfeld argued for a ten-year sentence for Papon in his closing statement before the court. This statement, or *plaidoirie*, was published as *Papon: Un verdict français*. Klarsfeld has subsequently published another book offering his overall assessment of the trial, titled *La Cour, les nains et le Bouffon*.

4 Varaut, *Plaidoirie de Jean-Marc Varaut*, p. 7.

5 Weill, "Penser le procès Papon," p. 108.

6 Henry Rousso, interviewed by Laurent Greilsamer and Nicolas Weill, "Le Tribunal de l'histoire a jugé Vichy depuis longtemps," *Le Monde*, 7 April 1988.

7 See Weill, "Penser le procès Papon," p. 100.

8 Among Chauvy's predecessors in making these accusations was Jacques Vergès, Klaus Barbie's lawyer.

9 For a succinct account of and commentary on the whole affair, see Rousso, *La Hantise du passé*, pp. 126–28.

10 Vidal-Naquet, *Le Trait empoisonné*, p. 93.

11 Pierre Péan, *Vies et mort de Jean Moulin* (Paris: Fayard, 1998). Péan has also written a biography of Swiss financier François Genoud, who funded Klaus Barbie's defense. In the summer of 1999, Péan published another book about the Moulin affair, titled *La Diabolique de Caluire* (Paris: Fayard). The book focuses on Lydie Bastien, mistress of René Hardy, who supposedly convinced Hardy to work with the Germans and betray Moulin.

12 Robert Paxton, foreword to Conan and Rousso, *Vichy: An Everpresent Past*, p. xiii. For more on the confiscation of Jewish property during the Occupation see the cover story of *Le Nouvel Observateur*, "La Spoliation des juifs de France," 3–9 December 1998, pp. 10–12.

13 Any number of books and articles have dealt with the films of Ophuls and Modiano's fiction (see here, chapters 2, 3, and 4). See especially Morris, *Collaboration and Resistance Reviewed* and Avni, *D'un passé l'autre*. As for Tournier's *Le*

Roi des Aulnes, Saul Friedlander argues convincingly that the novel, along with several other works of fiction and film produced at the time, offered new insights into the psychology of Nazism itself by stressing a dual obsession with kitsch and death. See his *Reflections of Nazism.* Tournier's own (disturbing) comments about the genesis and inspiration for his novel can be found in the chapter of *Le Vent paraclet* devoted to *Le Roi des Aulnes.*

14 Along these lines, see Garçon, "Le Retour d'une inquiétante imposture," 539–48, and Greene, "*La Vie en rose.*"

15 I strongly disagree with this assessment of the film. See my essay, "Claude Berri's *Uranus*: The Pitfalls of Representing Vichy in the 1990s," *Contemporary French Civilization* 22, no. 2 (summer/fall 1998): 285–301.

16 See Conan, "Enquête sur le retour d'une idéologie," and Guy Konopnicki, *Les Filières noires* (Paris: Denoël, 1996).

17 Paxton, foreword, pp. xii–xiii.

18 Rousso, *La Hantise du passé,* p. 118.

19 Rousso, *The Vichy Syndrome,* p. 10.

20 Along these lines, see Sartre's classic analysis of the collaborator in "Qu'est-ce qu'un collaborateur?" in *Situations III* (Paris: Gallimard, 1949), pp. 43–61.

21 For the repression of Jewish memory in the postwar period, see the conversation between Rousso and Klarsfeld, "Histoire et Justice," pp. 16–37.

22 See Rousso, *La Hantise du passé,* p. 28, and Todorov, *Les Abus de la mémoire.*

23 Valensi, "Présence du passé," 491.

24 See Rousso, *La Hantise du passé,* p. 73, Aron, *Histoire de Vichy,* and Jean-Pierre Azéma, "Vichy et la mémoire savante: Quarante-cinq ans d'historiographie," in *Le Régime de Vichy et les français,* ed. Azéma and Bédarida, p. 28.

25 Pascal Ory, "Comme de l'an quarante: Dix années de 'rétro satanas'," *Le Débat* 16 (1981): 110.

26 At a colloquium on Vichy held in honor of Paxton's retirement at Columbia University in September 1997, John Sweets delivered a fascinating—and amusing—lecture on the French reception of *La France de Vichy.* Proceedings of the conference are forthcoming.

27 Azéma, "Vichy et la mémoire savante," p. 28.

28 Paxton has subsequently compared the impact of his book on the French with what the impact would be on Americans if they were to discover that George Washington had been an agent of George III. See Deborah Marquardt, "The French Connection," *W&L: The Washington and Lee Alumni Magazine,* winter 1998, p. 16.

29 Valensi, "Présence du passé," p. 497.

30 Valensi, "Présence du passé," p. 494.

31 The proceedings of the conference were published under the title *Vichy et les français,* ed. Azéma and Bédarida.

32 Cited in Valensi, "Présence du passé," p. 499.

33 According to an article appearing in the 30 October–5 November 1997 issue of *L'Événement du jeudi*, Bergès had been "recuperated" by Papon and his allies. Among the latter were those in charge of the *Economica* publishing house, where Bergès's next two books would appear. See "Pourquoi Michel Bergès a-t-il 'trahi'?" p. 58.

34 Noiriel, *Sur la "crise" de l'histoire*, and Julliard, *Pour la Bosnie*, p. 25.

35 Nora, preface and introduction, *Realms of Memory*, pp. xv–xxiv, 1–21.

36 See the discussion of the Gayssot Law in chapter 7.

37 See the introduction to my *Memory, the Holocaust and French Justice*. See also the chapters on Touvier, Bousquet, and Papon here.

38 Conan, *Le Procès Papon*, p. 7.

39 Thibaud, "Un temps de mémoire," pp. 166–83.

40 See Weill, "Penser le procès Papon," p. 100. It is clear that Weill's criticism is aimed at, among others, Conan and Rousso, who had taken a position apparently similar to Weill's in *Vichy: An Everpresent Past*.

41 Nora, *Realms of Memory*, p. 3; Foucault quoted in Natalie Zemon Davis and Randolph Starn, introduction to *Representations* 26 (spring 1989): 2; Nora, *Realms of Memory*, p. 3.

42 All these issues are discussed in detail in chapter 5.

1. Memory and Justice Abused

1 I have culled this account of the murder of Bousquet from accounts published in Parisian newspapers, including *Le Monde*, *Libération*, *Le Figaro*, *L'Humanité*, and *Le Parisien*. It is interesting to note that all the accounts of the murder given by Didier and his exact words vary somewhat from newspaper to newspaper—hazards, perhaps, of the profession.

2 Conan and Rousso, *Vichy: An Everpresent Past*, p. 99.

3 The interview, titled "L'Affaire Papon révisée par Papon," was published in *Libération* on 6 March 1996. I would like to take this opportunity to express my gratitude to Annette Lévy-Willard for providing me with a copy of this interview as well as the transcript of Bousquet's 1949 trial, without which this chapter could not have been written.

4 For an excellent recent discussion of the Purge and the effectiveness of its judicial procedures and actions, see Rousso, "Une Justice impossible," pp. 745–70.

5 For a discussion of developments in French law concerning crimes against humanity, see the introduction to my *Memory, the Holocaust, and French Justice*, pp. 1–49.

6 Serge Klarsfeld, interview by Marie-Amélie Lombard, in *Le Figaro*, 9 June 1993.

7 See Mitterrand's comments to Olivier Wieviorka in *Nous entrerons dans la carrière*, p. 350.

8 See "C'était un voisin adorable," *Le Parisien*, 9 June 1993.

9 For details of Bousquet's life, see Froment, *René Bousquet*.

10 For a lengthier discussion of these issues, see the introduction to my *Memory, the Holocaust, and French Justice*.

11 Mitterrand and Wiesel, *Memoire à deux voix*. The conversations concerning Bousquet are on pp. 101–11 and will be discussed in greater detail in chapter 6.

12 Froment, *René Bousquet*, p. 493.

13 Golsan, *Memory, the Holocaust, and French Justice*, p. 17.

14 See Klarsfeld and Rousso, "Histoire et justice," pp. 24–25.

15 See Tournier, *The Wind Spirit*, pp. 62–63.

16 For contemporary newspaper accounts of and commentaries on the 1949 trial, see Froment, *René Bousquet*, pp. 500–514.

17 This is not to be confused with the *Libération* created in the wake of May 1968 by Sartre and Simone de Beauvoir, which will be cited in subsequent chapters.

18 All quotes are from Froment, *René Bousquet*, p. 514.

19 Froment, *René Bousquet*, p. 500. See also Tarr, *Henri Queuille en son temps*, pp. 328–29.

20 Froment, *René Bousquet*, p. 495.

21 For a discussion of Bousquet's anti-Communist activities during the Occupation, see Husson, "L'Itinéraire d'un haut fonctionnnaire," pp. 292–93. Curiously, the Acte d'Accusation of the 1949 trial stresses that Bousquet was *lenient* in his dealings with Communists.

22 Froment, *René Bousquet*, p. 494.

23 See Greilsamer, "Un 'collaborateur précieux.'"

24 For the text of the Bousquet-Oberg Accords, see appendix 5 in *Le Droit antisémite de Vichy*, pp. 593–98.

25 Rajsfus, *La Police de Vichy*, p. 92.

26 For a recent study in English of the roundups in Marseilles, see Ryan, *The Holocaust and the Jews of Marseille*.

27 Conan, "La Vraie Vie de René Bousquet," p. 32.

28 The text of the German résumé of the meeting is included in *Dossier Bousquet*, published by *Libération* as a supplement to their 13 July 1993 issue.

29 See the interview with Paxton conducted by Annette Lévy-Willard originally published in *Libération* and translated in Golsan, *Memory, the Holocaust and French Justice*, pp. 53–60.

30 Golsan, *Memory, the Holocaust and French Justices*, pp. 56–57.

31 Fax to the author, 31 January 1995.

32 Burrin, *La France à l'heure allemande,* p. 164.

33 Daladier, *Prison Journal, 1940–1945,* pp. 153–55.

34 Brinon, *Mémoires,* pp. 148–50.

35 Burrin, *La France à l'heure allemande,* p. 158.

36 One of the most famous photos of Bousquet taken during the war shows him smiling with a group of German officers. Holding a cigarette, Bousquet is wearing a coat with a large fur collar.

37 Cited in Conan, "La Vraie Vie de René Bousquet," p. 32.

38 Quoted in Burrin, *La France à l'heure allemande,* p. 162.

39 See the Klarsfeld interview, in *Le Figaro,* 9 June 1993.

40 Weill, "Penser le procès Papon," p. 100. Weill's principal target here is Jean de Maillard's interpretation of the Papon trial, "A quoi sert le procès Papon?"

41 For a discussion of the fictional portrayal of Bousquet in recent political potboilers published in France, see Whitney, "Presidential Fiction, French Style," p. 27.

2. History as Counterhistory

1 Patrick Modiano, *Dora Bruder* (Paris: Gallimard, 1997), p. 101.

2 Modiano, *Dora Bruder,* p. 65.

3 Modiano, *Dora Bruder,* pp. 72–73.

4 Nettelbeck, "Novelists and Their Engagement with History," p. 246.

5 Nettelbeck, "Novelists and Their Engagement with History," p. 246.

6 Modiano, *Dora Bruder,* pp. 51–52.

7 Modiano, *Dora Bruder,* p. 133.

8 Modiano, *Dora Bruder,* p. 10.

9 Modiano, *Dora Bruder,* p. 54.

10 Modiano, *Dora Bruder,* p. 67.

11 Colin Nettelbeck, "Getting the Story Right: Narratives of WW II in Post 1968 France," *Journal of European Studies* 15 (1985): 103. For further details on the Bonny-Laffont Gang, see Jacques Bonny, *Mon Père l'inspecteur Bonny* (Paris: Laffont, 1976).

12 See David Pryce-Jones, *Paris in the Third Reich: A History of the German Occupation* (New York: Holt Rinehart and Winston, 1981), p. 30.

13 Pryce-Jones, *Paris in the Third Reich,* p. 69.

14 The name Troubadour itself is, of course, suggestive of the character's rootlessness; the troubadours were wandering poets and minstrels who traveled and performed in the south of France and especially Provence from the twelfth through the fourteenth centuries. It should also be noted that, as a number of sources have pointed out, the name "Swing Troubadour" is actu-

ally the title of a famous 1941 song by Charles Trenet. Lines from the song are interspersed in Modiano's text. See especially Alan Morris, *Patrick Modiano* (Oxford and Washington: Berg, 1996), p. 50.

15 Patrick Modiano, *La Ronde de nuit* (Paris: Gallimard, 1969), p. 119.

16 In speaking of "a being without contours, undefinable, intangible, and invisible, an anonymous 'I' who is everything and nothing," Sarraute was of course referring to forms of characterization that would become typical of the New Novel. Modiano's characters have often been compared to those of the New Novelists, but Modiano himself rejects the comparison: "I am not interested in any experimental school and specifically reproach the New Novel with having neither tone nor life." Quoted in Morris, *Patrick Modiano,* p. 7.

17 Along these lines, see Kevin Telford, "Identity Is a Verb: Re-righting the Self in the Novels of Patrick Modiano," *French Forum* 19, no. 3 (September 1994): 347–56.

18 C. W. Nettelbeck and P. A. Hueston, "Anthology as Art: Patrick Modiano's *Livret de Famille*," *Australian Journal of French Studies* 21, no. 2 (1984): 179. Along similar lines, see more recently Willian VanderWolk, *Rewriting the Past: Memory, History, and Narration in the Novels of Patrick Modiano* (Amsterdam: Rodopi, 1997).

19 Patrick Modiano, *Livret de famille* (Paris: Gallimard, 1977), p. 116.

20 Nettelbeck, "Getting the Story Right," pp. 102–3. For details of Modiano's family, see, more recently, his letter to the author in Thierry Laurent, *L'Oeuvre de Patrick Modiano: Une autofiction* (Lyon: Presses Universitaires de Lyon, 1997), pp. 5–8, and Modiano's most recent book, *Dora Bruder.*

21 Marc Lambron, "Modiano ou la melancolie française," *Nouvelle Revue Française* 340 (May 1981): 92.

22 Gerald Prince, "Re-Membering Modiano, or Something Happened," *SubStance* 49 (1986): 37.

23 Modiano, *La Ronde de nuit*, p. 24.

24 Modiano, *La Ronde de nuit,* pp. 52–53.

25 Like his real-life model, Gerbère is a boyish-looking intellectual sporting horn-rimmed glasses, who generally hides his homosexuality behind tough profascist and anti-Semitic pronouncements.

26 In his letter to Thierry Laurent cited earlier, Modiano draws a sharp distinction between Jean Luchaire, a figure he describes as coming from "the Left" and who was "absolutely not an anti-Semite," and fanatical pro-Nazis like Robert Brasillach and Lucien Rebatet. Their "wartime adventures" as Modiano describes them had nothing in common. Luchaire, according to Modiano, "got lost in collaborationism through a certain weakness of character" (p. 6). Given these distinctions drawn in the letter to Laurent, it is interesting that they are part of the same, corrupt crowd in *La Ronde de nuit*.

27 Modiano, *La Ronde de nuit*, p. 108.

28 William Shirer, *The Collapse of the Third Republic* (New York: Simon and Schuster, 1969), p. 208.

29 Eugen Weber, *Action Française: Royalism and Reaction in Twentieth-Century France* (Stanford: Stanford University Press, 1962), p. 320.

30 Modiano, *La Ronde de nuit*, p. 139.

31 Modiano, *Dora Bruder*, p. 80.

32 Modiano, *Dora Bruder*, p. 147.

3. Collaboration and Context

1 Quoted in Garçon, "La Fin d'un mythe," p. 111.

2 A number of commentators have argued recently that the *mode rétro* continues today, a claim not at all unreasonable given the continuing obsession with the Occupation and the number of literary and cinematic works dealing with the period. For this perspective on the *mode rétro*, see the conclusion of Higgins's *New Novel, New Wave, New Politics,* and Morris, *Collaboration and Resistance Reviewed.* For my purposes here, I shall use the term in the more restrictive context of the period incorporating the fall of Gaullism and the rise of Giscardism in the mid-1970s because this period first produced the specific response to *Lacombe Lucien* that will be critiqued here.

3 Bonitzer and Toubiana, "Anti-Rétro," p. 5.

4 Zimmer, "La Paille dans le discours de l'ordre," p. 2495.

5 Zimmer, "La Paille dans le discours de l'ordre," p. 2495.

6 Bonitzer and Toubiana, "Anti-Rétro," p. 5.

7 Bonitzer, "Histoire de Sparadrap," p. 47.

8 Bonitzer and Toubiana, "Anti-Rétro," p. 10.

9 See Morris, *Collaboration and Resistance Reviewed*, chapter 2.

10 It is of interest to note that the "depoliticization" of the Occupation associated with the *mode rétro* does not jibe with the right-wing critiques of *Lacombe Lucien* mentioned above. These critiques note their displeasure with Lucien's *lack* of political idealism and commitment when he joins the Gestapo.

11 Bonitzer and Toubiana, "Anti-Rétro," p. 13.

12 For an excellent discussion of the genesis of the character of Lucien Lacombe, see Higgins, *New Novel, New Wave, New Politics,* p. 189.

13 In a discussion of *Lacombe Lucien* to which I shall return at the end of this chapter, Greene argues in *Landscapes of Loss* that Lucien's failure to understand what a Jew is after four years of Nazi and Vichy rule is implausible: "Is it possible that, after four years of propaganda and Occupation, anyone could still ask, as Lucien does, 'What is a Jew?'" (p. 75). I would argue that it is not only

possible but likely, given the isolation of the area that Lucien comes from and his lack of education. Besides, when Lucien asks the question to which Greene refers, he is indicating that he *is* aware of anti-Semitic propaganda, which he is trying to understand in his own, limited way: Vichy and Nazi propaganda taught hatred of the Jews without, of course, explaining who the Jews were in real, historical terms. Propaganda, by definition, distorts rather than instructs.

14 Quoted in Garçon, "La Fin d'un mythe," p. 116.

15 Malle and Andrieu, "*Lacombe Lucien* et l'Occupation," pp. 20–21.

16 Malle and Andrieu, "*Lacombe Lucien* et l'Occupation," p. 20.

17 Zimmer, "La Paille dans le discours de l'ordre," p. 2493.

18 For Malle's comments on Patrick Modiano's contributions to the film, see Nettelbeck and Hueston, *Patrick Modiano,* p. 55, and especially French, *Conversations avec Louis Malle,* p. 118.

19 Malle and Andrieu, "*Lacombe Lucien* et l'Occupation," p. 22.

20 In *Conversations avec Louis Malle,* Malle recounts an anecdote that encouraged him to make *Lacombe Lucien* and supports the view that extreme and rapid shifts in political allegiance were not uncommon during the Occupation, especially among young and impressionable boys. Malle's friend and a former Resistance fighter, Jean-Pierre Melville, was traveling from Bordeaux to Paris on the train in 1943 with a fellow member of the Resistance. In their compartment was a young man who announced he was off to join the Waffen ss to "fight for his country." By the time the train arrived in Paris, the two *résistants* had completely changed the young man's mind. He had decided to join them in the Resistance. See French, *Conversations avec Louis Malle,* pp. 126–27.

A number of historically documented instances also support the notion that radical swings from one political extreme to the other were not at all unusual in France during this period. The most obvious example is Jacques Doriot, who went from leader of the Parti Communiste in the early 1930s to leader of the fascist Parti Populaire Français (PPF) in the late 1930s and 1940s. Paul Jankowski documents fairly large numbers of similar conversions among the masses in his study of the PPF in Marseilles, *Communism and Collaboration.* Another example is Marcel Déat, a prewar Socialist turned pro-Nazi collaborationist during the Occupation.

21 It is curious that Malle discusses the Militia in this context, because Lucien is not a Militia member in the film, although a number of critics have mistakenly assumed that he is. For a discussion of the Militia in historical terms, see chapter 5 here dealing with the Touvier Affair. Jacob, "Entretien avec Louis Malle," p. 29.

22 Jacob, "Entretien avec Louis Malle," p. 29.

23 Malle and Andrieu, "*Lacombe Lucien* et l'Occupation," p. 20.

24 Malle, *Louis Malle par Louis Malle,* p. 9.

25 Malle, *Louis Malle par Louis Malle*, p. 9.

26 Malle, *Louis Malle par Louis Malle*, p. 13.

27 Malle's two films about the Occupation have often been compared, most recently by Lynn Higgins in "If Looks Could Kill: Louis Malle's Portraits of Collaboration," in *Fascism, Aesthetics, and Culture*, ed. Golsan, pp. 198–211. In an earlier review of *Au revoir les enfants* in the *New York Review of Books* (12 May 1988), Stanley Hoffmann discusses the two films and strongly expresses his preference for *Au revoir les enfants*, which, based on his personal experience of the Occupation, he considers far more convincing and authentic than the earlier film. Hoffmann also remarks on the theme of incest in *Au revoir les enfants* and the connection with *Le Souffle au coeur*, but he does not show how the link between familial themes and the Occupation slant of Malle's early views on *Lacombe Lucien*, as I have argued here.

As these remarks suggest, a more detailed comparison here of *Lacombe Lucien* and *Au revoir les enfants* would be superfluous. Nevertheless, I should like to state my own preference for *Lacombe Lucien* if for no other reason than the fact that the history of its reception reveals so much about the troubled memory of the Occupation. I shall also argue that the film's ambiguity makes it in many ways one of Malle's most representative works.

28 Malle, "Entretien exclusif avec Louis Malle," p. 6.

29 See Luchaire, *Ma Drôle de vie*. It is of interest to note that Luchaire's memoirs had long fascinated Patrick Modiano and influenced his own views on the Occupation. It is therefore not unlikely that they influenced the initial conception of the character of Lucien.

30 In *Conversations avec Louis Malle*, Malle notes that at the time of the making of the film he was aware of the fact that certain aspects of the film were not "politically correct" and were bound to stir up controversy. The example he cites is the inclusion of the black Gestapo member, Hippolyte. Malle was, however, totally unprepared for the general assault on the film's supposedly reactionary ideology. See French, *Conversations avec Louis Malle*, p. 126.

31 Or, as Zimmer argues, an ideology that determines its "formal perfection."

32 Bonitzer's comment along these lines is worth quoting in full: "[T]he blindness or paralysis . . . of the critics in dealing with the meaning of this film (a paralysis that one often finds expressed in the use of the word 'ambiguity,' this term, notably applied to the film by revisionist critics) always in reality reflects the position of the critic himself, who doesn't know if a negative judgment is in order or not: this serves to suspend the critical act" ("Histoire de Sparadrap," p. 43).

33 Delmas, "Sur les écrans," p. 34.

34 It is interesting to note that even those critics who are not particularly concerned with the film's politics or underlying ideology tend to strip the film of

its ambiguities in developing their interpretations. For example, François Garçon sees the film as being primarily a love story involving a "young *milicien*" and a "persecuted Jewess." In keeping with this reading of the film, he describes the scene involving Lucien's shooting of the German soldier and the flight of Lucien, France, and the grandmother in the following terms: "[I]n Lucien's presence, a German officer decides to take France and the grandmother as hostages. Without hesitating Lucien shoots the man with a burst of machine-gun fire and rushes out with the young girl" (p. 112). Needless to say, this is not what happens on screen.

35 All of these characters are borrowed from the early novels of Patrick Modiano. For a discussion of the impact of these works on the scenario of *Lacombe Lucien*, see my essay "Collaboration, Alienation, and the Crisis of Identity in the Film and Fiction of Patrick Modiano," pp. 107–22. For a discussion of Modiano's novels themselves, see chapter 2.

36 Cited in French, *Conversations avec Louis Malle*, p. 122.

37 Greene, *Landscapes of Loss*, p. 77.

38 Malle and Modiano, *Lacombe Lucien,* pp. 116–17.

39 Camber Porter, *Through Parisian Eyes*, p. 86.

40 French, *Conversations avec Louis Malle*, p. 122. These artistic concerns also apparently figured in the choice of Pierre Blaise to play the role of Lucien. Malle notes that "there was in him [Blaise] something very strong and very ambiguous. He could pass for the worst of traitors and at the same time he was very touching. Blaise was so good that he caused me a lot of trouble. *Many people almost thought the film was an apology for collaboration because Blaise was so moving and so troubling that it was impossible to hate him completely*" (French, *Conversations avec Louis Malle*, p. 122, emphasis mine).

41 Camber Porter, *Through Parisian Eyes,* p. 86.

42 Malle, *Louis Malle par Louis Malle*, p. 31.

43 Camber Porter, *Through Parisian Eyes,* p. 84.

44 Hoffmann, "Cinquante ans après," p. 39.

45 Quoted in Camber Porter, *Through Parisian Eyes*, p. 11. In *Conversations avec Louis Malle*, Malle notes that he was aware that Ophuls had been "shocked" by precisely the film's ambiguity. Malle goes on to suggest that Ophuls's discomfort with *Lacombe Lucien* stems from divergent ambitions on the part of the two directors in making their respective films, *Lacombe Lucien* and *Le Chagrin et la pitié*:

> *Le Chagrin et la Pitié* is an ideological film. Ophuls wanted to make a demonstration, show what had happened in a provincial town, Clermont-Ferrand. He wanted to expose things that had been covered up. He was trying to prove something and denounce collaboration. He was making a moral judgment. For me, the demonstration had been made. I wanted to

move beyond it. Rather than judge, I wanted to study a type of comportment that is despicable and without doubt difficult to understand. After
all, if people are shocked by ambiguity, they shouldn't go to see my films.
Ophuls's films and *Lacombe Lucien* function on entirely different levels.
(pp. 129–30)

46 See Greene, *Landscapes of Loss*, pp. 74–77.

4. Revising *The Sorrow and the Pity*

1 In *The Vichy Syndrome*, Rousso describes the film as "a deliberate effort of
demystification on a grand scale" (p. 111).

2 Rousso, *The Vichy Syndrome*, p. 106.

3 Rousso notes that the only woman to testify as a participant in the events
is the hairdresser whose head is shaved at the time of the Liberation. In
"Whose Sorrow? Whose Pity? Whose Pleasure? Framing Women in Occupied France," Miranda Pollard offers a thorough critique of the film for
failing to include women. Pollard rightly asserts that this absence seriously
compromises the film's representation of the historical realities of the period.
Pollard's essay is included *Gender and Fascism in Modern France*, ed. Hawthorne
and Golsan, pp. 141–55.

4 Quoted in Greene, *Landscapes of Loss*, p. 70.

5 The commentaries on *The Sorrow and the Pity* cited here are all provided in
Rousso, *The Vichy Syndrome*, pp. 106–8.

6 Camber Porter, *Through Parisian Eyes*, p. 12.

7 Ophuls, "Joy to the World," p. 42.

8 Ophuls, "Joy to the World," p. 43.

9 Higgins, *New Novel, New Wave, New Politics*, p. 192.

10 Greene, *Landscapes of Loss*, p. 90.

11 Ophuls, "Joy to the World," p. 42.

12 Higgins, *New Novel, New Wave, New Politics*, p. 192.

13 Colombat, *The Holocaust in French Film*, pp. 226, 230.

14 Ophuls, "The Sorrow and the Laughter," p. 113.

15 Ophuls, "The Sorrow and the Laughter," p. 112.

16 Camber Porter, *Through Parisian Eyes*, p. 15.

17 Nichols, *Representing Reality*, p. 52.

18 In an article titled "Marcel Ophuls on Barbie: Reopening the Wounds of War"
published in the *New York Times* on 2 October 1988, Ophuls is quoted as
saying that he does not believe in collective guilt. He points out that his wife, a
German native, was in the Hitler Youth and that his brother-in-law was in the
Herman Goering Division. Ophuls's comments appear to be at odds with the

very negative portrait of the Germans as a whole in the film, a portrait that does seem to imply some form of a national collective guilt.

19 Ophuls, "Joy to the World," p. 43.

20 For an excellent discussion of the Bitburg incident and its place in the German national memory of the Nazi period, see Rabinach, "Beyond Bitburg," pp. 187–218.

21 For a discussion of the role of Genoud in the Barbie Affair, see Paris, *Unhealed Wounds,* esp. pp. 140–43. As noted in the introduction, Mitterrand's biographer Pierre Péan has also recently written a book on Genoud.

22 In an article written at the time of the Touvier trial, Henry Rousso disagrees with this assessment of the similarities between Touvier and Barbie. See his article "Klaus Barbie and Paul Touvier," pp. 155–56.

5. The Trial of Paul Touvier

1 The details of Touvier's life are included in any number of books in French, among the most reliable being Rémond et al., *Paul Touvier et l'Église,* and Greilsamer and Schneidermann, *Un Certain Monsieur Paul.* In English, see the introduction to my *Memory, the Holocaust, and French Justice,* and Ted Morgan, "The Last War Criminal: The Trial of Paul Touvier," *New York Times Magazine,* 22 May 1994.

2 See Greilsamer and Schneidermann, *Un Certain Monsieur Paul,* pp. 105–11.

3 For the history of the Chevaliers de Notre Dame and the support the group offered Touvier over many years, see Rémond et al., *Paul Touvier et l'Église,* pp. 302–8.

4 Rémond et al., *Paul Touvier et l'Église,* pp. 295–98.

5 Conan and Rousso, *Vichy: An Everpresent Past*, pp. 92–93.

6 Vidal-Naquet, *Réflexions sur le génocide,* p. 266.

7 This claim is not entirely accurate. As Philip Watts observes, during the Purge several statutes including Article 83 of the penal code, which punished "national indignity," were applied retroactively. See Watts, *Allegories of the Purge*, p. 19.

8 Vergès and Bloch, *La Face cachée du procès Barbie,* p. 13.

9 The Katyn episode as presented by Trémolet during Touvier's trial is discussed in Todorov's "The Touvier Trial," p. 174.

10 Finkielkraut, *Dispatches from the Balkan War*, p. 80.

11 Bernard-Henri Lévy, *La Pureté dangereuse* (Paris: Grasset, 1994), p. 204.

12 Wieviorka, *Nous entrerons dans la carrière*, p. 350.

13 I am indebted to Annette Lévy-Willard for providing me with a copy of Getti's indictment.

14 Touvier's attendance at Uriage is reported in Getti's indictment and also in Rémond et al., *Paul Touvier et l'Église,* p. 71. For a discussion of the Uriage experiment, see John Hellman, *The Knight-Monks of Vichy.*

15 See Delperrié de Bayac, *Histoire de la milice, 1918–1945.*

16 Sternhell was found guilty on two of seven counts by a French judge, but the offending passages from which the implication was made, *Ni droite, ni gauche,* were not ordered stricken from current or future editions. For a fuller discussion of the affair, see Wohl, "French Fascism, Both Right and Left," pp. 91–98.

17 Kiejman, "L'Histoire devant ses juges," pp. 112–13. It is interesting that, as stated in the Introduction, during the Papon trial the situation was in fact the reverse. The historians called to offer their expert opinions were compromised in their testimony because, unlike the members of the court, they did not have access to the criminal dossier. See Rousso, *La Hantise du passé,* p. 101.

18 Bredin, "Le Droit, le juge, et l'historien," p. 93.

19 Kiejman, "L'Histoire devant ses juges," p. 122.

20 See Golsan, *Memory, the Holocaust, and French Justice,* pp. 38–39.

21 Gros, "Un droit monstrueux," p. 561.

22 Wexler, "The Interpretation of the Nuremberg Principles," p. 349.

23 Quoted in Golsan, *Memory, the Holocaust, and French Justice,* p. 110.

24 Portions of the April 1992 verdict are produced in Bédarida, *Touvier, le dossier de l'accusation.* The passage cited here is on p. 316.

25 In order to understand the extent of Vichy anti-Semitism, it is important to look at Vichy's anti-Semitic laws rather than Pétain's speeches. For a thorough recent assessment, see Weisberg, *Vichy Law and the Holocaust in France.*

26 Bédarida, *Touvier, le dossier de l'accusation,* pp. 314–21.

27 Bédarida, *Touvier, le dossier de l'accusation,* p. 316.

28 Conan and Rousso, *Vichy: An Everpresent Past,* p. 91.

29 Bédarida, *Touvier, le dossier de l'accusation,* pp. 25–26.

30 The same line of reasoning has been followed by historians and legal experts. Among the most recent examples, see Weisberg, *Vichy Law and the Holocaust in France.*

31 See Bredin, "History and Justice Abused," pp. 109–13.

32 Bédarida, *Touvier, le dossier de l'accusation,* p. 16.

33 Vidal-Naquet, *Réflexions sur le génocide,* p. 252.

34 Tigar et al., "Paul Touvier and the Crime against Humanity," p. 285.

35 Tigar et al., "Paul Touvier and the Crime against Humanity," p. 285.

36 Delarue admitted after the trial that he changed his testimony because to someone of his generation, seeing Touvier acquitted or partially vindicated was "unacceptable." See Conan and Rousso, *Vichy: An Everpresent Past,* p. 122.

37 Wexler, "The Interpretation of the Nuremberg Principles," p. 367.

38 Finkielstein, "Changing Notions of State Agency in International Law," pp. 262–82.

39 Wexler, "The Interpretation of the Nuremberg Principles," p. 296.

40 Guéry, "Une Interrogation après le procès Touvier," p. 119.

41 See Taylor, *The Anatomy of the Nuremberg Trials*, p. 294.

42 See Colin, *Le Crime contre l'humanité*.

6. Mitterrand's Dark Years

1 The *dépôt légal* is September 1994.

2 Reported in *Le Monde*, 11–12 September 1994.

3 *Le Monde*, 11–12 September 1994.

4 Thibaud, "L'Homme au-dessus des lois," p. 116.

5 Thibaud, "L'Homme au-dessus des lois," p. 133.

6 Mongin, "La France de Mitterrand ou le royaume de l'anachronisme," p. 88.

7 In the second volume of his recently published biography of Mitterrand, *Mitterrand: Une histoire de Français,* p. 533, Lacouture argues that Mitterrand suffered from a memory lapse in making this statement because he was in a great deal of physical pain during the television interview.

8 Judt, "Truth or Consequences," 11–12. For further commentary on the scandal in this country, see especially Singer, "Mitterrand le Petit," pp. 380–82.

9 Andrieu, "Réponse d'une historienne," p. 206.

10 Andrieu, "Réponse d'une historienne," p. 207.

11 Andrieu, "Réponse d'une historienne," p. 107.

12 Mongin, "La France de Mitterrand ou le royaume de l'anachronisme," p. 96.

13 Fiterman's comments are recorded in *Le Monde*, 11–12 September 1994.

14 These comments by Socialist leaders were quoted in *Le Monde*, 9 September 1994.

15 Lacouture, *Mitterrand,* p. 585.

16 Nay, *Le Noir et le rouge*. The English translation, *The Black and the Red: François Mitterrand, the Story of an Ambition* (New York: Harcourt Brace Jovanovitch), appeared in 1987.

17 Faux, Legrand, and Perez, *La Main droite de Dieu*. The *dépôt légal* for this book is the same as the *dépôt légal* for *Une Jeunesse française*: September 1994.

18 In an interview with Jean Lacouture on 13 March 1998, Jacques Chirac continued to express anger over Mitterrand's cynical promotion of the National Front in order to weaken opposition from the republican right. For Chirac, this was proof that Mitterrand's republican convictions "were not very solid." See Lacouture, *Mitterrand,* p. 578.

19 This translation is an updated version of the French text with a new preface by Robert Paxton.

20 In the *Prolongements* section of the 1996 folio edition of the book, Conan and Rousso hasten to point out that despite the reactions of some readers of the book, it was not their intention to suggest that France should simply "turn the page" on Vichy or throw the veil of forgetfulness over it, as Pompidou had suggested in his 1971 press conference on his pardon of Touvier. It is interesting that Conan and Rousso should feel obliged to make this statement, since it suggests there is no middle ground between obsession and forgetfulness where Vichy is concerned.

21 Paxton's comments are included in "A Symposium on Mitterrand's Past," pp. 19–21.

22 For the Grossouvre affair, see Plenel, *Un temps de chien*, pp. 13–38.

23 Laughland, *The Death of Politics*.

24 "A Symposium on Mitterrand's Past," pp. 19–20.

25 "A Symposium on Mitterrand's Past," pp. 19–21. All the issues Paxton alludes to are discussed in Conan and Rousso, *Vichy: An Everpresent Past*, chapters 1 and 4.

26 Péan, *Une Jeunesse française,* p. 113.

27 Péan, *Une Jeunesse française,* p. 150.

28 Péan, *Une Jeunesse française,* p. 171.

29 Péan, *Une Jeunesse française,* pp. 163–64.

30 Péan, *Une Jeunesse française,* p. 162.

31 Péan, *Une Jeunesse française,* p. 183.

32 The complete text of the essay is provided as an appendix at the end of *La Main droite de Dieu,* pp. 235–39.

33 Péan, *Une Jeunesse française,* p. 194.

34 Péan, *Une Jeunesse française,* p. 203.

35 For Pétainisme's emphasis on remorse and repentance, see Claude Chabrol's brilliant compilation of Vichy's propaganda films, *L'Oeil de Vichy.*

36 Péan, *Une Jeunesse française,* p. 523.

37 See Hoffmann's comments in "A Symposium on Mitterrand's Past," p. 7.

38 Péan, *Une Jeunesse française,* p. 84.

39 Péan, *Une Jeunesse française,* p. 85.

40 Montherlant, *Essais*, pp. 242–43.

41 Montherlant, *Essais,* pp. 956–57.

42 Guéhenno, *Journal des années noires*, p. 207.

43 Quoted in Péan, *Une Jeunesse française,* p. 118.

44 In a striking example of Montherlantian misogyny, Mitterrand lamented in a letter written from Vichy in the summer of 1942: "Je m'humanise, et donc me féminise" (Péan, *Une Jeunesse française,* p. 198).

45 For years, scholars of French fascism have debated whether or not the Croix de Feu movement can be defined as fascist. For a recent and compelling argument in favor of the movement being labeled fascist, see Soucy, *French Fascism.*

46 Péan, *Une Jeunesse française,* p. 75.

47 Péan, *Une Jeunesse française,* pp. 63–64.

48 Montherlant, *Essais,* p. 244.

49 Mitterrand and Wiesel, *Mémoire à deux voix*, p. 110. Mitterrand's arrogant and unapologetic attitude toward his friendship with Bousquet also manifested itself in a shocking outburst recorded by Laure Adler. Asked by Adler if he wished to condemn Bousquet for the record and if he wished to express his horror over the Vél d'Hiv roundups, Mitterrand replied, "I find you disgusting, you and all the journalists. I want no more relations with you. I find your attitude shameful." Quoted in Lacouture, *Mitterrand,* p. 532.

50 Conan and Rousso, *Vichy: An Everpresent Past,* p. 227.

7. Denying the Holocaust in France

1 The term "negationism" was coined by Rousso in *The Vichy Syndrome* to distinguish between "revisionism," which, as Rousso argues, usually refers to "a normal phase in the evolution of historical scholarship" and the denial of the Holocaust, where "what is at issue is a system of thought, an ideology, and not a scientific or even critical approach to the subject" (p. 151). More recently, in the context of the Roger Garaudy–Father Pierre affair, Robert Redeker has argued that, although some in France still insist on a distinction between the two terms in discussing the Holocaust, the distinction is a false one and only serves the purposes of the deniers. Redeker argues that the end pursued in both cases is the same, the only difference being that negationism moves directly toward its goal whereas revisionism adopts a more subtle strategy of minimization rather than outright denial. See Redeker, "La Toile d'arraignée," p. 1.

2 According to Pierre-André Taguieff, Guillaume announced the publication of Garaudy's book to members of the press in November 1995 and sent a similar announcement to "Friends of *La Vieille Taupe*" on December 15. See Taguieff, "L'Abbé Pierre et Roger Garaudy," p. 210.

3 Henceforth I will use the French term "negationist" for the Holocaust deniers rather than the American term "revisionist." The French term is more concise and accurate.

4 The edition of the book for sale to the general public was published at Garaudy's expense. On the cover of the book and on the binding, Garaudy

lists the publisher as "Samizdat Garaudy." The use of the word "Samizdat" clearly suggests an effort to draw a comparison between Garaudy's book and those "self-published"—"samizdat"—works by East European dissidents protesting communist oppression.

5 Garaudy, *Le Procès du sionisme israélien,* p. 100.

6 Denunciations of Israeli and American racism have of course regularly been part and parcel of "negationism" in France, especially since Chomsky's defense of Faurisson, an episode to which we shall return. But earlier negationist texts by Faurisson and Paul Rassinier concern themselves primarily with the details of what might be called the denial itself: contesting testimony by witnesses and victims, alternative explanations for the uses of the gas chambers, etc.

7 The strategy of conflating Nazi crimes with those committed by "whites"— Americans, Europeans, and Israelis—against people of color in the Third World and former colonies was also, of course, used by Jacques Vergès in his defense of Klaus Barbie in the mid-1980s. For a discussion of the trial and Vergès's strategy, see Finkielkraut, *Remembering in Vain.*

8 Taguieff, "L'Abbé Pierre et Roger Garaudy," p. 210.

9 Veil, "Ils ont profité de nos erreurs," p. 22. The Gayssot Law was passed in the wake of the desecration of a Jewish cemetery in the southern town of Carpentras in May 1990. The desecration produced a wave of national indignation, including massive demonstrations in Paris and elsewhere. Despite the good intentions which prompted its passage, the Gayssot Law has been severely criticized from the beginning. In 1991, Tzvetan Todorov insisted that the criminalization of tendentious interpretations of history was "grotesque" and continued: "Truth does not need a law in order to be protected; if law becomes necessary, it's because the legislator has doubts about it being the truth." See Todorov, "Letter from Paris: Racism," p. 49.

10 See Redeker, "La Toile d'arraignée," p. 3.

11 The details of Father Pierre's biography as described here are taken from Eric Conan and Sylviane Stein, "Ce qui a fait chuter l'Abbé Pierre," *L'Express,* 2–8 May 1996.

12 Founded after the Liberation under the leadership of the Resistance leader Maurice Schumann, the MRP was liberal and impeccably *résistant*, but attracted many conservative votes among former Pétainists because of its Catholic affiliation and because no true right-wing party existed at the time in French politics.

13 In an interesting and ironic twist, Pierre Vidal-Naquet, one of negationism's fiercest denouncers whose work will be discussed shortly, states in his recently published *Mémoires 2, le trouble et la lumière, 1955–1998* that he voted for

Garaudy and his Communist list at the time because of their opposition to the French military presence in Algeria.

14 Father Pierre's comments discussed here are included in a pamphlet published in June 1996 titled *Le Secret de l'Abbé Pierre*. The authors, Michel-Antoine Burnier and Cécile Romane, were present at discussions between Abbé Pierre and Bernard Kouchner, which were published in book form as *Dieu et les hommes* in 1993. I would like to thank my colleague Nathan Bracher for calling my attention to *Le Secret de l'Abbé Pierre*.

15 Father Pierre's comments are quoted in Taguieff, "L'Abbé Pierre et Roger Garaudy," p. 211.

16 In their essay in *L'Express*, Eric Conan and Sylviane Stein note that Father Pierre backed away from his support of Garaudy when LICRA threatened to remove him from its honorary board.

17 A poll conducted at the height of the controversy indicated that 64 percent of Frenchmen had not changed their opinion of Father Pierre as a result of his support of Garaudy. Twenty-four percent were less sympathetic to Father Pierre than before the incident, whereas 9 percent were more sympathetic to him afterward.

18 See Perrault, "La Victoire des révisionnistes," pp. 18–19.

19 Along these lines, see Redeker, "La Toile d'arraignée," p. 1.

20 The term is used by Taguieff and implies a fear of a worldwide Jewish or, in its modern garb, Israeli-American conspiracy for domination and control. See his "L'Abbé Pierre et Roger Garaudy," p. 211. See Finkielkraut, "Le Siècle de la négation," p. 24.

21 Vidal-Naquet, quoted in Perrault, "La Victoire des révisionnistes," p. 16.

22 Redeker, "La Toile d'arraignée," p. 2.

23 Quoted in Young, *The Texture of Memory*, p. 1.

24 Finkielkraut, "Le Siècle de la négation," p. 24.

25 Along these lines, see Maier, *The Unmasterable Past*, esp. pp. 1–34.

26 The claims made by Bardèche in *Nuremberg ou la terre promise* are enumerated in Seidel, *The Holocaust Denial*, p. 95.

27 The details provided here concerning Rassinier's life and career are taken from Brayard's excellent recent study of Rassinier and negationism in France, *Comment l'idée vint à M. Rassinier*.

28 Vidal-Naquet, "Paul Rassinier ou la dérive retardée," pp. 9–16.

29 Faurisson, *Mémoire en défense*.

30 Faurisson's comments are included in Brigneau, *Mais qui est donc le professeur Faurisson?* They are cited in Brayard, *Comment l'idée vint à M. Rassinier*, pp. 419–22. It is noteworthy that Brigneau is a former collaborator and currently a right-wing activist who has written for such extremist reviews as *Le Choc du mois*, recently defunct.

31 A detailed discussion of the critical reception of Faurisson's article on Rimbaud's poem can be found in Brayard, *Comment l'idée vint à M. Rassinier,* pp. 422–27.

32 Brayard, *Comment l'idée vint à M. Rassinier,* p. 430.

33 Quoted in Brayard, *Comment l'idée vint à M. Rassinier,* p. 434.

34 See Fresco, "Les Redresseurs de morts," p. 2154.

35 Vidal-Naquet, *Assassins of Memory,* pp. 21–23.

36 Bridonneau, *Oui, il faut parler des négationnistes,* p. 41.

37 Faurisson had been forced to leave his post at the University of Lyons II because the university administration could no longer guarantee his safety. He had also been beaten up near his home in Vichy.

38 The petition is quoted in its entirety in Thion et al., *Vérité historique ou vérité politique,* p. 163.

39 Chomsky's preface is in *Mémoire en defense,* pp. ix–xv. For discussions and critiques of Chomsky's preface and his role in the Faurisson Affair, see especially Seidel, *The Holocaust Denial,* pp. 102–4, and Vidal-Naquet, *Assassins of Memory,* pp. 65–73.

40 For a discussion of the charges brought against Faurisson, see Seidel, *The Holocaust Denial,* pp. 106–7.

41 Vidal-Naquet, *Assassins of Memory,* p. xxiv.

42 Quoted in Perrault, "La Victoire des révisionnistes," p. 23.

43 Seidel, *The Holocaust Denial,* p. 110.

44 Taguieff, "L'Abbé Pierre et Roger Garaudy," p. 216.

45 For Finkielkraut's background and education, see especially Friedlander, *Vilna on the Seine,* pp. 92–106.

46 Finkielkraut, "Le Siècle de la négation," p. 24.

47 Garaudy, *Le Procès du sionisme israélien.*

48 Denis, "Abbé Pierre," pp. 94–99.

8. From Vichy to Sarajevo

1 Wallon, "La Guerre de Sarajevo," p. 376.

2 Lévy, *Le Lys et la cendre,* pp. 10–11.

3 Lévy, *Le Lys et la cendre,* p. 10.

4 Wallon, "La Guerre de Sarajevo," p. 376.

5 Judt, "Paris and the Tribes of Europe," 34–39.

6 For a brief if somewhat apologetic overview of French governmental attitudes toward the war in the former Yugoslavia, see Lepick, "French Perspectives," pp. 76–86.

7 Finkielkraut, *Dispatches from the Balkan War,* pp. 20–21.

8 Finkielkraut, "Le Goût perdu de la liberté," p. 7.

9 Tanner, *Croatia*, p. 223.

10 Julliard, *Ce fascisme qui vient*, pp. 19–20.

11 For Lévy's comments along these lines, see *La Pureté dangereuse*, p. 10.

12 Morin, *Les Fratricides,* pp. 74–76.

13 Morin, *Les Fratricides*, p. 99.

14 Finkielkraut, "Europe," pp. 219–20.

15 Finkielkraut, *Dispatches from the Balkan War*, p. 32.

16 Bruckner, *La Tentation de l'innocence*, p. 210.

17 Mitterrand's efforts to incriminate the Croats in the current conflict by recalling their Ustacha past were roundly condemned by the majority of the intellectuals under discussion here. See in particular Finkielkraut's comments in *Dispatches from the Balkan War*, pp. 80–82.

18 Intellectuals in countries other than France have also expressed their indignation over the fact that Western leaders knew of the Balkan genocide and still did nothing. This is suggested by the title of an excellent recent collection of essays edited by Cushman and Mestrovic, *This Time We Knew*.

19 See Lévy, *Le Lys et la cendre*, p. 232.

20 Finkielkraut, *Dispatches from the Balkan War*, p. 63.

21 Finkielkraut, *Dispatches from the Balkan War,* p. 88.

22 Bruckner, *La Tentation de l'innocence*, p. 242. This is a reference to Ernst Nolte's position during the "Historian's Debate" in Germany during the mid-1980s.

23 Baudrillard, "No Pity for Sarajevo," pp. 80–84.

24 Finkielkraut, *Dispatches from the Balkan War*, p. 87.

25 Lévy, *La Pureté dangereuse*, pp. 199–204.

26 Finkielkraut, *Dispatches from the Balkan War*, p. 86.

27 Julliard, *Ce fascisme qui vient,* pp. 128–29.

28 Lévy, *Le Lys et la cendre*, pp. 98–99.

29 Lévy, *Le Lys et la cendre*, p. 515.

30 See Todorov, "La Mémoire et ses abus," pp. 39–42.

9. Memory's Time Bombs

1 Daeninckx, *Meurtres pour mémoire*, p. 64.

2 Daeninckx, *Meurtres pour mémoire,* p. 72.

3 Daeninckx, *Meurtres pour mémoire,* p. 95.

4 For Mitterrand's role in the revelation of Papon's role in the deportation of Jews during the Occupation, see Bernard Violet, *Le Dossier Papon* (Paris: Flammarion, 1997), p. 13.

5 Baruch, like many other historians of Vichy, would later testify at Papon's trial.

6 Alain Finkielkraut, "Papon, trop tard," *Le Monde*, 14 October 1997.

7 For a survey and commentary on this issue, see Rousso, "Pour les jeunes."

8 For the text of Chirac's statement and a discussion of its merits, see Conan and Rousso, *Vichy: Un passé qui ne passe pas*, pp. 425–57.

9 As will be recalled, Vergès wished to muddy the waters during the Barbie trial by labeling French crime in the colonies crimes against humanity. See Finkielkraut, *Remembering in Vain*.

10 For this testimony, see *Libération*, 16 October 1997, and *Le Monde*, 17 October 1997.

11 See the introduction to Conan and Rousso, *Vichy: Un passé qui ne passe pas*.

12 Boulanger, *Maurice Papon*.

13 Violet, *Le Dossier Papon*, p. 53.

14 Violet, *Le Dossier Papon*, p. 74.

15 Violet, *Le Dossier Papon*, p. 83.

16 Violet, *Le Dossier Papon*, p. 85.

17 Jean-Luc Einaudi, *La Bataille de Paris. 17 octobre 1961* (Paris: Seuil, 1991), p. 48.

18 Boulanger, *Maurice Papon*, p. 237.

19 Quoted in Violet, *Le Dossier Papon*, pp. 89–90.

20 According to Boulanger, Papon saw Pflimlin as a "loser" and, always careful to be on the winning team, regardless of the price, chose to turn down the cabinet post offered. See Boulanger, *Maurice Papon*, p. 237.

21 For the August 1958 roundups, see Einaudi, *La Bataille de Paris*, pp. 52–53.

22 Boulanger, *Maurice Papon*, p. 239.

23 Einaudi, *La Bataille de Paris*, pp. 54–55.

24 Einaudi, *La Bataille de Paris*, p. 55.

25 Einaudi, *La Bataille de Paris*, p. 83.

26 For the full text of the curfew, see Einaudi, *La Bataille de Paris*, p. 85.

27 Quoted in Einaudi, *La Bataille de Paris*, p. 86.

28 Quoted in Eunaudi, *La Bataille de Paris*, p. 235.

29 Benjamin Stora, *La Gangrène et l'oubli: La mémoire de la guerre d'Algérie* (Paris: La Découverte, 1992), p. 95.

30 Quoted in Einaudi, *La Bataille de Paris*, p. 84.

31 Quoted in Violet, *Le Dossier Papon*, p. 116.

32 Einaudi, *La Bataille de Paris*, pp. 154–55.

33 See Einaudi, "Le Papon des ratonnades," p. 53.

34 In his memoirs, Papon claims that he not only witnessed the occasional attacks by police on Algerians in the courtyard but also quickly descended into the courtyard to put a halt to these acts. It is also clear that he felt such

attacks were justified, given earlier attacks on the police. See Maurice Papon, *Le Chevaux du pouvoir: Le préfet de police du général de Gaulle ouvre ses dossiers 1958– 1967* (Paris: Plon, 1988), p. 212.

35 Quoted in Einaudi, *La Bataille de Paris,* p. 165.

36 For the testimony of one of these doctors, see Einaudi, *La Bataille de Paris,* pp. 200–203.

37 Einaudi, *La Bataille de Paris,* p. 227.

38 Einaudi, *La Bataille de Paris,* pp. 184–85.

39 Einaudi, *La Bataille de Paris,* p. 195.

40 Einaudi, *La Bataille de Paris,* p. 197.

41 Quoted in Einaudi, *La Bataille de Paris,* p. 225.

42 Quoted in Stora, *La Gangrène et l'oubli,* p. 98.

43 Quoted in Einaudi, *La Bataille de Paris,* p. 256.

44 Boulanger, *Maurice Papon,* p. 246.

45 Quoted in Einaudi, "Le Papon des ratonnades," p. 53.

46 Quoted in Einaudi, "Le Papon des ratonnades," p. 53.

47 Boulanger, *Maurice Papon,* p. 220.

48 Boulanger, *Maurice Papon,* p. 222.

49 Boulanger, *Maurice Papon,* p. 209.

50 Boulanger, *Maurice Papon,* p. 207.

51 Boulanger, *Maurice Papon,* p. 211.

52 Bredin, "Le Droit, le juge et l'historien," p. 94.

53 See the interview with Pierre-Vidal Naquet, "Ce qui accable Papon," *Le Nouvel Observateur,* 23–29 October 1997, pp. 56–57.

54 Rousso, *The Vichy Syndrome,* p. 75.

55 Jean-Luc Einaudi, "Octobre 1961: Pour la vérité, enfin," *Le Monde,* 20 May 1998.

Selected Bibliography

Andrieu, Claire. "Réponse d'une historienne." *Esprit* (December 1994): 206.

Aron, Robert. *Histoire de Vichy, 1940–1944*. Paris: Fayard, 1954.

Assouline, Pierre. *L'Epuration des intellectuels 1944–1945*. Brussels: Éditions Complexe, n.d.

Avni, Ora. *D'un passé l'autre: Aux portes de l'histoire avec Patrick Modiano*. Paris: L'Harmattan, 1997.

Aycock, Wendell, and Michael Schoenecke, eds. *Film and Literature: A Comparative Approach to Adaptation*. Lubbock: Texas Tech University Press, 1988.

Azéma, Jean-Pierre, and François Bédarida, eds. *Le Régime de Vichy et les français*. Paris: Fayard, 1992.

Baruch, Marc Olivier. *Servir l'état français: L'administration en France de 1940 à 1944*. Paris: Fayard, 1997.

Baudrillard, Jean. "No Pity for Sarajevo." In *This Time We Knew: Western Responses to Genocide in Bosnia*, ed. Thomas Cushman and Stjepan Mestrovic, 80–84. New York: New York University Press, 1996.

Bédarida, François. *Touvier, le dossier de l'accusation*. Paris: Seuil, 1996.

Bertin, Célia. *Femmes sous l'Occupation*. Paris: Stock, 1993.

Best, Geoffrey. *War and Law since 1945*. Oxford: Oxford University Press, 1995.

Billig, Joseph. *Le Commissariat général aux questions juives (1941–1944)*. 3 vols. Paris: Éditions du Centre, 1955.

Bonitzer, Pascal. "Histoire de Sparadrap." *Cahiers du cinéma* 250 (May 1974): 47.

Bonitzer, Pascal, and Serge Toubiana. "Anti-Rétro: Entretien avec Michel Foucault." *Cahiers du cinéma* 251–52 (July–August 1974): 5.

Boulanger, Gérard. *Maurice Papon: Un technocrate français dans la collaboration*. Paris: Seuil, 1994.

——. *Papon: Un intrus dans la République*. Paris: Éditions du Seuil, 1997.

Brayard, Florent, ed. *Comment l'idée vint à M. Rassinier*. Paris: Fayard, 1996.

Bredin, Jean-Denis. "Le Droit, le juge, et l'historien." *Le Débat* 32 (November 1984): 93.

——. "History and Justice Abused." In *Memory, the Holocaust and French Justice: The Bousquet and Touvier Affairs*, ed. Richard J. Golsan, 109–13. Hanover NH: University Press of New England, 1996.

Bridonneau, Pierre. *Oui, il faut parler des négationnistes*. Paris: Les Éditions du Cerf, 1997.

Brigneau, François. *Mais qui est donc le professeur Faurisson? Une enquête, un portrait, une analyse*. Paris: François Brigneau, 1992.

Brinon, Fernand de. *Mémoires*. Paris: La Page Internationale, n.d.

Bruckner, Bruckner. *La Tentation de l'innocence*. Paris: Grasset, 1995.

Bruno, Jean, and Frédéric de Monicault. *L'Affaire Papon: Bordeaux: 1942–1944*. Paris: Éditions Tallandier, 1997.

Burnier, Antoine, and Cécile Romane. *Le Secret de l'abbé Pierre*. Paris: Editions Mille et Une Nuits, 1996.

Burrin, Philippe. *La France à l'heure allemande*. Paris: Seuil, 1995.

——. "La France et le fascisme." *Le Débat* 32 (November 1984): 52–72.

Carpi, Daniel. *Between Mussolini and Hitler: The Jews and the Italian Authorities in France and Tunisia*. Hanover NH: University Press of New England, 1995.

Carroll, David. *French Literary Fascism: Nationalism, Anti-Semitism, and the Ideology of Culture*. Princeton: Princeton University Press, 1995.

"C'était un voisin adorable." *Le Parisien,* 9 June 1993.

Chabrol, Claude. *L'Oeil de Vichy*. Paris: TF1 Video, 1993.

Cobb, Richard. *French and Germans, Germans and French: A Personal Interpretation of France under Two Occupations, 1914–1918 / 1940–1944*. Hanover NH: University Press of New England, 1983.

Cohen-Grillet, Philippe. *Maurice Papon: De la collaboration aux assises*. Bordeaux: Le Bord De L'Eau, 1997.

Colin, Marcel, ed. *Le Crime contre l'humanité*. Ramonville Saint-Agne: Éditions Érès, 1996.

Colombat, Pierre-André. *The Holocaust in French Film*. Metuchen NJ: Scarecrow, 1993.

Conan, Eric. "A lire en marge du procès." *L'Express,* 2 October 1997, 56.

——. "Le Casse-tête juridique." *L'Express,* 2 October 1997, 54–56.

——. "Enquête sur le retour d'une idéologie." *L'Express,* 17–23 July 1992, 27.

——. "Papon, les Français et Vichy." *L'Express,* 2 October 1997, 28–31.

——. *Le Procès Papon: Un journal d'audience*. Paris: Gallimard, 1998.

——. "Un Vichysto-résistant parmi d'autres." *L'Express,* 2 October 1997, 48–50.

——. "La Vraie Vie de René Bousquet." *L'Express,* 5 October 1990, 32.

Conan, Eric, and Henry Rousso. *Vichy: An Everpresent Past*. Trans. Nathan Bracher. Hanover NH: University Press of New England, 1998. Originally published as *Vichy, un passé qui ne passe pas* (Paris: Fayard, 1994).

Le Crime contre l'humanité: Mesure de la responsabilité? Actes du cycle des conférences Droit, Liberté et Foi, June 1997. École Cathédrale, Institute de Formation Continue du Barreau de Paris. Paris: CERP, 1998.

Cushman, Thomas, and Stjepan Mestrovic, eds. *This Time We Knew: Western Responses to Genocide in Bosnia*. New York: New York University Press, 1996.

Daeninckx, Didier. *Meurtres pour mémoire*. Paris: Gallimard, 1984.

Daladier, Edouard. *Prison Journal, 1940–1945*. Boulder: Westview Press, 1995.

Delmas, Jean. "Sur les écrans." *Jeune Cinéma* 77 (March 1974): 34.

Delperrié de Bayac, Jacques. *Histoire de la milice, 1918–1945*. Paris: Fayard, 1969.

Denis, Jean-Pierre. "Abbé Pierre." *Panoramiques* 35 (1998): 94–99.

Dossier Bousquet. Libération. Supplement. 13 July 1993.

Le Droit antisémite de Vichy. Paris: Seuil 1996.

Dumay, Jean-Michel. *Le Procès de Maurice Papon: La chronique de Jean-Michel Dumay.* Paris: Fayard, 1998.

Einaudi, Jean-Luc. "Le Papon des ratonnades." *L'Express,* 2 October 1997, 53–54.

Faurisson, Robert. *Mémoire en défense: Contre ceux qui m'accuse de falsifier l'histoire.* Paris: La Vieille Taupe, 1980.

Faux, E., T. Legrand, and G. Perez. *La Main droite de Dieu.* Paris: Seuil, 1994.

Finkielkraut, Alain. *Dispatches from the Balkan War and Other Writings.* Trans. Peter S. Rogers and Richard Golsan. Lincoln: University of Nebraska Press, 1999. Originally published as *Comment peut-on être Croate?* (Paris: Gallimard, 1992).

——. "Europe: La crise de conscience (Entretien avec Alain Finkielkraut)." *Politique Internationale* 69 (1995): 219–20.

——. *The Future of a Negation: Reflections on the Question of Genocide.* Trans. Mary Byrd Kelly. Lincoln: University of Nebraska Press, 1998.

——. "Le Goût perdu de la liberté." *Le Messager européen* 8 (1994): 7–31.

——. *Remembering in Vain: The Klaus Barbie Trial and Crimes against Humanity.* Trans. Roxanne Lapidus. New York: Columbia University Press, 1992.

——. "Le Siècle de la négation." *L'Evénement du jeudi,* 27 June–3 July 1996, 24.

Finkielstein, Claire. "Changing Notions of State Agency in International Law: The Case of Paul Touvier." *Texas International Law Journal* 30, no. 2 (1995): 261–84.

Francos, Ania. *Il était des femmes dans la Résistance.* Paris: Stock, 1978.

French, Phillip. *Conversations avec Louis Malle.* Paris: Denoël, 1993.

"The French New Right: New Right-New Left-New Paradigm." *Telos* (fall 1993–winter 1994): 98–99.

Fresco, Nadine. "Les Redresseurs de morts." *Les Temps modernes* 589 (1996): 2154.

Friedlander, Judith. *Vilna on the Seine: Jewish Intellectuals in France since 1968.* New Haven: Yale University Press, 1990.

Friedlander, Saul. *Reflections of Nazism.* Bloomington: Indiana University Press, 1993.

Froment, Pascale. *René Bousquet.* Paris: Stock, 1994.

Frossard, André. *Le Crime contre l'humanité.* Paris: Laffont, 1987.

Garaudy, Roger. *Le Procès du sionisme israélien.* Paris: Éditions Vent du Large, 1998.

Garcon, François. "La Fin d'un mythe." *Vertigo* 2 (April 1989): 111.

——. "Le Retour d'une inquiétante imposture: *Lili Marlene* et *Le Dernier Métro.*" *Les Temps modernes* 422 (September 1981): 539–48.

Glucksmann, André. *De Gaulle, où es-tu?* Paris: Editions Lattès, 1995.

Goldhagen, Daniel Jonah. *Hitler's Willing Executioners: Ordinary Germans and the Holocaust*. New York: Knopf, 1996.

Golsan, Richard J. "Collaboration, Alienation, and the Crisis of Identity in the Films and Fiction of Patrick Modiano." In *Film and Literature: A Comparative Approach to Adaptation,* ed. Wendell Aycock and Michael Schoenecke, 107–22. Lubbock: Texas Tech University Press, 1988.

——. "Memory's *bombes à retardement*: Maurice Papon, Crimes against Humanity, and 17 October 1961." *Journal of European Studies* 28, nos. 1–2 (March–June 1998): 153–72.

——. "Que reste-t-il de l'affaire Touvier? Mémoire, histoire et justice." *The French Review* 72, no. 1 (October 1998): 102–12.

Golsan, Richard J., ed. *Fascism, Aesthetics, and Culture*. Hanover NH: University Press of New England, 1992.

——. *Memory, the Holocaust, and French Justice: The Bousquet and Touvier Affairs*. Hanover NH: University Press of New England, 1996.

Golsan, Richard J., and Jean-François Fourny, eds. "The Occupation in French Literature and Film, 1940–1992." *L'Esprit Créateur* 33, no. 1 (1993).

González, Shirley Mangini. *Memories of Resistance: Women's Voices from the Spanish Civil War*. New Haven: Yale University Press, 1995.

Gravier, Bruno, and Jean-Marc Elchardus, eds. *Le Crime contre l'humanité*. Paris: Édition Erès, 1996.

Greene, Naomi. *Landscapes of Loss: The National Past in Postwar French Cinema*. Princeton: Princeton University Press, 1999.

——. "*La Vie en rose*: Images of the Occupation in French Cinema." In *Auschwitz and After: Race, Culture, and "the Jewish Question" in France,* ed. Lawrence Kritzman, 283–98. New York: Routledge, 1995.

Greilsamer, Laurent. "Un 'collaborateur précieux.'" *Le Monde*, 9 June 1993.

Greilsamer, Laurent, and Daniel Schneidermann. *Un Certain Monsieur Paul: L'Affaire Touvier*. Rev. ed. Paris: Fayard, 1992.

Gros, Dominique. "Un Droit monstrueux?" In *Le Droit antisémite de Vichy*. Le genre humain 30–31. Ed. Maurice Olender, 561. Paris: Seuil, 1996.

Guéhenno, Jean. *Journal des années noires*. Paris: Gallimard, 1947.

Guéry, Christian. "Une Interrogation après le procès Touvier: Le crime contre l'humanité existe-t-il?" In *Juger sous Vichy*. Le genre humain 28. Ed. Maurice Olender, 119. Paris: Seuil, 1994.

Haget, Henri. "Paroles de victimes." *L'Express,* 2 October 1997, 38–44.

Hawthorne, Melanie, and Richard J. Golsan, eds. *Gender and Fascism in Modern France*. Hanover NH: University Press of New England, 1997.

Hellman, John. *The Knight-Monks of Vichy France: Uriage, 1940–1945*. Montreal: McGill-Queen's University Press, 1993.

Higgins, Lynn A. "If Looks Could Kill: Louis Malle's Portraits of

Collaboration." In *Fascism, Aesthetics, and Culture*, ed. Richard J. Golsan, 198–211. Hanover NH: University Press of New England, 1992.

——. *New Novel, New Wave, New Politics: Fiction and the Representation of History in Postwar France*. Lincoln: University of Nebraska Press, 1996.

Hoffmann, Stanley. "Cinquante ans après." Special issue. *Esprit* 181 (May 1992): 39.

——. Review of *Au revoir les enfants*, by Louis Malle. *New York Review of Books*, 12 May 1988.

——. "A Symposium on Mitterrand's Past." *French Politics and Society* 13, no. 1 (winter 1995): 7.

Husson, Jean-Pierre. "L'Itinéraire d'un haut fonctionnaire: René Bousquet." In *Vichy et les Francais*, ed. Jean-Pierre Azéma and François Bédarida, 292–93. Paris: Fayard, 1992.

Jacob, Gilles. "Entretien avec Louis Malle (à propos de Lacombe Lucien)." *Positif* 157 (March 1974): 29.

Jankélévitch, Vladimir. *L'Imprescriptible: Pardonner? Dans l'honneur et la dignité*. Paris: Seuil, 1986.

Jankowski, Paul. *Communism and Collaboration: Serge Sabiani and Politics in Marseille*. New Haven: Yale University Press, 1989.

Jeanneney, Jean-Noël. *Le Passé dans le prétoire: L'historien, le juge et le journaliste*. Paris: Éditions du Seuil, 1998.

Judt, Tony. "Paris and the Tribes of Europe." *French Politics and Society* 10, no. 2 (spring 1992): 34–39.

——."Truth or Consequences." Review of *Une Jeunesse française: François Mitterand, 1934–1947*, by Pierre Péan. *New York Review of Books*, 3 November 1994, 11–12.

Julliard, Jacques. *L'Année des fantômes: Journal 1997*. Paris: Bernard Grasset, 1998.

——. *Ce fascisme qui vient* . . . Paris: Seuil, 1994.

——. *Pour la Bosnie*. Paris: Seuil, 1996.

Kaplan, Alice Yaeger. *Reproductions of Banality: Fascism, Literature, and French Intellectual Life*. Minneapolis: University of Minnesota Press, 1986.

Kiejman, Georges. "L'Histoire devant ses juges." *Le Débat* 32 (November 1984): 112–13.

Klarsfeld, Arno. *La Cour, les nains et le Bouffon*. Paris: Éditions Robert Laffont, 1998.

——. *Papon: Un verdict français*. Paris: Éditions Ramsay, 1998.

——. *Touvier: Un crime français*. Paris: Fayard, 1994.

Klarsfeld, Serge. Interview with Marie-Amélie Lombard. *Le Figaro*, 9 June 1993.

——. *Vichy-Auschwitz: Le role de Vichy dans la solution finale de la question juive en France*. 2 vols. Paris: Fayard, 1985.

Klarsfeld, Serge, and Henry Rousso. "Histoire et justice: Débat entre Serge Klarsfeld et Henry Rousso." *Esprit* 181 (May 1992): 16–37.

Kouchner, Bernard, and Abbé Pierre. *Dieu et les hommes*. Paris: Ed. Corps 16, 1993.

Kupferman, Fred. *Le Procès de Vichy: Pucheu, Petain, Laval*. Brussels: Éditions Complexe, 1980.

Lacouture, Jean. *Mitterand: Une histoire de Français. Tome 2: Les vertiges du sommet*. Paris: Seuil, 1998.

Lambert, Bernard. *Dossier d'accusation: Bousquet, Papon, Touvier*. Paris: FNDIRP, n.d.

Laughland, John. *The Death of Politics: France under Mitterrand*. London: Michael Joseph, 1994.

Lebovics, Herman. *True France: The Wars over Cultural Identity, 1900–1945*. Ithaca: Cornell University Press, 1992.

Lepick, Olivier. "French Perspectives." In *International Perspectives on the Yugoslav Conflict*, ed. Alex Danchev and Thomas Halverson, 76–86. New York: St. Martin's, 1996.

Lévy, Bernard-Henri. *L'Idéologie française*. Paris: Grasset, 1981.

———. *Le Lys et la cendre: Journal d'un écrivain au temps de la guerre de Bosnie*. Paris: Grasset, 1996.

———. *La Pureté dangereuse*. Paris: Grasset, 1994.

Luchaire, Corinne. *Ma Drôle de vie*. Paris: Sun, 1949.

Maier, Charles. *The Unmasterable Past: History, the Holocaust, and German National Identity*. Cambridge MA: Harvard University Press, 1988.

Maillard, Jean de. "A quoi sert le procès Papon?" *Le Débat* 32 (November 1998): 32–42.

Malle, Louise. "Entretien exclusif avec Louis Malle." *Cahiers Roger Nimier: Ascenseur pour l'échafaud* 6 (1989): 6.

———. *Louis Malle par Louis Malle*. Paris: l'Athanor, 1978.

Malle, Louis, and René Andrieu. "Lacombe Lucien et l'Occupation: Louis Malle s'explique, René Andrieu conteste." *L'Humanité dimanche*, 3 April 1974, 20–21.

Malle, Louis, and Patrick Modiano. *Lacombe Lucien*. Paris: Gallimard, 1974.

"Marcel Ophuls on Barbie: Reopening the Wounds of the War." *New York Times*, 2 October 1988.

Marrus, Michael, and Robert Paxton. *Vichy France and the Jews*. New York: Schocken Books, 1983.

Mason, Tim. *Nazism, Fascism and the Working Class*. Cambridge: Cambridge University Press, 1995.

Matisson, Maurice-David, and Jean-Paul Abribat. *Psychanalyse de la collaboration: Le syndrome de Bordeaux, 1940–1945*. New York: William Morrow, 1990.

Mayer, Arno J. *Why Did the Heavens Not Darken? The "Final Solution" in History*. New York: Pantheon, 1990.

Mehlman, Jeffrey. *Legacies of Anti-Semitism in France*. Minneapolis: University of Minnesota Press, 1983.

Milza, Pierre, and Serge Bernstein. *Dictionnaire historique des fascismes et du nazisme*. Brussels: Éditions Complexe, 1992.

Mitterrand, François, and Elie Wiesel. *Mémoire à deux vois*. Paris: Odile Jacob, 1995.

Mizejewski, Linda. *Divine Decadence: Fascism, Female Spectacle, and the Makings of Sally Bowles*. Princeton: Princeton University Press, 1992.

Le Monde. 9, 11–12 September 1994.

Monestier, Marianne. *Elles étaient cent et mille: Femmes dans la Résistance*. Paris: Fayard, 1972.

Monferrand, Hélène de. *Les Amies d'Héloïse*. Paris: Éditions de Fallois, 1990.

———. *Journal de Suzanne*. Paris: Éditions de Fallois, 1991.

Mongin, Olivier. "La France de Mitterrand ou le royaume de l'anachronisme." *Esprit* (November 1994): 88.

Montherlant, Henry de. *Essais*. Paris: Gallimard, Éditions de la Pléiade, 1963.

Morgan, Ted. *An Uncertain Hour: The French, the Germans, the Jews, the Barbie Trial, and the City of Lyon, 1940–1945*. New York: William Morrow, 1990.

Morin, Edgar. *Les Fratricides: Yougoslavie-Bosnie, 1991–1995*. Paris: Arléa, 1995.

Morris, Alan. *Collaboration and Resistance Reviewed: Writers and the "Mode Rétro" in Post-Gaullist France*. New York: Berg, 1992.

Musil, Robert. "Ruminations of a Slow-Witted Mind." *Critical Inquiry* 17, no. 1 (autumn 1990): 46–61.

Nay, Catherine. *Le Noir et le rouge*. Paris: Grasset et Fasquelle, 1984.

Nettelbeck, Colin. "Novelists and Their Engagement with History: Some Contemporary French Cases." *Australian Journal of French Studies* 35, no. 2 (1998): 246.

Nettelbeck, Colin, and P. A. Hueston. *Patrick Modiano: Piéces d'identité*. Paris: Lettres Modernes, 1986.

Nichols, Bill. *Representing Reality: Issues and Concepts in Documentary*. Bloomington: Indiana University Press, 1991.

Noiriel, Gérard. *Sur la "crise" de l'histoire*. Paris: Belin, 1996.

Nora, Pierre. *Realms of Memory: The Construction of the French Past*. Vol. 1: *Conflicts and Divisions*. Trans. Arthur Goldhammer. New York: Columbia University Press, 1996.

Novick, Peter. *The Resistance versus Vichy: The Purge of Collaborators in Liberated France*. New York: Columbia University Press, 1968.

Ophuls, Marcel. "Joy to the World! An Interview with Marcel Ophuls." *American Film*, September 1988, 42.

———. "The Sorrow and the Laughter." *Premier*, November 1988, 112–13.

Papon, Maurice. "L'Affaire Papon révisée par Papon." Interview by Annette Lévy-Willard. *Libération,* 6 March 1996.

Paris, Erna. *Unhealed Wounds: France and the Klaus Barbie Affair.* New York: Grove Press, 1985.

Paxton, Robert O. Interview with Annette Lévy-Willard. In *Memory, the Holocaust, and French Justice: The Bousquet and Touvier Affairs,* ed. Richard J. Golsan, 53–60. Hanover NH: University Press of New England, 1996.

——. "A Symposium on Mitterrand's Past." *French Politics and Society* 13, no. 1 (winter 1995): 19–21.

——. *Vichy France: Old Guard and New Order, 1940–1944.* New York: Columbia University Press, 1982.

Payne, Stanley G. *A History of Fascism, 1914–1945.* Madison: University of Wisconsin Press, 1996.

Péan, Pierre. *Une Jeunesse française: François Mitterand, 1934–1947.* Paris: Fayard, 1994.

Perrault, Gilles. Interview with Claude Askolovitch and Philippe Cohen. "La Victoire des révisionnistes." *L'Événement du jeudi,* 27 June–3 July 1996, 18–19.

Plenel, Edwy. *Un Temps de chien.* Paris: Stock, 1994.

Poirot-Delpech, Bertrand. *Papon: Un crime de bureau.* Paris: Éditions Stock, 1998.

Pollard, Miranda. "Whose Sorrow? Whose Pity? Whose Pleasure? Framing Women in Occupied France." In *Gender and Fascism in Modern France,* ed. Richard J. Golsan and Melanie Hawthorne, 141–55. Hanover NH: University Press of New England, 1997.

Porter, Melinda Camber. *Through Parisian Eyes: Reflections on Contemporary French Arts and Culture.* Oxford: Oxford University Press, 1986.

Poznanski, René. *Être juif en France pendant la Seconde Guerre Mondiale.* Paris: Hachette, 1994.

Le Procès de Maurice Papon. Compte Rendu Sténographique. 2 vols. Les Grands Procès Contemporains. Paris: Éditions Albin Michel, 1998.

Rabinach, Anson. "Beyond Bitburg: The Place of the 'Jewish Question' in German History after 1945." In *Coping with the Past: Germany and Austria after 1945,* ed. Cathy Harms, Lutz R. Reuter, and Volker Dürr, 187–218. Madison: University of Wisconsin Press, 1990.

Rajsfus, Maurice. *La Police de Vichy: Les forces de l'ordre au service de la Gestapo.* Paris: Cherche Midi, 1995.

Rassat, Michèle-Laure. *La Justice en France.* Paris: Presses Universitaires de France, 1985.

Redeker, Robert. "La Toile d'arraignée du révisionnisme." *Les Temps modernes* 589 (August–September 1996): 1.

Reisman, W. Michael, and Chris T. Antoniou, eds. *The Laws of War*. New York: Vintage, 1994.

Rémond, René, et al. *Paul Touvier et l'Église: Rapport de la commission historique instituée par le cardinal Decourtray*. Paris: Fayard, 1992.

Rémy, Dominique, ed. *Les Lois de Vichy: Actes dits "lois" de l'autorité de fait se prétendant "gouvernement de l'état français."* Paris: Éditions Romillat, 1992.

Rousso, Henry. *La Hantise du passé: Entretien avec Philippe Petit*. Paris: Textuel, 1998.

——. "Une Justice impossible: L'épuration de la politique antijuive de Vichy." *Annales* 48, no. 3 (May–June 1992): 745–70.

——. "Klaus Barbie and Paul Touvier." In *Memory, the Holocaust, and French Justice: The Bousquet and Touvier Affairs*, ed. Richard J. Golsan, 155–57. Hanover NH: University Press of New England, 1996.

——. "Pour les jeunes, un passé très présent." *L'Express*, 2 October 1997, 32–34.

——. *The Vichy Syndrome: History and Memory in France since 1944*. Cambridge: Harvard University Press, 1991. Originally published as *Le Syndrome de Vichy: De 1944 à nos jours* (Paris: Seuil 1987).

Ryan, Donna F. *The Holocaust and the Jews of Marseille*. Urbana: University of Illinois Press, 1996.

Schneidermann, Daniel. *L'Étrange procès*. Paris: Fayard, 1998.

Seel, Pierre. *Moi, Pierre Seel, déporté homosexuel*. Paris: Calmann-Lévy, 1994.

Seidel, Gill. *The Holocaust Denial: Antisemitism, Racism, and the New Right*. Leeds, Eng.: Beyond the Pale Collective, 1986.

Singer, Daniel. "Mitterrand le Petit." *The Nation*, 10 October 1994, 380–82.

Sirinelli, Jean-François. *Histoire des droites en France*. Paris: Gallimard, 1992.

Slitinsky, Michel. *L'Affaire Papon*. Paris: Alain Moreau, 1983.

——. *Procès Papon: Le devoir de justice*. Paris: Éditions de l'Aube, 1997.

Soucy, Robert. *Fascism in France: The Case of Maurice Barrès*. Berkeley: University of California Press, 1972.

——. *Fascist Intellectual: Drieu la Rochelle*. Berkeley: University of California Press, 1979.

——. *French Fascism: The First Wave*. New Haven: Yale University Press, 1986.

——. *French Fascism: The Second Wave, 1933–1939*. New Haven: Yale University Press, 1995.

Stephenson, Jill. *Women in Nazi Society*. London: Croom Helm, 1975.

Sternhell, Zeev. *Maurice Barrès et le nationalisme Français*. Paris: A. Colin, 1972.

——. *Neither Right nor Left: Fascist Ideology in France*. Berkeley: University of California Press, 1986. Originally published as *Ni droite ni gauche: L'idéologie fasciste en France* (Paris: Seuil, 1983).

Sternhell, Zeev, Mario Sznajder, and Maia Ahersi. *The Birth of Fascist Ideology:*

From Cultural Rebellion to Political Revolution. Princeton: Princeton University Press, 1994.

Suleiman, Susan Rubin. *Authoritarian Fictions: The Ideological Novel as a Literary Genre*. Princeton: Princeton University Press, 1992.

Sweets, John. *Choices in Vichy France: The French under Nazi Occupation*. New York: Oxford University Press, 1986.

———. *The Politics of Resistance in France, 1940–1944: A History of the Mouvements Unis de la Résistance*. Dekalb: Northern Illinois University Press, 1976.

Taguieff, Pierre-André. "L'Abbé Pierre et Roger Garaudy: Négationnisme, antijudaïsm, antisionisme." *Esprit* (August–September 1996): 210.

Tanner, Marcus. *Croatia: A Nation Forged in War*. New Haven: Yale University Press, 1997.

Tarr, Francis de. *Henri Queuille en son temps*. Paris: La Table Ronde, 1995.

Taylor, Telford. *The Anatomy of the Nuremberg Trials: A Personal Memoir*. Boston: Little, Brown, 1992.

Thalmann, Rita, ed. *Femmes et fascismes*. Paris: Tierce, 1986.

———. *La Mise au pas: Idéologie et stratégie sécuritaire dans la France occupée*. Paris: Fayard, 1991.

Theweleit, Klaus. *Male Fantasies*. Vol. 1: *Women, Floods, Bodies, History*. Minneapolis: University of Minnesota Press, 1987. Vol. 2: *Male Bodies: Psychoanalyzing the White Terror*. Minneapolis: University of Minnesota Press, 1989.

Thibaud, Paul. "L'Homme au-dessus des lois." *Le Débat* (September–November 1994): 116.

———. "Un Temps de mémoire?" *Le Débat* 96 (September–October 1997): 166–83.

Thion, Serge, et al. *Vérité historique ou vérité politique? Le dossier de l'affaire Faurisson la question des chambres à gaz*. Paris: La Vieille Taupe, 1980.

Tigar, Michael, et al. "Paul Touvier and the Crime against Humanity." *Texas International Law Journal* 30, no. 2 (1995): 286–310.

Todorov, Tzvetan. *Les Abus de la mémoire*. Paris: Arléa, 1995.

———. "Letter from Paris: Racism." *Salmagundi* 88–89 (fall 1990–winter 1991): 3.

———. "La Mémoire et ses abus." *Esprit* 193 (July 1993): 39–42.

———. "The Touvier Trial." In *Memory, the Holocaust, and French Justice: The Bousquet and Touvier Affairs*, ed. Richard J. Golsan, 169–78. Hanover NH: University Press of New England, 1996.

Tournier, Michel. *The Wind Spirit: An Autobiography*. Boston: Beacon, 1988.

Trémolet de Villers, Jacques. *Paul Touvier est innocent*. Paris: Éditions Dominique Martin Morin, 1990.

Tucker, William R. *The Fascist Ego: A Political Biography of Robert Brasillach*. Berkeley: University of California Press, 1975.

Union des femmes français. *Les Femmes dans la Résistance*. Paris: Editions du Rocher, 1977.

Valensi, Lucette. "Présence du passé, lenteur de l'histoire: Vichy, l'Occupation, les juifs." *Annales: Economies, Sociétés, Civilisations* 48, no. 3 (May–June 1993): 491–500.

Varaut, Jean-Marc. *Plaidoirie de Jean-Marc Varaut devant la cour d'assises de la Gironde au procès de Maurice Papon, fonctionnaire sous l'occupation*. Paris: Plon, 1998.

Veil, Simone. "Ils ont profité de nos erreurs." *L'Evénement du jeudi,* 27 June– 3 July 1996, 22.

Veillon, Dominique. *Vivre et survivre en France, 1939–1947*. Paris: Payot, 1995.

Verdès-Leroux, Jeanine. *Refus et violences*. Paris: Gallimard, 1996.

Vergès, Jacques, and Étienne Bloch. *La Face cachée du procès Barbie*. Paris: Samuel Tastet, 1983.

Vidal-Naquet, Pierre. *Assassins of Memory: Essays on the Denial of the Holocaust*. Trans. Jeffrey Mehlman. New York: Columbia University Press, 1992.

——. *Mémoires 2, le trouble et la lumiére, 1955–1998*. Paris: Seuil/La Découverte, 1998.

——. "Paul Rassinier ou la dérive retardée." In *Comment l'idée vint à M. Rassinier*, ed. Florent Brayard, 9–16. Paris: Fayard, 1996.

——. *Réflexions sur le génocide: Les juifs, la mémoire, et le présent. Tome III*. Paris: Seuil, 1995.

——. *Le Trait empoisonné: Réflexions sur l'affaire Moulin*. Paris: Éditions La Découverte, 1993.

Wallon, Emmanuel. "La Guerre de Sarajevo a vraiment eu lieu. Notes sur l'engagement des artistes et des intellectuelles." *Les Temps modernes,* 587 (March-April-May 1996): 374–99.

Watts, Philip. *Allegories of the Purge: How Literature Responded to the Postwar Trials of Writers and Intellectuals in France*. Stanford: Stanford University Press, 1999.

Weber, Eugen. *The Hollow Years: France in the 1930s*. New York: Norton, 1994.

Weill, Nicolas. "Penser le procès Papon." *Le Débat* 103 (January–February 1999): 100–110.

Weisberg, Richard H. *Vichy Law and the Holocaust in France*. New York: New York University Press, 1996.

Wexler, Leila Sadat. "The Interpretation of the Nuremberg Principles by the French Court of Cassation: From Touvier to Barbie and Back Again." *Columbia Journal of Transnational Law* 32, no. 2 (1994): 349.

Whitney, Craig R. "Presidential Fiction, French Style." *New York Times Book Review,* 4 February 1996, 27.

Wieviorka, Olivier. *Nous entrerons dans la carrière. De la Résistance á l'exercice du pouvoir*. Paris: Seuil, 1994.

Wohl, Robert. "French Fascism, Both Right and Left: Reflections on the Sternhell Controversy." *Journal of Modern History* 63 (March 1991): 91–98.

Young, James E. *The Texture of Memory: Holocaust Memorials and Meaning*. New Haven: Yale University Press, 1993.

Zimmer, Christian. "La Paille dans le discours de l'ordre." *Les Temps modernes* 336 (July 1974): 2495.

Zuccotti, Susan. *The Holocaust, the French, and the Jews*. New York: Basic Books, 1993.

Index

Hoffmann, Stanley, 118, 193 n.27; on the "*Lacombe Lucien* myth," 19, 70–72, 146

Holocaust: apology from French Catholic Church for, 160; collective guilt for, 195 n.18; duty to memory of, 15, 183–84; moral complexity of, 12; uniqueness of, 77–78, 86. *See also* Final Solution; negationism

Holocaust denial. *See* negationism

Hueston, P. A., 50, 192 n.18

humanitarianism, 78, 129, 149–50

L'Humanité, 25, 31, 74, 165, 173, 187 n.1

L'Humanité dimanche, 61–62

Husson, Jean-Pierre, 188 n.21

Institut d'Histoire du Temps Présent (IHTP), 10, 12

Israel: Father Pierre's attack on, 128, 129–30, 202 n.20; Faurisson's attack on, 138, 201 n.6; Garaudy's attack on, 125–27, 201 n.7; Rassinier's attack on, 132, 201 n.6

Izetbegovitch, Alija, 149

Jäckel, Eberhard, 10; *La France dans l'Europe d'Hitler*, 11–12

Jacob, Gilles, 63, 192 n.21

Jacob, Madeleine, 30–31

Jamet, Fabienne, 49

Jankowski, Paul, 192 n.20

Jeantet, Gabriel, 115, 117

Je suis partout, 53

Jospin, Lionel, 109, 161

Jouve, Pierre, 119

Jouvenel, Bertrand de, 93

Judt, Tony, 106; *Past Imperfect*, 144–45

Julliard, Jacques, 14–15, 144, 145, 149, 154; *Ce fascisme qui vient . . .*, 8, 147–48, 152–53

Karadic, Radovan, 145

Kiejman, Georges, 28–29, 93–94, 197 n.17

Kerillis, Henri de, 120

Klarsfeld, Arno, 185 n.3

Klarsfeld, Serge, 12, 26–27, 40, 75–76, 185 n.3, 186 n.21

Knochen, Helmut, 32

Korman, Charles, 138–39

Kosovo, 182–83. *See also* Balkan conflict

Kouchner, Bernard, 202 n.14

Kriegel, Annie, 5

Lacombe Lucien (Malle), 57–72; ambiguity of, 66–72, 193 n.27 n.32 n.34, 194 n.40 n.45; director's response to criticisms of, 62–65, 69–70, 193 n.30; early critical reception of, 6, 21, 57–58, 61–62, 191 n.10; later critical reception of, 68–69, 70–72, 193 n.13; Modiano's involvement in, 62, 192 n.18, 193 n.29, 194 n.35; as "myth," 19, 70–72, 146; political trajectory of hero of, 61–63, 121, 191 n.12, 192 n.20 n.21

Lacoste, Robert, 162

Lacouture, Jean, 109, 198 n.7 n.18, 200 n.49

Laffont, Henri. *See* Bonny-Laffont gang

Lagrange, Madame, 83

Lambron, Marc, 51, 55; *1941*, 7

Lang, Jack, 104

Lanzmann, Claude, 12, 75, 76

Laughland, John: *The Death of Politics*, 112

Laurent, Jacques: *Le Petit canard*, 65, 66

Laurent, Thierry, 190 n.20 n.26